D1611630

The
Orient of the Boulevards

NEW CULTURAL STUDIES

Series Editors

Joan DeJean
Carroll Smith-Rosenberg
Peter Stallybrass
Gary A. Tomlinson

A complete list of books in the series
is available from the publisher.

The Orient of the Boulevards

Exoticism, Empire, and Nineteenth-Century French Theater

Angela C. Pao

PENN

University of Pennsylvania Press
Philadelphia

10 9 8 7 6 5 4 3 2 1

Published by
University of Pennsylvania Press
Philadelphia, Pennsylvania 19104-4011

Library of Congress Cataloging-in-Publication Data
Pao, Angela Chia-yi.
The Orient of the boulevards : exoticism, empire, and nineteenth-century
French theater / Angela C. Pao.
p.   cm. — (New cultural studies)
Includes bibliographical references and index.
ISBN 0-8122-3425-1 (alk. paper)
1. French drama—19th century—History and criticism.   2. Orient—In literature.
3. Exoticism in literature.   4. Theater—France—History—19th century.
I. Title.   II. Series.
PQ543.P36   1998
842'.709325—dc21   97-29126
                                                                    CIP

TO MY PARENTS,
for having always given this fish water

Contents

Illustrations

Introduction: From the Orient as Theater to the Orient in the Theater

> The idea of representation is a theatrical one; the Orient is the stage on which the whole East is confined. On this stage will appear figures whose role it is to represent the larger whole from which they emanate. The Orient then seems to be, not an unlimited extension beyond the familiar European world, but rather a closed field, a theatrical stage affixed to Europe.
>
> (Said 63)

THE THEATRICAL METAPHOR IS A central and recurrent one in Edward Said's *Orientalism*. In drawing this comparison, Said was interested in stressing two attributes of theatrical representation in particular: the total and unidirectional control the author, *metteurs en scène*, performers, and audience exercise over the characters and setting displayed on the stage; and the reductionism inherent in the process of staging. A second passage further develops the parallel between the operations of Orientalism and the workings of the theater:

Underlying all the different units of Orientalist discourse—by which I mean simply the vocabulary employed whenever the Orient is spoken or written about—is a set of representative figures, or tropes. These figures are to the actual Orient—or Islam, which is my main concern here—as stylized costumes are to characters in a play; they are like, for example, the cross that Everyman will carry, or the particolored costume worn by Harlequin in a *commedia dell'arte* play. In other words, we need not look for correspondence between the language used to depict the Orient and the Orient itself, not so much because the language is inaccurate but because it is not even trying to be accurate. What it is trying to do . . . is at one and the same time to characterize the Orient as alien and to incorporate it schematically on a theatrical stage whose audience, manager, and actors are *for* Europe, and only for Europe. (71)

As Said's analogies suggest, the relationship between the Orient and European theater has indeed been a long and dynamic one. By no means, however, has it been a purely metaphorical one. From the entrance of the Magi in the medieval Passion cycles to the introduction of Turkish characters into the commedia dell'arte, from the inclusion of Moorish figures in Renaissance and Baroque tragedy to the Asiatic casts of characters in nineteenth-century melodrama, the Orient has had a significant presence in European drama. In each period, this presence takes a different shape, sometimes subtly and sometimes radically altered from previous representations. But whatever the changes, they are always framed by the triple context of the historical and material relations between the two regions; the prevailing social, political, and intellectual concerns in France; and, last but not least, the dominant theatrical practices and dramatic conventions of the time.

Theories and Methods

The publication of *Orientalism* in 1978 sparked a proliferation of studies on Orientalism in the literature, arts, and academic discourses of the West. These works were distinguished from earlier studies by their effort to insert Orientalism into a political and colonialist tradition rather than to consider it as a purely thematic and aesthetic phenomenon. The central question to be answered had been posed by Said in his introduction to *Orientalism*:

The kind of political questions raised by Orientalism, then, are as follows: What other sorts of intellectual, aesthetic, scholarly, and cultural energies went into the making of an imperialist tradition like the Orientalist one? How did philology, lexicography, history, biology, political and economic theory, novel-writing, and lyric poetry come to the service of Orientalism's broadly imperialist view of the world? (15)

Until relatively recently, the examination of aesthetic or imaginative texts has been confined to narrative prose and lyric poetry.[1] The relationship between theater and colonialist or imperialist enterprise began to receive serious attention only in the 1990s, with the publication of two major anthologies on the subject.[2] Any omission of theater from studies on colonialist discourse would, in fact, be a critical one given the status of theater as the dominant visual mass medium of the late eighteenth to mid-nineteenth centuries. In its quality as an institutional activity closely regulated by centralized official censorship until 1906, theater offers a highly visible illustration of the ties that exist between public discourses and the political and socioeconomic institutions that enable those discourses. As a manifestly commercial activity dependent on wide public appeal, the theater presents a valuable record of "the statements proliferating out of Orientalism into the general culture" (Said 15) and a vivid demonstration of the imaginary functions fulfilled by cultural exoticism.

In undertaking a study of Orientalism and nineteenth-century theater, one cannot automatically adopt the methodology, categorizations, and time frame applied to prose forms and their governing institutions. The extensive social, political, and artistic machinery involved in bringing a production to the stage and the vast scale of collective reception require a separate consideration of the textual and extratextual structures and practices, constraints, and expectations that control the production of meaning and affect. Chief among the factors that set theater apart from other forms considered for their participation in overseas engagement and expansion is the unique status of nineteenth-century theater as a source at once of entertainment and information, with neither term corresponding perfectly to twentieth-century concepts of these classifications. Even over the course of the nineteenth century, these designations, along with those of fiction and reality, were characterized by a fluidity and an evolution dependent as much on political climate and audience composition as on generic development.

The richness and variety of nineteenth-century theatrical activity made several initial choices necessary. First, I had to decide whether to consider the state-subsidized Grands Théâtres or the independent theaters of the boulevards. Here, boulevard theater, with the broad social base supporting these organizations and the sensitivity to public mood and demand dictated by the commercial interests of these theaters, clearly promised the more revealing terrain. The boulevard theaters, moreover, were the site of major scenic innovations in the first half of the nineteenth century, particularly in the realm of the *pièces à grand spectacle* that most often featured exotic subject matter.

On the boulevards, the Orient served as a common theme for several types of plays: melodramas, dramas, vaudevilles, comedies, *féeries*, military tableaux and plays, *pantomimes dialogués*, and still other genres. Of these I

decided for several reasons to consider only the dramatic plays, broadly defined to include all those works that relied primarily on plot, character, and
prose dialogue to engage the audience or to generate "de l'intérêt," to use
the terminology of the period. While these were not the only plays to carry
topical treatments of the Orient—vaudevilles, for instance, provide some
of the most pointed and telling commentaries on political and military
events of the day—it is this body of work that reflects a clear transformation of form and content in response to changing overseas developments.

The often violent instability of the sociopolitical order in nineteenth-
century France and the heterogeneous nature of the theater of this period
call for a methodological approach that recognizes the complex interplay
of social, political, and cultural interests at the same time that it takes
into account the functioning and effects of institutional structures and
conventions of representation. These issues are addressed to varying degrees by almost all scholars currently working in what can broadly be
described as the field of cultural studies, whether they align themselves
most closely with Foucauldian, Marxist, New Historicist, or cultural ma-
terialist approaches. These approaches, however, were initially intended to
deal with verbal discourses and only later were expanded to include the
analysis of visual images—both of which endure in some material form.
Consequently, not all features of these models are ideally suited to accommodate a cultural form such as theater, the most essential part of which—
the actual performance—is ephemeral. Whereas all cultural critics dealing with the past must engage in the reconstruction of the conditions of
production and reception and posit contemporary interpretations, theater
scholars must first attempt to piece together the object that constitutes the
core of their analysis. The specific nature of theatrical production also requires that a problem peculiar to theater—the relationship of the text and
the performance—be taken into account. The most effective treatment of
these problems involves the articulation and synthesis of theories developed by literary and sociocultural critics with those developed by theater
and film semioticians, whose primary concern it is to understand dramatic
forms as systems of communication. The goal was to devise a composite
approach that would (1) view the material conditions of production and
reception as inseparable from representational strategies; (2) understand
production and reception as being equally engaged in the process of signification; (3) analyze cultural activity in terms of various relationships of
power; and (4) be designed to respect the need for both historical and
theatrical specificity. Always it must be understood that the text, images,

sounds, and gestures themselves are held to be meaningless and of neutral value outside a given cultural and historical context.

Beginning at the most fundamental level, this investigation of Orientalism in nineteenth-century French boulevard theater is grounded in a concept of culture that stresses the idea that cultural activity is not localized in a particular area of practice or production. Rather, it is considered inseparable from economic, social, and political conditions and relations. The relationship of the cultural to these other domains, moreover, is not conceived of as one of reflection or dependence. All areas of human activity are understood to be similarly aligned and organized by the tensions—not necessarily socioeconomic in nature—between antagonistic groups or interests. This is in essence the argument developed by Pierre Bourdieu during the 1970s and most thoroughly explicated in his *La Distinction: Critique social du jugement* (1979) and *Le Sens pratique* (1980).

According to Bourdieu, societies are organized into various fields—political, educational, scientific, economic, theatrical, medical, literary, and so forth. Each field has a certain autonomy, operates in its own structured space(s), and functions according to its own principles or laws. All fields in a given society make manifest the relations of power that characterize the social order as a whole. At any given moment each field offers a set of positions, the number and arrangement of which are open to continual modification, to be occupied by members of the society. Individuals are not envisioned as completely passive social subjects, as many structuralist and poststructuralist theories imply, but instead have the option of exercising a degree of agency to compete for control of the interests and resources particular to each field. These acts of agency, however, are understood to be contained by socially constituted mental structures or dispositions that operate in conjunction with the rules governing the field itself. Building on Erwin Panofsky's notion of *habitus*—which can be summarized as "the mental habit, the group of unconscious schemas, of internalized principles that give unity to an epoch's way of thinking" (Chartier, "Intellectual History" 20)—Bourdieu writes:

The conditionings associated with a particular class of conditions of existence produce *habitus*, systems of durable, transposable dispositions, structured structures predisposed to function as structuring structures, that is, as principles which generate and organize practices and representations that can be objectively adapted to their outcomes without presupposing a conscious aiming at ends or an express mastery of the operations necessary in order to attain them. Objectively "regulated" and "regular" without being in any way the product of obedience to rules, they can be collectively orchestrated without being the product of the organizing action of a conductor. (*Logic* 53)

According to Bourdieu's *théorie de la pratique*, practices themselves become the primary carriers of ideologies. Ideological systems are no longer seen only as the abstracted reflections or the intellectual continuations of social conflicts. Instead of being viewed exclusively as disembodied principles and beliefs that can only be verbally expressed, established ideologies are understood to be realized and transmitted most effectively through institutional structures and practices. Belonging to a particular social category is not seen to be solely or even primarily a matter of sharing the same professed beliefs, but more deeply of applying the same *logic* to various situations and relationships. These logics put into play the mental and sensorial schemas of perception and appreciation generated by an individual's experiences with various institutions and practices. They are sometimes shared by the society as a whole and sometimes confined to a specific group.

While certain aspects of Bourdieu's theories have been found to be problematic,[3] one of the most attractive aspects of this model for the present study is that it places theatrical institutions on par with legislative bodies or industrial complexes. At the same time, the model's blurring of the boundaries between individual and collective social behavior prepares the way for understanding the relationship between the individual spectator and the collective audience. Furthermore, the model's emphasis on the nonverbal and nonintellectual transmission of ideologies creates a hospitable environment for acknowledging all areas of theatrical production and performance—the nonverbal as well as the verbal—as potentially significant producers of meaning. This perspective makes impossible a dismissive attitude toward forms of theater and drama where the authors are not preoccupied with the literary qualities of their work and have as their primary aim the successful reproduction of a generic product rather than the creation of a (more or less) unique play.[4] The habitual and the commonplace, in whatever social or cultural context, become prime shapers of subjectivity.

Theories of practice are rendered even more receptive to interfacing with theories of theatrical communication in the revised versions of Bourdieu's model developed by Michel de Certeau. De Certeau took exception to the primarily unconscious nature of social behavior and relationships assumed by Bourdieu's notion of habitus. He objected to the fact that in

Bourdieu's scheme of things "there is no choice among several possibilities, and thus no 'strategic intention'; there is no introduction of correctives due to better information, and thus not 'the slightest calculation'; there is no prediction, but only an 'assumed world' as the repetition of the past" (56). In a move significant for this study of Orientalism (since Foucault's notion of discourse is central to Said's definition of Orientalism), de Certeau's critique of Bourdieu in *L'Invention du quotidien* (*The Practice of Everyday Life*) is paired with a critique of Foucault. Basing his comments primarily on *Surveiller et punir*, de Certeau points out that Foucault's models of institutions, discursive practices, and technologies inevitably privilege *les appareils producteurs*, the productive apparatuses that exercise power. While having no quarrel with many, perhaps most, of Foucault's conclusions, de Certeau points out:

If it is true that the grid of "discipline" is everywhere becoming clearer and more extensive, it is all the more urgent to discover how an entire society resists being reduced to it, what popular procedures (also "miniscule" and quotidian) manipulate the mechanisms of discipline and conform to them only in order to evade them, and finally, what "ways of operating" form the counterpart, on the consumer's (or "dominee's"?) side, of the mute processes that organize the establishment of socioeconomic order. (xiv)

In order to reveal "the clandestine forms taken by the dispersed, tactical and makeshift creativity of groups or individuals already caught in the nets of 'discipline'" (xiv–xv), de Certeau shifts the focus of investigation. Instead of knowledge, habitus, rules, strategies, apparatuses or institutions, it is the *uses* actually made of these and other cultural representations by various social groups—and not only those who control their production and regulation—that are to be examined:

The presence and circulation of a representation (taught by preachers, educators and popularizers as the key to socioeconomic advancement) tells us nothing about what it is for its users. We must first analyze its manipulation by users who are not its makers. Only then can we gauge the difference or similarity between the production of the image and the secondary production hidden in the processes of its utilization. (xiii)

De Certeau characterizes this daily engagement as the opposition of "strategies" of production and "tactics" of consumption. In the study of nineteenth-century theater, these distinctions become highly pertinent, considering the surveillance exercised over public theaters by the bureau of censorship, and will be discussed in detail in Chapter 3.

Besides breaking down the central dichotomy between creation and production on the one hand and consumption and reception on the other, the redirection of investigative focus onto practices and usages entails the questioning of other fundamental definitions and divisions formerly used to structure the field of cultural activity. One that is particularly pertinent to the present project concerns the definition of "popular culture" in a specifically French context. Traditionally, a clear distinction has been posed between popular forms of culture (*culture populaire*) and behavior on the one hand and elite or learned forms (*culture savant*) on the other.[5] These distinctions inevitably were seen to correspond to class divisions. Detailed examinations of specific cultural materials, however, have exposed the shortcomings of the classic notion of popular culture as a theoretical and working concept. In his study on *The Cultural Uses of Print in Early Modern France*, sociocultural historian Roger Chartier isolates three basic presuppositions of this traditional categorization which must be called into question:

[F]irst, that it is possible to establish exclusive relationships between specific cultural forms and particular social groups; second, that the various cultures existing in a given society are sufficiently pure, homogeneous, and distinct to permit them to be characterized uniformly and unequivocally; and third, that the category "the people" or "the popular" has sufficient coherence and stability to define a distinct social identity that can be used to organize cultural differences in past ages according to the simple opposition of *populaire* versus *savant*. (3)

Instead of these neat divisions and hierarchical correspondences, Chartier uncovered "evidence of fluid circulation, practices shared by various groups, and blurred distinctions," whether genres, objects, motifs, or ideas were being considered (3). His findings bear out the premises of de Certeau's model of cultural dynamics, attesting to "intricate cultural mixtures of discipline and invention, reutilizations and innovations, models imposed (by the state, the church, or the market), and freedoms preserved" (4). Where marked divergences in practices were apparent, they were as likely to be founded upon membership in sexual, territorial, or religious groups as upon socioeconomic or socioprofessional position. In the realm of theatrical activity, recent studies such as Robert M. Isherwood's book on popular entertainment in eighteenth-century Paris, *Farce and Fantasy* (1986), have similarly overturned claims that theatrical diversions—whether performed in the streets or indoors—were organized along fairly strict class lines. To operate, then, from the outset with the classic assumptions regarding "popular" texts, beliefs, modes of conduct, and so forth would be to assume the validity of divisions that, in fact, have yet to be established for any given object of study. Chartier concludes: "When, on the one hand, the concept of popular culture obliterates the bases shared by the whole of society and when, on the other, it masks the plurality of cleavages that differentiate cultural practices, it cannot be held as pertinent to a comprehension of the forms and materials that characterize the cultural universe of societies in the modern period" (5).

The call for a reconfigured notion of popular culture and with it that of the "public"—be it one of readers or spectators—has produced a new conception that has proved increasingly useful as societies have become more and more heterogeneous. As described by Jean-Marie Goulemot, the moment of reading or viewing is one in which a work is submitted to "a confrontation with a body, a time, and an acquired culture" (98). This "acquired culture" of the reader or spectator is of a dual nature: it consists of (1) mental and sensorial schemas that are internalized as the result of various group affiliations (Bourdieu's habitus in essence) and then organized into "a cultural narrative," and (2) particular competencies and memories associated with a given cultural practice. In the case of readers, the cultural competencies consist of their memories of previous readings and factors such as the genre of the book, its place of publication, critical reviews, scholarly knowledge, and so forth. These acquired competencies and memories are called into play in given instances of reading or viewing. The specificity of each situation—in which the reader participates as a physical as well as an intellectual subject—underlies each transaction as it occurs. While Goulemot emphasizes the active role of reception, he leaves room for the guidelines instituted during the processes of writing and publishing. The reader is positioned not only by qualities of the narrative, but by structural features of the text and of the printed object as well. These features, which may be introduced by either the author or the editor, include the book format; typography (e.g., capitalization, italics, or underlining); length of chapters or paragraphs; titles and subtitles; illustrations (the strategic placement of which applies different forms of anchoring); and prefaces and introductions. He concludes his survey of "reading as the production of meaning" by noting that "it is also true that the book commands a positioning of the reader it interpellates," and stipulates that it is on the basis of this positioning of the reader that the production of meaning is organized.

In many respects, this emphasis on the physiological and material aspects of the process of reception has had less of a transformative impact on theater studies than on literary studies. Due to the public prominence of the encounter between spectator and performance (as opposed to the predominantly private nature of the act of reading, at least since the nineteenth century), theater critics have long since made consideration of the physical or material an integral part of their analyses. Another of Goulemot's characterizations of the reader is even more compatible with concepts of the spectator developed primarily by theater semioticians. His statement noting that "[t]he reader, in relation to the text, is defined by a physiology, a history, and a library" (91) is one that can very easily be revised to read "[t]he spectator, in relation to the performance, is defined by a physiology, a history, and a repertory." For Goulemot, "Everything can be included under the term history, if one gives it successively a physiological, affective, cultural, or political content." Theater practitioners, critics, and theoreticians have, of necessity, been attentive to physiological and affective aspects of performance since spaces were first designated specifically for dramatic productions.

The most congenial meeting ground for the concepts of sociocultural historians and those of theoreticans of theater is provided by the work of theater semioticians who, following developments in literary semiotics and textual linguistics, have adopted a pragmatic rather than a structuralist approach. Among these scholars, Anne Ubersfeld and Marco De Marinis have developed the most comprehensive models. The compatibility of these models with those described above, and, indeed, some of their common origins, are immediately evident in De Marinis's description of what he calls "the coordinates of a pragmatic approach":

In order to shift from the taxonomic approach characteristic of structuralism to a pragmatic one . . . textual analysis must break (provisionally) into two parts: *co-textual* and *contextual*:

(1) Co-textual analysis is concerned with the "internal" regularities of the performance text, with its material and formal properties . . . and its levels of structure (codes, textual structures).

(2) Contextual analysis deals with the "external" aspects of the performance text, which can, in turn be broken down into (a) *the cultural context*, or the relationship that can be discerned between the text in question . . . and other texts, whether performances or not, belonging of the same cultural synchrony; (b) *the context of performance*, by which is meant all the practical situations in which the performance text occurs, as well as the circumstances of its enunciation and reception, including the various phases of its coming into being (rehearsals and the like), and all other theatrical activities which encompass and produce the moment of performance. (3–4)

Like Goulemot, Ubersfeld and De Marinis place final control over the production of meaning in the hands of the spectator and connect this control to the acquired competency of the spectator as a theatergoer. Ubersfeld points out in fact that the intervention of the spectator occurs at not one but two critical moments: the moment of production as well as that of reception.

The spectator is coproducer of the performance at two critical moments: at the start and at the finish. One could say that it is not *the same* spectator at the start and at the finish, during the planning and at the moment of reception. And the gap separating spectator A who was foreseen by the transmitters and spectator B who actually attends the performance is a measure of the unpredictability of reception. In the beginning, the spectator is present in the spectacle to the extent that the various *énonciateurs* (writer, director, designer, actor) take into account the referential universe of the spectator, or rather his universe*s*: that of his experience as well as that of his culture. (*Ecole* 304)

Acknowledging the distinction between the spectators envisioned by the producers of a theatrical work and the ones who actually attend forestalls abstract speculation as to the reception of a work—speculation that in the past has all too often been based on the producers' self-interested accounts of the intended public. This distinction is of particular significance in the case of nineteenth-century French theater—as we shall see. It was in fact this "unpredictability of reception" ("l'aléa de la réception") that the censors sought to minimize if not completely eliminate. By joining sociocultural historians in designating both lived experience and culturally acquired perceptions and competencies of the spectator as coequal determinants of reception, Ubersfeld lays the groundwork for understanding representations of the Orient through the interaction of changing historical and generic contexts.

Ubersfeld uses the analogy of a contract to describe the links between practitioners and audience that guarantee the very possibility of performance. In stressing the joint participation of theatrical producers and consumers, both more or less experienced, at all levels and stages of creation, she parallels de Certeau's and Chartier's rejection of a unidirectional model of influence and control: "The very fact of the performance assumes a previous *agreement*, a sort of past *contract* between the practitioners and the spectators, a contract that not only specifies the very fact of the performance, with its socioeconomic conditions, but the mode of representation, and the code of perception of the spectacle (in general in the form of the unsaid)." As the case of the formalization of the national or military tableaux, pantomimes, melodramas, and dramas will demonstrate, the construction of this contract for any given genre and any modification of its terms had to be a gradual process of joint negotiation, at least as far as mode of representation and code of reception were concerned. As the same case shows, with the razing of the Boulevard du Temple in 1862 and the subsequent banning of military spectacle in the rebuilt theater district, the socioeconomic conditions of representation could nevertheless be drastically altered through political control of the physical spaces of performance.

While several complex and illuminating models of theater as a system of communication have been proposed—the work of Erika Fischer-Lichte and Patrice Pavis comes to mind in addition to that of Ubersfeld and De Marinis—these models have been least concerned with performance situations where generic conventions and commercial interests are the most powerful structuring elements. Instead, as De Marinis acknowledges, it has been film theoreticians who have dominated in this area. This seems quite understandable when one considers that, in the late twentieth century, film scholars have a far greater investment in understanding popular genres than do theater theoreticians. Since the late nineteenth and early twentieth centuries, the authority and vision of the director and the quest for a unique interpretation of the text have taken precedence over generic prescriptions as the central force in shaping a theatrical production. At the same time, of course, cinema has replaced live theater as the dominant medium for presenting popular dramatic genres—almost all of which were developed in nineteenth-century theaters—to large general audiences. By and large, the most detailed investigations of generic forms have therefore been conducted by film rather than theater semioticians.

The work of Roger Odin is particularly valuable in providing useful concepts for reconstituting the cultural contexts and competencies associated with nineteenth-century theater. Particularly pertinent are his discussions of institutions and the mode of entry of the spectator into the fiction of the representation. Odin defines the institution as "a structure articulating a cluster of determinations" ("Pour une sémio-pragmatique" 71). Institutional determinations, as opposed to those which derive from the cultural space in its entirety, are confined to the theatrical or cinematographic field. In film the main institutions include the fictional film, experimental cinema, silent movies, the documentary, industrial and educational films, and home movies. While exact parallels cannot be drawn for eighteenth- and nineteenth-century French theater, comparable divisions would include the tragedies, comedies, and dramas of the Comédie-Française and Odéon; the grand operas of the Opéra; the melodramas, comedies, and vaudevilles of secondary boulevard theaters; equestrian dramas and spectacles; fairground shows; the entertainment of the cafés-concerts; and the revolutionary festivals. It is the designation of the institution as the fundamental unit of analysis and the concomitant emphasis on specificity and context that place semio-pragmatic approaches in a parallel relation to the most recent methodologies of cultural history. The strong affinities between the premises of semio-pragmatics and those of sociocultural history are readily apparent in the following statements:

[O]nly the act of communication considered in its own institutional framework can be considered as the basic unit of semiology. . . . [C]inema as a homogeneous and unique institution does not exist; only cinemas dependent on different institutions exist. . . .

The consequence of this splitting of the cinematographic institution is as follows: if it is the institution that gives, as we have claimed, meaning to the internal figures of the filmic text . . . then it is illusive to attempt to construct *the* grammar of *the* cinema. Each of the cinemas (institutionally defined) having its specific signifying functioning, it is appropriate to construct the grammar of *a* type, of *a* cinematographic genre. ("Rhétorique" 368–69)

The very presence of the spectator in the theater poses three critical questions dealing with that individual's identity as a spectator. In all of the following statements the word "theater" or "play" can readily be substituted for "movies," "film," or "cinema." Drawing on Christian Metz, Odin notes that the first question to be asked concerns the decision to attend the movies at all: "It is essential . . . to find out what, 'in a social system where the spectator is not physically forced to go to the movies,' can indeed induce an individual to do such a thing. . . . The problem posed is, we can see, that of the construction of the entity 'film spectator' " ("L'Entrée" 6). Borrowing from Metz again, Odin confirms that this entity is the product of economic, financial, sociological, and psychic mechanisms. This granted, the second question that arises concerns the choice of film or play to see. Most important in Odin's commentary on this point are his observations regarding the "apparatuses" that guide this choice:

[T]he "choice" of a film is always less free than we would like to think. First of all, what criteria does one use to "choose" a film? For, obviously, one always "chooses" a film without having seen it. Here again, very definitely, "apparatuses" exist that must be analyzed: cinematographic publicity, criticism, the distribution arrangements, the geographical location of the theaters (for it is often the movie theater that determines the "choice" of a film). ("L'Entrée" 199)

This last point is particularly relevant for nineteenth-century theater, where licensing practices restricted the genres that could be included in a given theater's repertory. This practice created theatergoers who were habitués of favorite theaters. Spectators would adopt a specific *régime de conscience* (order of consciousness) appropriate to the theater and genre selected. In stressing the importance of genre in installing the *régime de conscience* and more, De Marinis cites E. D. Hirsch: "A generic conception is not simply a tool that can be discarded once understanding is attained . . . because understanding itself is genre-bound. The generic conception serves both a heuristic and a constitutive function" (qtd. in De Marinis 178).

Institution and genre cooperate in indicating to the spectator, who is assumed to possess the appropriate cultural competencies, what protocols of spectatorship to apply to the reception of a work. Although they are always supported by institutional conventions (e.g., most simply, the darkening of house lights or the playing of an overture), individual works must bear the final responsibility for ensuring the entry of the spectator into the particular order of fiction or reality they are promoting. It is incumbent upon the opening scene—simultaneously employing visual, auditory, and verbal sign systems—to position an already prepared spectator in relation to a theatrical experience that can never be exactly repeated nor completely controlled. Throughout the duration of the performance the audience as a whole will continually be positioned and possibly repositioned as a result of deliberate or accidental occurrences both on the stage and in the auditorium. At this point, it might be useful to recall the insights of Michel de Certeau regarding the potential of the user, consumer, and—in this case—spectator to circumvent convention through tactical manipulations and in the process alter institutional practices, perhaps permanently. For example, as we shall see, the renegotiation of acceptable limits of repositioning as they related to the mixing of genres (e.g., by asking the audience to shift between tragic and comic modes of reception during a single performance) or to the interjection of contemporary political commentary into a fictional universe were vital matters in nineteenth-century popular theater.

Sources and Structure

Any effort to reconstruct nineteenth-century theater as a cultural institution and to replace the representations of the Middle East and North Africa in their original context must of course rely on a variety of documentary sources. Those I have consulted include contemporary theatrical treatises and dictionaries, critical reviews from daily newspapers and specialized theatrical journals, censors' reports and censored manuscripts, police reports on disturbances in the theaters, reports of the *comités de lecture* of boulevard theaters, annotated prompter's copies of plays, costume and set illustrations, personal memoirs, and theater histories and biographies written during the nineteenth century. These sources furnish more or less detailed descriptions of actual or ideal performances, present perspectives on particular aspects of theatrical activity, and illustrate various phases in the processes of production and reception. While many sources may seem to be more useful in reconstituting the performance as a produced as opposed to a received object or text, it should be kept in mind that the two processes of production and reception are always articulated one on the other and so are never entirely independent. Evidence regarding the production of a play is therefore often (although certainly not always) evidence regarding its reception. Whatever the source being interrogated, it was with the awareness that information gathered from such historical sources can never be analyzed apart from the conditions of their own production. Whether the document in question is a censorship report, a critical review, a personal memoir, or a theatrical treatise, special interests or constraints were involved in its production—interests and constraints that selected and shaded the information being transmitted. In short, the documents being consulted to contextualize the plays were in themselves texts that needed to be similarly contextualized. Accordingly, in the third and sixth chapters, I have first given necessarily abbreviated accounts of the adjacent institutions of the Bureau of Censorship and the journalistic press, including the positionings of the censors and critics as social subjects, before going into my readings of the censorship reports and the critical reviews.

The two parts of the book—the first on historical melodrama and the second on military or national drama—are not perfectly symmetrical. Each genre raises its own set of issues, which are to a certain degree defined by the sources themselves as well as by the institutions and usages attached to each form. Both parts begin with an overview of institutional history. Chapters 2 and 7 take close looks at allied textual forms, eighteenth-century classical tragedy and nineteenth-century journalistic accounts of Middle Eastern and North African campaigns, which participated in particularly close intertextual exchanges with historical melodrama and national drama, respectively. Chapters 3 and 6 deal with issues that the archival sources indicate were critical to understanding the process of representation and mode of reception applied to the Orient. For melodrama, the problem to be explored was the exotic as a historically and institutionally specific notion. In the case of national drama, the pertinent question was the process of fictionalization and narrativization, the transformation of actuality into drama.

Finally, I singled out two works for close analysis. They were chosen from among the plays that were the most enthusiastically acclaimed, had unusually long initial runs, and were subsequently revived with great success. One was chosen from among those plays that were entirely imaginary in subject matter or based on incidents drawn from ancient history. The other is representative of those works that used events that had occurred within the living memory of many if not all of the spectators as the primary subject matter or as a background for a fictional narrative. Guilbert de Pixerécourt's *Les Ruines de Babylone* (1810) and Victor Séjour's *Les Massacres de Syrie* (1860) represent the fullest and most successful realizations of their respective genres. They also reveal a surprising range of modalities and features of representation of the Orient. Even as they resist reduction, these works provide an account of the functioning of the dramatic theater of the boulevards in the context of domestic and overseas relations. The fifty years separating the writing and staging of these pieces mark the time span during which there matured an Orient whose appeal to theater audiences no longer relied on its attractions as an imaginary realm but on its qualities as a representation of actuality.

Note on Translations

In general, to accommodate the largest number of readers, I have quoted all material in English translation in the main body of the text. The original French version of primary sources is included in the endnotes. If the original text was composed in verse, however, the passage will be cited in French and the translation supplied in the notes. All translations are my own unless otherwise indicated.

PART I

DOMESTIC EXOTICISM

It was at Sceaux, in a charming house, gleaming white, amid the greenery of the grounds; noble refuge of friendship, elegant temple of the arts. The master of the place liked to withdraw here from the cares of public affairs among a circle of intimate friends . . . ; the chatelaine came here from the Empress's court to hold her own court of friends; . . .

That day, Madame the Countess Duchâtel did not play any music. . . . Instead she led us into the second salon, and asked you for *Les Ruines de Babylone*, smiling as the manuscript fell open of its own accord. The guests took their places on large ottomans; the master and mistress of the house had at their feet, on silk cushions, their young children. . . . From scene to scene, from act to act, the interest poured forth and grew among the assembled listeners, just as it did in your work. . . . I doubt that the three hundred performances of *Les Ruines de Babylone* in Paris and the reports of its successes in the provinces and on all foreign stages could, for you, have matched this first triumph, this elite matinée.

—Letter from Emile Deschamps to
Guilbert de Pixerécourt, May 4, 1841 [1]

The charming and elegant scene described in this passage would seem to be far removed from the boisterous and turbulent environment generally associated with the popular theaters of nineteenth-century Paris. The commercial theaters then concentrated along the Boulevard du Temple have often been represented as providers of entertainment for the working-class populace, who in turn have typically been portrayed as rowdy and credulous consumers. It has frequently been assumed that when the middle- or upper-class bourgeois or even aristocrats attended these theaters their excursions were undertaken as a form of "slumming" rather than out of any appreciation for the fare being offered. The first critics to propagate this view were contemporaries of Pixerécourt, and their opinions have subsequently been repeatedly cited to support models of popular theatrical genres as simplistic forms appropriate only for unsophisticated audiences. But Deschamps's recollections challenge this conception by showing that the enjoyment of melodrama had become an integral part of upper-class cultural practices and patterns of sociability by 1810. Discounted at the same time are assumptions that the extraordinary appeal of melodrama is to be accounted for in terms of modes of experience and susceptibilities unique to the lower classes of society. Clearly, the trials and tribulations of the Asiatic heroes and heroines of *Les Ruines de Babylone* were a source of fascination for a very broad audience.

Historians and theorists of popular theater in general and of melodrama in particular have been steadily removing the derogatory or pejorative aspects of the terms "popular" and "melodramatic" since the 1960s. Studies on melodrama by Eric Bentley, James Rosenberg, Robert Heilman, and James Smith were the first to seriously consider the source of melodrama's enduring appeal across national boundaries and over several centuries. Peter Brooks's *The Melodramatic Imagination* broke with the ahistorical perspectives of these scholars and defined melodrama as a genre particular to a secular age. Michael Booth, David Grimsted, Bruce McConachie, and Jeffrey Mason have placed English and American melodramatic forms and the theatrical organizations that presented them in the context of prevailing social values and contemporary crises. French scholars including Jean-Marie Thomasseau and Julia Przybos have employed structuralist and poststructuralist theories in their analyses of melodrama. Christine Gledhill, E. Ann Kaplan, and others have brought together insights from the fields of cinema and women's studies to shed light on questions of gender and melodrama in the nineteenth century as well as in the twentieth. The extent of scholarly interest in melodrama in the 1970s and 1980s was reflected in several special issues of journals devoted to the topic.[2]

French boulevard theater itself was the subject of a spate of studies published around the first decade of the twentieth century, with works by Maurice Albert, Henri Beaulieu, Georges Cain, and Louis-Henry Lecomte appearing in quick succession. While several specialized studies—for instance, on theater and the French Revolution, on provincial theaters, and on particular aspects of production—would be produced over the subsequent decades, new comprehensive treatments of popular theater in Paris would not appear until the 1970s when Marvin Carlson's book on the French stage of the nineteenth century was published. Full revitalization of the field would occur in the 1980s with critical attention being focused first on eighteenth-century popular performance. Major works by Robert Isherwood, Michele Root-Bernstein, and Martine de Rougemont appeared at roughly two-year intervals. Finally, in the early 1990s, nineteenth-century popular theater received fresh consideration as a sociopolitical institution and industry in outstanding studies by F. W. J. Hemmings and John McCormick.

Some of the most creative work on popular theater and melodrama has emerged from a number of conferences organized around popular culture in theater, film, and television. The first of these, on "Performance and Politics in Popular Drama," took place at the University of Kent in 1977 and was the broadest in scope, considering "Aspects of Popular Entertainment in Theatre, Film, and Television 1800–1976," to quote the subtitle of the collection of published papers. The 1990 "Themes in Drama" conference held in Riverside, California, chose melodrama as its focus, and a 1992 international conference held in London emphasized interdisciplinary approaches to the study of melodrama. This last event—entitled "Melodrama: Stage Picture Screen"—in particular confirmed the transformation of melodrama's status from a lowly form of mass entertainment to a complex cultural phenomenon.

In this resurgence of interest, questions of race, ethnicity, and relations between Western and non-Western societies have received varying degrees of attention, depending largely on the national tradition being considered. As would be expected given U.S. history, such issues have been most consistently treated in studies of American melodrama and popular theater. In addition to discussions in the three full-length studies on American melodrama already mentioned, a number of articles have been published on African and Native Americans in nineteenth-century American theater, with many of these focusing on *Uncle Tom's Cabin*, *Metamora*, various plays about Pocahontas, or *The Octoroon*.[3] Whereas the focus in American cultural studies has been on internal interracial relations, scholars looking at nineteenth-century British theater understandably have been primarily concerned with racial tensions connected with imperialist and colonialist enterprises. In *Acts of Supremacy: The British Empire and the Stage, 1790–1930*, several essays coauthored by J. S. Bratton, Richard Allen Cave, Breandan Gregory, Heidi J. Holder, and Michael Pickering analyze the impact of nationalism and imperialism on theatrical representations. In France, the interest generated by work on colonialist discourses has provided an impetus for studies on twentieth-century postcolonial theater and film rather than for reexaminations of the stage of the previous century. When cultural and racial differences in nineteenth-century French theater have been discussed, they have been treated for the most part in terms of a purely aesthetic or thematic exoticism. Connections between the building of an overseas empire and theatrical representations have been considered only in relation to Napoleon's career. The staging of the exotic in nineteenth-century France has yet to be considered as a sociopolitical act.[4]

I

Nineteenth-Century
Popular Theater

Institutions and Practices

> How vast is the domain of melodrama! To say nothing of the resources
> offered by foreign theaters or of the lode a hundred times richer that
> authors who have dedicated their pens to the writing of melodramas find
> in their imagination, melodrama exploits in turn the history of all times
> and of all countries, and the tales consecrated by various mythologies.
> (*Le Journal de Paris*, no. 6, January 6, 1814) [1]

Boulevard Theaters

The proper place to begin an investigation of the intersections of history,
theater, and exoticism is with an overview of the theatrical institutions
and genres that were the prime generators of representations of the Orient. Theatrical activity first moved from the Saint Germain, Saint Laurent,
and Saint Ovide fairgrounds to the Boulevard du Temple on what was
then the northern edge of Paris in the late 1750s and the 1760s. Here the
fairground troupes, most notably those led by Nicolas-Médard Audinot
and Jean-Baptiste Nicolet, were able to move into more or less permanent
structures situated amid a wide variety of street performers, carnival sideshows, puppet shows, cafés, gambling dens, and brothels. At their new
location on the Boulevard du Temple, these theaters shared in the general
popularity of the entertainment offered to a very diverse public. In Robert
Isherwood's words,

[T]he boulevards cracked the social stratification separating the highborn and low-
born. In the streets, cafés, and *petits spectacles*, all the ranks mingled openly and

freely. Certainly, it was not an equality of wealth, occupation, or education; but it was one of pleasure, of taste. The culture of the people's marketplace—the streets—engulfed nearly the whole city by 1780. . . . The taste of *le bas peuple* spread through the ranks of *le monde*, creating one society and one culture, a counterculture to the officially sanctioned world of court and city. (216)

At the insistence of the state-subsidized Grands Théâtres—the Comédie-Française, the Comédie-Italienne and the Opéra—restrictions were imposed to curb the competition offered by these aggressive new entrepreneurs: the minor or *petits théâtres* were prevented from presenting fully dialogued plays and had to compensate the Opéra for using musicians, singers, or dancers in their productions.

The French Revolution of 1789 brought an end to the licensing system of the ancien régime which restricted the number of theaters that could operate in Paris as well as regulated the type of performances that could be offered at each. On January 19, 1791, the National Assembly issued a decree declaring that any citizen had the right to establish a public theater and to present works of any genre as long as the municipal authorities were notified in advance. The same decree placed supervision of the public theaters in the hands of city officials, who were restrained in their powers to shut down any theater or to prohibit the performance of any given play. During this phase of freedom, dozens of new theaters opened, although most closed fairly quickly. Some regulation of the theaters was reinstituted under the Directory, but there was no immediate return to the restrictive conditions that preceded the Revolution.

In 1807 Napoleon set about restructuring the national theater system. By that time the number of theaters in the capital had already declined to seventeen. Napoleon's decree reduced that number to eight: four nationally subsidized theaters and four secondary ones. The four official theaters (and the type of performances they were authorized to present) were the Comédie-Française or Théâtre de l'Empereur (tragedy and comedy), the Odéon or Théâtre de l'Impératrice (lesser forms of drama including many of the plays from the old Comédie-Italienne repertory), the Opéra (grand opera and ballet), and the Opéra-Comique (light opera and comic ballet). The four secondary theaters that were allowed to continue operations were the Théâtre de l'Ambigu-Comique (founded by Audinot), the Théâtre de la Gaîté (Nicolet's theater), the Théâtre du Vaudeville, and the Théâtre des Variétés. Of these, the Ambigu-Comique and the Gaîté were authorized to perform melodramas, pantomimes, and *féeries*, while the Vaudeville and the Variétés could offer shorter plays (notably the *genre poissard*,

VUE DU CIRQUE OLYMPIQUE DE M.M. FRANCONI :
avec plusieurs Scènes du Tailleur.

Figure 1. Performance of *Le Tailleur anglais* at the first Cirque Olympique (1815–1816). Engraving from Mme. B***, *Les Animaux savants*. By permission of the Houghton Library, Harvard University.

which drew on the lives of the working-class populace for its material), parodies, and musical entertainments known as vaudevilles or *comédies-en-vaudeville*. One of the theaters that had been closed by the 1807 decree was the Théâtre de la Porte-Saint-Martin, which had staged melodramas and ballet-pantomimes since 1802. After petitioning for two years, the theater finally received permission to reopen in 1810 as the Théâtre des Jeux Gymniques but overstepped the limitations of its licensed repertory (historical tableaux, military spectacles, prologues, and acrobatics); it was shut down the next year. Following the restoration of the Bourbon monarchy in 1815, the theater resumed operations under its old name. Originally constructed as a temporary home for the Opéra from 1781 to 1794, the Porte-Saint-Martin, with its deep stage and a large auditorium that could seat eighteen hundred spectators, provided an ideal venue for the *pièces à grand spectacle* that flourished in the nineteenth century.

With only a few exceptions, the plays that form the focus of the present study were performed at the Ambigu-Comique, the Gaîté, the Porte-Saint-Martin, and the Cirque Olympique, descendant of the first permanent circus amphitheater in Paris. Founded by the Englishman Philip Astley in 1783, this establishment was taken over by Antonio Franconi ten years later. The company was originally licensed only to display feats of equestrian skill, but its owners sought to transgress these boundaries from the outset. By December 1807, when the troupe moved into new quarters and became known as the Cirque Olympique, it was already presenting dramatic pantomimes in which horses and other animals figured prominently (Figure 1). Nevertheless, perhaps because a large part of the repertory glorified the military accomplishments of Napoleon's Grande Armée, the site escaped classification as a secondary theater in 1807 and would remain active through 1862, when its third home was demolished along with the other theaters of the Boulevard du Temple (Figure 2). During the last twenty to thirty years of its existence, the Cirque Olympique was formally licensed to perform plays of two, three, or four acts. But long before that (by the time of the fall of the First Empire, in fact), to quote Maurice Albert, "the mimes [of the Cirque Olympique] were speaking fluently" (268).

The Restoration brought a relaxation in the regulation of the public theaters and, with it, the revival of old theaters such as the Associés and the Jeunes-Artistes, as well as the opening of new ones including the Panorama-Dramatique, the Funambules, the Théâtre-Historique, the Nouveautés, the Délassements-Comiques, and many more. The competi-

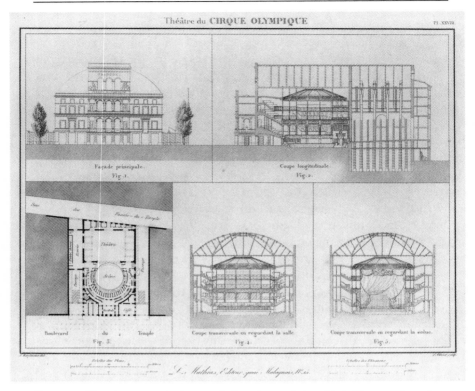

Figure 2. Façade, ground plan, and elevations of the third Cirque Olympique (1840). *Architectonographie des théâtres*, 2nd series. From the Rare Book and Special Collections Division, Library of Congress,

tion created a great demand for new works. According to statistics cited by Carlson, between 1815 and 1830 369 new comedies, 280 new melodramas, 200 new comic operas, and 1,300 new vaudevilles were performed on the stages of the Boulevard du Temple (*The French Stage* 53). This extraordinary proliferation of theatrical activity was brought to an abrupt end in 1862, when all seven of the active theaters were demolished along with neighboring buildings.

The razing of the Boulevard du Temple was part of a larger plan for restructuring the center of Paris.[2] The master plan was devised by Napoleon III with Georges Eugène Haussman, whose official title was prefect of the Seine and whose assignment it was to transform the central sectors of the city into fashionable districts. When the popular theaters had first moved to this area in the middle of the eighteenth century, the population of the city of Paris was a little over a half million. The Boulevard du Temple, then only partially paved and notoriously muddy, bordered on one of the more densely populated but poorer quarters of the city. By midcentury the population of the city had doubled, and the popular entertainment district was no longer on the outskirts but near the center of the city. In addition to making the center of the capital more attractive, the system of wide boulevards planned by Baron Haussman would eliminate many of the narrow streets that had been so easily barricaded by insurrectionists during the Revolution of 1848 and other violent uprisings. The repertories, price structures, and seating arrangements of the fine new theaters that were rebuilt on the reconfigured site courted a more prosperous audience than their predecessors had. The street entertainments and sideshows had already begun to disappear in the 1830s, and the 1862 program of urban renewal completed the process of gentrification. Furthermore, as John McCormick points out (85), the destruction of the working-class character of the neighborhoods surrounding the theaters altered the nature of the theatergoing experience for many of the proletarian spectators. No longer were they attending a community institution situated on their territory. A trip to the theater became an event separated from the everyday life of the lower-class spectator. Henceforth, the term "boulevard theater" would increasingly come to mean "bourgeois theater."

While the gradual embourgeoisement of selected theaters had been evident for some time,[3] this process had not significantly altered boulevard culture as a whole. The physical reconfiguration of the urban landscape, however, effectively erased a site of popular cultural activity. No longer conjoined under the rubric of the third estate as they had been under the ancien régime and no longer allied by an ambition to wrest power away from the aristocracy and the church, the bourgeoisie and the working classes occupied a shrinking common ground both figuratively and literally.

The increasing distance between the two groups as it related to theatrical institutions has been captured by Louis-Léopold Boilly, an artist best known for his portrayals of everyday life in Napoleonic France, in a painting exhibited at the 1819 salon. The work depicts the entrance to the Ambigu-Comique on the occasion of a free performance (Figure 3). In the artist's treatment, a bourgeois family watches a pushing, shoving proletarian crowd fighting its way through the theater entrance and knocking over a gentleman in the process.[4] The head of the family, like other members of his class pictured on the far right of the painting, regards the small mob with disapproval, even disdain. Meanwhile, his wife and children have

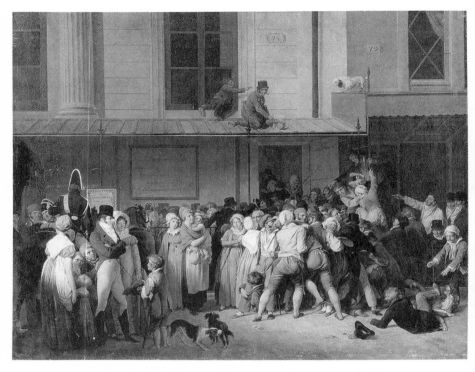

Figure 3. Louis-Léopold Boilly, *The Entrance to the Théâtre de l'Ambigu-Comique for a Free Performance* (1819). Oil on canvas, 66.5 x 80.5 cm. Museé du Louvre, Département des peintures, Paris.

drawn close to him as if for protection. A barefoot beggar boy standing before them is ignored. In 1819, the audience's separation into different seating sections within the same auditorium apparently afforded sufficient distance between members of different classes. By 1862, it would seem that this degree of separation no longer provided a comfortable buffer zone between the antagonistic groups.

Even after the radical changes of 1862, bourgeois and working-class culture could not be totally divorced one from the other. The links were too strongly forged, and not only as a result of the mixing of cultures on the boulevards. The world of the Grands Théâtres also figured in the theatrical experience of members of all classes. It has long been recognized that the vociferous parterres of the state theaters were filled with spectators who were not members of the aristocracy or the grande bourgeoisie. While the regular presence of more or less isolated members of the lower classes

in the parterres has been widely recognized, the exclusion of "le peuple"—
the common masses—as a class from this cultural field has generally been
assumed. In *The Theatre Industry in Nineteenth-Century France*, Hemmings
devotes considerable space to the free performances that were offered by
the state-subsidized theaters as well as by the secondary ones. His research
reveals a national theatrical heritage shared by representatives of all classes.
While only sporadically offered under the ancien régime to celebrate occasions such as the birth of a royal heir, "représentations de par et pour le
peuple" (performances in the name of and for the people)—were more frequent occurrences during the years of the Revolution and the Directory.
Napoleon continued this tradition to mark significant events such as his
birthday, his coronation, his marriage to Marie-Louise of Austria, and the
birth of his long-awaited son, as well as major victories and the signing of
important treaties.

One of the richest accounts of these free performances has been recorded by Etienne de Jouy in an essay dated December 4, 1813. Hemmings
surmises that the event being commemorated was the emperor's coronation. Jouy relates that the day of the would-be spectator began at dawn
when crowds gathered at the walls reserved for the posting of theater bills.
The literate would read aloud the titles of the works being performed at
various theaters for the benefit of those who did not know how to read.
Jouy notes that some of the more unfamiliar titles were rather grossly mis-
pronounced. Contrary to what this observation might suggest, however,
the crowds seeking to take advantage of the free performances were not
entirely composed of uninitiated theatergoers. As Jouy's account goes on
to note, "[A]long the embankments and at the central market . . . it is de-
lightful to listen to the arguments about the merits of each play, the actors'
talents and the preference to be given to the various types of entertainment" (qtd. in Hemmings, *Theatre Industry* 118).

The theaters that excited the most interest seem to have been those
that under ordinary circumstances were least accesssible to the general
populace, namely, the Théâtre-Français and the Opéra. It would seem that
on the day Jouy picked to record for posterity, the play being offered at the
Théâtre-Français was Voltaire's Oriental tragedy, *Zaïre*. These were Jouy's
conclusions regarding the performance he witnessed:

The audience on those days of "no charge for admission," by the very fact that it
can seldom afford to go to the theatre, brings to bear on the performance a concen-
tration of attention that nothing can disturb, a keenness of judgement that nothing
can blunt. Taken separately, not one of the individuals composing it could perhaps
have understood a single line of *Zaïre*; but this mass of men, as unenlightened the

one as the other, like a pile of damp hay that ignites spontaneously in a loft, is suddenly endowed with a warmth of sentiment and a purity of taste which permit it
to discern all the beauties of the work and to appreciate all the efforts of the actors.
(Qtd. in Hemmings 119)

The rather unflattering comparison of "le peuple" to "damp hay" and the
likening of their response to spontaneous combustion probably says more
about Jouy's biases (biases shared by many of his class) regarding the lower
classes than about what actually transpired in the auditorium. Judging by
what Jouy himself said, it seems far more likely that the audience was of
mixed composition and that many were perfectly capable of understanding
Zaïre—just as general audiences of Shakespeare's time were able to appreciate *Othello*, the work that inspired *Zaïre*.

It was undoubtedly true that the majority of those who filled the
theaters on free admission days lacked any formal literary education; but
many, perhaps even most, would have been educated as spectators by their
familiarity with the historical melodramas of boulevard theater. The same
Boilly painting mentioned above provides visual documentation of the
working-class audience's eagerness to see a historical melodrama with an
Oriental setting. As we can see from the poster outside the theater, the
play being offered to the public for free was a revival of *Les Machabées*, a
historical melodrama set in the Ancient Near East. This play earned a typically backhanded compliment from one of the critics of *Le Camp volant*
not only for its splendid, even magical, set decoration and impressive use
of stage machinery but for the dramatic qualities of the text. On March 31,
1819, "J." wrote that the play was "one of the finest examples of its genre
that has been written for a long time and perhaps the only one where the
connection between ideas corresponds to the sequence of incidents."[5]

Both the perceptions and the misapprehensions of Jouy's reading of
the free performance are echoed in another passage cited by Hemmings,
this one attributed to the great tragedian Talma:

[Y]ou should come along to one of those free admission days, you would see how
[the audience] responds to every hint, how it applauds at all the right places, how
warmly and with just the right measure. It grasps every nuance, nothing escapes it;
it is nature in the raw, if you will, but it is nature, and if the actor is truthful, the
working-class audience, which is truth personified, responds immediately. (Qtd. in
Theatre Industry 119)

His account clearly attests to a high degree of theatrical competency on the
part of the audience. At the same time, it reflects an Enlightenment and

Romantic perception of social "others"—whether they be non-Europeans, women, or members of the working class—as behaving more naturally, or being closer to nature, than the European bourgeois male. Talma, like most of the philosophers, writers, and artists who placed "le peuple" beyond the grasp of denaturalizing and deforming sociocultural processes, intended the gesture as a compliment. (As has been well documented, of course, the same arguments could and would be turned against these groups to justify their exclusion from power.)

Rather than assuming that members of different classes were subject to radically different processes of cultural formation, however, we would be more consistent if we were to credit this special audience's regard for Talma's performances to an informed appreciation of his talents, which they could compare to those of the artists they had watched in the boulevard theaters.[6] Talma, after all, was renowned for his fiery and passionate style of acting. In an assessment of the great actor's talents that was meant to be disparaging, the prominent drama critic Geoffroy spoke of "his distorted features, his wild eyes, his quivering voice, his sombre, lugubrious tone, his taut muscles, his trembling, his convulsions" (qtd. in Carlson, *The French Stage* 24). Even if the tragedies he was appearing in were composed in *alexandrins*, the highly expressive and emotive style of acting advocated by Talma abridged the distance between the performance of tragedy and melodrama. Whether on the stages of the Grands-Théâtres or those of the secondary boulevard theaters, the serious dramatic genres shared a common trajectory toward greater realism in production and greater expressivity in performance.

Another area in which there have been common misperceptions regarding nineteenth-century popular theater as a cultural apparatus has involved the relationship between print and oral cultures.[7] While the recent concern of theater critics and theoreticians has been, very rightly, to emphasize that the staged performance is not merely the extension, translation, or illustration of the literary text, it should also be realized that in the nineteenth century there was a great demand for the printed texts of even moderately successful plays. Such was the demand that publishers were known to employ stenographers to transcribe the text during a live performance.

Nor was this demand confined to the literate members of society and certainly not to any particular class. Studies of nineteenth-century reading practices have revealed that the reading aloud of a wide range of texts—newspapers, stories, political and religious tracts, and even philosophical

writings—had long participated in patterns of sociability that gave the illiterate access to published material. When theater, especially melodrama, of
the first half of the nineteenth century is examined, the tendency has been
to emphasize the third of the public that was *not* literate.[8] In keeping with
this bias, Guilbert de Pixerécourt has been constantly cited for his remark
"J'écris pour ceux qui ne savent pas lire" (I write for those who cannot
read). What is rarely recalled is that Pixerécourt also wrote, "Melodrama
purified the language of the people who, after seeing it played, borrowed
it for two sous and read it until they knew it by heart" (qtd. in Brown
90). It is certainly true that this reading cannot be considered apart from
the performance. The postperformance reading of a playscript or screen-
play stimulates an imaginary representation which, in Anne Ubersfeld's
words, "privileges what is already inscribed in the memory of the reader"
(*Ecole* 11). The verification of this interdependence, and therefore of the
status of the printed text as historical evidence, is critical, since for most
nineteenth-century plays this printed text—frequently illustrated after the
mid-1830s—is the only part of the original work that has survived intact.

Melodrama

As with any genre, there was considerable variation among the hundreds of
plays that were labeled melodramas. Out of this diversity, critics have generally acknowledged a broad distinction between so-called classical melodrama, which dominated the scene from the 1790s to around 1830, and
social melodrama, which flourished from the 1830s through the 1850s. John
McCormick offers one of the most thorough discussions in a single volume of both types of melodrama, integrating accounts of literary features
with descriptions of acting styles, musical accompaniment, spectacular elements, staging practices, and critical and audience response. Very broadly
and somewhat crudely speaking, classical melodrama promulgated the
Manichean allegory of a world caught up in a constantly renewed struggle
between vice and virtue. This struggle was embodied in the figures of a
young hero or heroine persecuted by a villain whose identity evolved in
response to changing social conditions. Social melodrama, as the name implies, addressed pressing social issues of the time. Action that was formerly
driven by the desire for personal vindication in the face of individual persecution was supplanted by a call to correct systemic social injustices that

oppressed the less fortunate members of society. Given the removal in time and space and, most importantly, the different relationship to reality that inevitably accompanied plays with Oriental subject matter, it is not surprising that Orientalist representations found no place in social melodrama.

This is not to say that the issues raised in social melodramas were unrelated to French colonialist expansion into North Africa and the Middle East. The poverty and deplorable social conditions depicted in works by authors such as Emile Souvestre, Frédéric Soulié and Félix Pyat were largely a consequence of the same Industrial Revolution that provided a major impetus for colonization. It goes beyond mere coincidence that the establishment of the bourgeois July Monarchy (which replaced the ultra-royalist regime installed by the Restoration) and the conquest of Algiers took place within weeks of each other (see Chapter 7), and that it was under the July Monarchy that social melodrama evolved. Nevertheless, the focus of this study will remain the paradigms of the Orient as they appeared in the context of classical melodrama. It is in the constrast between these representations and those fostered in national drama or military epic that the relationship between historical events and popular cultural representations of the Middle East and North Africa are most strikingly illustrated.

Most helpful to this project are analyses that not only have considered melodrama's formal properties but have also aimed at defining the functions of the genre, the rhetorical and theatrical strategies used to support those functions, and the modes of reception attached to it. The most powerful argument regarding the source of melodrama's sustained appeal has been advanced by Peter Brooks in *The Melodramatic Imagination*. Unlike many earlier authors who were preoccupied with the origins of melodrama, Brooks approaches melodrama as "a mode of conception and expression, as a certain fictional system for making sense of experience, as a semantic field of force" (xiii). He contends that classical French melodrama performed a vital cultural function by confirming the existence of a moral order in a universe that had been irretrievably secularized by the social, intellectual, political, and economic movements leading up to the 1789 Revolution. The stylistic excesses of melodramatic writing, acting, and staging were not, as others have suggested, either a matter of bad taste or an accommodation to the limited competencies of lower-class spectators. In Brooks's words, melodramatic excess—"the spectacular excitement, the hyperbolic situation, and the grandiose phraseology" (25)—applied pressure to the surface of reality in an effort to make the world of representation yield up a world of signification. Mimesis was openly acknowledged as "a signifying and significant enterprise" rather than one aimed at a mechanical reproduction of reality (148).

Brooks further argues that the alternative to the Sacred proposed by melodrama contributed to the formation of a modern sense of self, a conception of the individual ego as the fundamental social unit. This development, which has been most thoroughly described in relation to Romanticism, was evident in the diegetic universe envisioned by melodrama. In that universe, Brooks argues, "[T]he promulgation of ethical imperatives had to depend on an individual act of self-understanding that would then . . . be offered as the foundation of a general ethics. . . . From amid the collapse of other principles and criteria, the individual ego declares its central and overriding value, its demand to be the measure of all things" (16). On the stage, this act of self-understanding invariably came as one of the notorious coups de théâtre that involved the revelation of true identities. Contradicting critics who have generally decried these revelations as being contrived and artificial, Brooks recognized that these moments were not about verisimilitude but about "virtue made visible and acknowledged, the drama of recognition" (27).

If the individual subject was henceforth to be recognized as the fundamental social unit, the institution that bore the primary responsibility for the formation of that subject was the nuclear family. Eighteenth-century dramatic forms—bourgeois tragedy, bourgeois drama, and the *comédie larmoyante*—had already registered the emerging dominance of the bourgeoisie. In this new order a hierarchy of moral worth and natural sensibility was substituted for the social status conferred solely by aristocratic lineage. The primary responsibility for preparing middle-class young men to participate in public life was removed from religious and educational institutions, which were still tied to the preservation of the feudal order, and installed in the family. Accordingly, the tragedy of members of the noble ruling class being tested by destiny, political intrigues, and their own failings was joined on the stage by the drama of middle-class patriarchs seeking to preserve the moral integrity and the financial prosperity of their families. The new bourgeois plays of the early and mid-eighteenth century by Destouches, La Chaussée, Diderot, Sedaine, and others focused on redefining the father-child relationship as one based equally on paternal authority and affection. Some, like Marivaux's *La Mère confidente*, assigned mothers the role of friend and confidante, dedicated to ensuring the happiness of her children by placing their natural feelings and emotions over impersonal social conventions.

Beginning near the end of the eighteenth century and throughout the nineteenth, the maternal role was further defined as one that demanded self-sacrifice for the sake of children. E. Ann Kaplan has linked the emergence of what came to be called the maternal melodrama to the withdrawal of the middle-class woman from the public economy as Industrial Age factories took over the manufacture of textiles and other domestic provisions. Kaplan cites Linda Kerber, who points out that "the domestic function of the preindustrial woman had not needed ideological justification; it was implicit in the biological and political economy of her world. Someone had to keep the spinning wheel turning and the open-hearth fire constantly tended, and the nursing mother who could not leave her infant was the obvious candidate." Industrialization, however, changed the "terms of domesticity" and "began to free middle-class women from some of their unremitting toil and to propel lower-class women more fully into the public economy" (qtd. in Kaplan 115). Henceforth, the most important duty of the middle-class woman was to raise her children to take their places as productive members of society in the fashion prescribed respectively for men and women. In order to properly carry out this mission, mothers were themselves required to lead morally impeccable lives. The sad tales of "fallen women" who failed to meet this standard would figure prominently in popular fiction, drama, and film of the mid-eighteenth through the mid-twentieth century.

Whether in eighteenth-century bourgeois drama or nineteenth-century melodrama, representations of the family were rendered with an excess of sentiment.[9] As Anne Vincent-Buffault has demonstrated in *L'Histoire des larmes*, the recasting of the bourgeois family in a sentimental mold must be seen in the light of contemporary attitudes concerning the expression of emotions. In dramatic scenes, novels, and memoirs of the period, "respect, sense of duty and the honour of families was mixed with the love between parents and children, giving a significant character to tears" (20). Tears shed in the privacy of the home—whether to mark paternal love, maternal love, filial piety, or fraternal devotion—were seen as a celebration of the intimacy of the family. The exchange of tears in acts of mutual consolation or reconciliation was believed to cement familial bonds of affection. Outside the family, too, the moral superiority of characters was measured not only by their thoughts and actions but by their capacity to be moved to tears by the misfortunes of others or by the generous actions of friends and strangers.

Similar standards were applied to members of the audience. Spectators who could be moved to tears of joy or compassion were both exhibiting and refining their sensibilities—sensibilities that identified them as members of the new elite of innate worth which was to supplant the old elite of noble birth. It was further optimistically believed by many that the communal shedding of tears could make the theatrical experience a morally affirming one. As Vincent-Buffault concludes,

> The theatre as a setting for tears shared in mutual recognition, allowed everyone to prove his natural bounty through tenderness, and all to prove the excellence of their relationships which pushed them to fling themselves into each other's arms. . . . The observation and the participation of others multiplied the moral effects. The tears which were shed revived the sensibility and were a commitment to virtue. (67–68)

She notes that some eighteenth-century philosophers and critics (Rousseau being the most notable exception) saw the theater as competing with the church as an institution of moral instruction. The advantage of the theater was that it combined "the love of virtue . . . with a delicious collective emotion" (68). Nineteenth-century boulevard theater would continue to capitalize on this advantage, but as practitioners then and critics now have recognized, spectators who filled the seats of popular theaters had not come solely or even primarily in search of moral edification. However gratifying a production might prove to be in that respect, it also had to succeed as entertainment and as a theatrical event. Performance, spectacle, and music were as much the guarantors of this success as the dramatic qualities of the text. Nonverbal elements were called upon both to support the meaning of the verbal text and to exceed it in making an impact on the audience.

Bodies, Speech, Sound, and Spectacle

Brooks's work marks an advance over previous approaches in that he takes into account the significance of nonverbal and nonliterary elements. To him, melodrama involves the complex play of signs, "played out across a whole scale, or staff, of codes—or perhaps more accurately, a set of different registers of the sign, which can reinforce and also relay one another. Melodrama tends toward total theater, its signs projected, sequentially or simultaneously on several planes" (46). One of the key sites for projection of these signs was of course the actors' bodies. As Brooks notes in a recent article entitled "Melodrama, Body, Revolution": "The melodramatic body is a body seized by meaning. Since melodrama's simple, unadulterated messages must be made absolutely clear, visually present, to the audience, bodies of villains and victims must unambiguously identify their status" (18). Not only is the body the bearer of distinctive gestures (e.g., gaits, posture, mannerisms) and features (birthmarks, scars, etc.), it provides a channel for expression that can more readily escape psychic, social, or circumstantial repressions than the preferred carrier of meaning: the voice.[10] As Brooks notes, during the late eighteenth and early nineteenth centuries, gesture was seen as "the first and ultimately the most passionate form of communication, that which comes to the fore when the code of verbal language lapses into inadequacy. . . . Only the body can speak for the soul at such moments" ("Melodrama" 19–20) (Figure 4).

The investment of meaning in the melodramatic body followed in a tradition of linking theories of acting and drama to theories of the emotions and passions that date to the Middle Ages. One of the works on this subject that had a significant impact on nineteenth-century theater practices was written in German by J. J. Engels in 1785–1786 and translated into French under the title *Idées sur le geste et l'action théâtrale* in Year 3 of the Republican calendar. The translator's preface suggests how the relationships among emotion, gesture, music, theatrical utility, and social organization were conceptualized in the 1790s. Postrevolutionary French society was seen as being divided into two broad classes: those who were destined to work for a living and those who had been endowed with wealth. For very different reasons, both groups were in a position to profit greatly from the right kind of theatrical performance. For the former, the theater was to serve as a means of relaxation and diversion after a day of productive labor; for the latter, it was a way to revive sensibilities jaded by overindulgence in less constructive pleasures. While these characterizations are highly suspect in their simplistic matching of function and class, a point worth making is that, whatever the different interests or needs of various segments of the audiences, these needs were to be met by perfecting the same theatrical apparatus. Costumes and props were to be rendered with the most scrupulous accuracy, since the truthfulness of a play—that is, the sense of reality it conveyed—relied to a large extent on the exact reproduction of physical and visual details. The actors were called upon to perform their roles as naturally as possible, by rigorously applying a manner of playing appropri-

ACTE II, 2e TABLEAU, SCÈNE VII.

DGENGUIZ-KAN,
ou
LA CONQUÊTE DE LA CHINE,
PIÈCE EN TROIS ACTES ET SIX TABLEAUX,

Par M. Anicet Bourgeois,

REPRÉSENTÉE POUR LA PREMIÈRE FOIS, A PARIS, SUR LE THÉATRE DU CIRQUE-OLYMPIQUE, LE 30 SEPTEMBRE 1837;

MISE EN SCÈNE DE M. FERDINAND LALOUE,

DÉCORATIONS DE MM. FILASTRE ET CAMBON, BALLETS DE M. RAGAINE.

Figure 4. Oriental bodies seized by meaning. Title illustration for *Dgenguiz-Kan, ou la Conquête de la Chine*, by Anicet Bourgeois (1838). *Magasin Théâtral*, vol. 19. The New York Public Library; Astor, Lenox and Tilden Foundations.

ate to the characters and situations. The ultimate goal was the creation of "une illusion parfaite" (3). The actor's qualities demanded by modern authors were "a fiery soul that feels and expresses the passions; a gentle and persuasive sensibility that will appeal to all who are listening; and a physiognomy that is the faithful interpreter of each of these in turn" (8).[11] The facial expressions and bodily movements of the actor were believed to act as a kinesthetic trigger that would activate a series of affective memories in the spectator (22–23).

The privileged place held by the embodied expression of emotions was shared by another nonverbal form of communication, the musical accompaniment that was integrated into dramatic productions.[12] Music was recognized as an invaluable magnifier of affect that was, as the very name of the genre indicates, essential for producing the desired effects of melodrama. Originally used primarily for the overture, the ballets, and scene changes between acts, music was skillfully employed to underscore dramatic tensions, establish mood or local color, heighten the urgency of rapid physical action, and identify characters and themes through the use of leitmotivs. While the scoring could be largely formulaic, some authors collaborated with composers to introduce innovative uses of music. Important as these nonverbal means of expression were, however, it was understood that as conveyers of meaning they were subordinated to the verbal text. The relationship of the three critical elements—words, gestures, and music—was set out by Engels's translator:

We believe that pantomime should be restricted to treating familiar subjects, in the same way that music in lyric drama must accompany the spoken word: both can and must reinforce feeling. But if these two arts assume the right to try and express by the means proper to them completely unknown subjects, the one becomes vague and insipid gesticulation, and the other a series of tones, which, if well ordered will charm the ear, but will nevertheless have an ambiguous meaning that each person can vary and interpret according to his fancy. (28) [13]

In other words, the dramatic and narrative context was needed to anchor the meaning of the nonverbal agents of communication; or, to borrow Peter Brooks's words, the function of music was to confer additional legibility on the melodramatic text (*Melodramatic Imagination* 48).

When implemented by practitioners in the popular theaters, these theories and ideas were brought into contact with the active traditions of pantomime and acrobatics, as well as with more conventional styles of acting. The *pantomime dialoguée*, devised to circumvent licensing restrictions on the use of language, played an important part in developing a style of performance that relied largely on broad, unambiguous facial expressions and gestures to communicate with the audience. Many of the performers who appeared in these pantomimes would also act in melodramas. Furthermore, when melodramas were first performed, they were featured on a mixed bill that included comic pantomimes and even acrobatic interludes; often the same performers were featured in the different types of entertainment. As could only be expected, the end result fell short of the "perfect illusion" of reality envisioned by the theorists. Instead what resulted was a fictional plot that could have no equivalent in reality, characters who were clearly theatrical constructs, and actors who performed in an exaggerated manner. Paradoxically, these elements, which had no equivalents outside the theater, were framed by sets, costumes, props, and furnishings that sought to be perfect iconic imitations of their real-world counterparts.

Speech participated in this process of negotiating between the real and the imaginary in a similarly ambivalent fashion. The dialogue of melodrama could hardly be said to reproduce actual conversations people were likely to have at home or in the streets. Compared to the declaimed verses of classical tragedy or the abbreviated exchanges of pantomimes, however, the language itself could be said to more nearly approximate everyday speech. Pixerécourt, for one, found fault with his immediate predecessors for making all characters speak in the same manner (a manner of speaking, moreover, that resembled that of a professor of rhetoric) regardless of their station in life. In keeping with the trajectory of eighteenth- and nineteenth-century theater, he called for drama and performance that would be "une représentation exacte et véridique de la nature" (an accurate and truthful representation of nature ["Dernières" 494]). Despite Pixerécourt's aims, there was undeniably a hyperbolic cast to the speech acts of melodramatic characters. As Brooks so persuasively argues, it was precisely this "rhetoric of excess" that distinguished melodrama from other dramatic genres. The exaggerations and excesses for which melodrama has been criticized are the very qualities that "make the world we inhabit one charged with meaning, one in which interpersonal relations are not merely contacts of the flesh but encounters that must be carefully nurtured, judged, handled as if they mattered" (*Melodramatic Imagination* 22).

It could be said that the reproduction of material reality and the approximation of everyday speech cast an "impression of reality" over the purely theatrical aspects of the performance and created a mode of reception unique to melodrama. The question of *l'effet du réel* (the reality effect) generated by a medium becomes highly pertinent if we are to go beyond merely describing nineteenth-century representations of the Orient and attempt to assess how these representations might have been received and used by those who saw them. The problem of *l'effet du réel* was first treated by Roland Barthes in relation to narrative and still photography and was then taken up by Christian Metz in connection with cinema.[14] While the nature of this effect would be particular to each medium, many of the questions Barthes and Metz raise are pertinent to nineteenth-century theater at a time when new standards for realism were set.

At the heart of the problem is the feeling of credibility that is generated by an apparatus that produces visual, narrative, and/or auditory fictions. This feeling of credibility cannot be invoked without the affective and perceptual participation of the spectator. According to Metz, such participation is encouraged by a medium operating in a mode of presence. To him, the filmic mode is the mode of presence par excellence, whereas in theater "[t]he actor's bodily presence contradicts the temptation one always experiences during the show to perceive him as a protagonist in a fictional universe, and the theater can only be a freely accepted game played among accomplices. Because the theater is too real, theatrical fictions yield only a weak impression of reality" (9–10). To a certain extent, what Metz says is true. Theater scholars have long recognized that the "here and now" quality of live performance as opposed to the "there and then" quality of the novel or film is the characteristic that sets theater apart from other forms designed to produce narrative fictions. It should also be considered, however, that Metz's remarks seem to assume a perceptual organism that has experienced advanced cinematic representation, which would not have been the case for nineteenth-century audiences. Even photographic representation was not available to provide a contrasting experience against which audiences of the original classical melodrama could measure the degree of reality provided by the theater. I would suggest that the real presence not only of bodies but of tables, chairs, carpets, bridges, fountains, and the like only became "too" real following the perfection of the cinematic apparatus. (Twentieth-century theater practitioners, in fact, have learned to capitalize on this newly acquired "excess of presence" to compete with film.)

Although standards for realism in the theater need to be considered in relation to practices of writing and staging known to theater audiences, the work of scholars interested in the relationship between nineteenth-century theater and twentieth-century cinema have provided valuable insights into what might have constituted the bases for a "realistic" theatrical experience for nineteenth-century audiences. To a large extent the impression of reality was defined by staging practices. Going beyond the most easily cited demand for authenticity of costume and design as gauges of realism, Nicholas Vardac and Hassan El-Nouty have demonstrated how theatrical forms and staging practices moved toward creating an impression of reality that relied on seamless narrative continuity and the reproduction of bodily mobility and eye movements. These effects would eventually be most successfully realized by filming and editing techniques such as tracking, panning, dissolves, fades, parallel editing, and so on. But what could easily be accomplished through camera movements on location and through cutting and splicing in the editing room was a far more cumbersome and elaborate affair in the theater.

In a chapter devoted to "The Spectacle Stage" in *From Stage to Screen: Theatrical Method from Garrick to Griffith*, Vardac has detailed the complex arrangements and movements of painted flats, platforms, cycloramas, treadmills, traps, and other scenic elements that created a moving picture within the frame of the stage proscenium. El-Nouty's *Théâtre et pré-cinema: Essai sur la problèmatique du spectacle au XIXe siècle* presents a detailed and enlightening account of nineteenth-century French theater as the outcome of the promotion of visual or optical spectacle and the search for the perfect illusion. Rather than separating the traditions of the official and popular theaters, he emphasizes their close association through the designers and studios that produced work for both venues. Special effects, such as those that had first been developed during the latter part of the eighteenth century in Philippe de Loutherbourg's miniature Eidophusikon or Louis-Jacques Daguerre's experiments in the early 1820s with manipulating light through a system of shutters onto painted scrims and backdrops, were increasingly integrated into dramatic productions.[15] The retention of gas lighting in theaters well into the century helped sustain the illusions created by painters, carpenters, and machinists. By the middle of the century, these scenic ambitions were being accommodated by the structural organization of plays into tableaux (indicating set changes) as well as by the action-based acts and scenes.

In Vardac's scheme, the demand for "pictorial sensationalism" and the impulse toward "photographic realism" represented divergent trajectories that intersected in melodrama through the middle of the nineteenth century, only to separate during the latter part of the decade as realistic and naturalistic drama, which eschewed spectacular if not dramatic sensation, came into favor. Vardac's argument could be expanded in the manner suggested by Roger Odin for cinema and Marco De Marinis for theater to say that there was not one intersection but a range of intersections or alliances of the sensational and real in nineteenth-century theatrical genres. Accordingly, it will be important to understand that modern strategies for staging the Islamic societies of the Middle East and North Africa were formulated under the alliances of the sensational and the real that were particular to historical melodrama on the one hand and national drama and military epic on the other.[16]

Archival sources indicate that nineteenth-century audiences did indeed turn to melodrama expressly, although not exclusively, to experience its powerful assault on the senses. Whether the comments were admiring or disparaging, critical reviews consistently attest to the public's attraction to the spectacular elements of production and the management's willingness to accommodate that desire. The powerful draw of visual spectacle had been recognized and promoted since the beginning of the century. A new level of achievement in the production of scenic effects was realized in 1802 with Pixerécourt's *Pisarre, ou la Conquête du Pérou*. The premiere of the play on September 27 was also the inaugural performance of the Théâtre de la Porte-Saint-Martin. Monsieur B***, the *Courrier* reviewer who covered this opening, did not seem to see any contradiction in the purposeful development of rich visual and spectacular elements and the desire to please the public, on the one hand, and "l'amour des arts"—at least in their theatrical incarnations—on the other:

What's more, the pomp of the stage, the beauty of the sets, the richness of the costumes, and all the brilliance that is particularly suited to melodrama, everything demonstrates how much the directors are animated by love of the arts and the desire to please the public; and in this respect the melodrama of *Pisarre* surpasses perhaps all of the finest that has been seen in this genre.[17]

Theaters competed to present the grandest spectacles in order to attract larger audiences. When the Porte-Saint-Martin was seeking to establish itself as a successful rival of the Ambigu-Comique, B***'s colleague, F. J. B. P. G***, gave his advice to the directors of the new theater and with it his assessment of the tastes and demands of the audience. Above all, he stressed the need for variety and for productions of impressive scale, exhorting the administration "to redouble its efforts to vary the pleasures of a public that does not like to be presented with the same thing all the time." He finished by noting that "[a]bove all, the public requires great effects" (*Courrier des Spectacles*, no. 2035, October 1802).[18]

The analysis of nonintellectual and noncognitive aspects of theater has posed unique challenges to critics. While Peter Brooks's arguments broke new ground in understanding melodrama as a complex system of signs, not all of which were verbal, he does not entertain the possibility that the verbal, visual, gestural, and auditory excesses of melodrama operated in excess of meaning, outside of discourse. As film critic Tom Gunning puts it, "Brooks in effect 'tames' this spectacular excess by defining it as 'expressive,' a process of rendering meanings unambiguous and impressive" (51). Acknowledging the validity of Brooks's model for classical melodrama,

Gunning suggests that the subsequent evolution of melodrama and the variety of forms it has spawned demands a more encompassing conceptual framework. In his view, melodrama must be understood in terms of the physical and emotional sensations addressed to the body and the senses, and not just in terms of the moral cognition offered to the psyche:

Melodrama might be best seen as a dialectical interaction between moral signifi-cance and an excess aimed precisely at non-cognitive affects, thrills, sensations, and strong affective attractions. The very longevity of melodrama as a form demands a historical treatment in which the proportions of this combination as well as the specific nature of the significance and thrills it offers must be specified for each period and each dramatic form. (51)

Anne Ubersfeld offers one of the most flexible models for understand-ing a performance text that uses the full range of "languages of the stage" at the same time that it leaves room for those that exceed any form of narrative or symbolic discourse. Her definition of the theatrical sign pro-poses that

Every theatrical "sign" has the same status as any other artistic sign: (1) it delivers an intellectual message, it says something in relation to the other signs; (2) it acts as a stimulus: the gesture of fear of an actor induces the emotion in the spectator, the color red excites or stimulates him; (3) it is an element in an aesthetic whole and as such it contributes to the pleasure of the receiver in the same way as a like pictorial sign, cinematographic frame or sequence, or line of a poem. The sum of effects produced along these three axes can be called meaning. (*Ecole* 27)

While her second category would include the "tamed" elements Brooks focuses on, the third category, if "pleasure" is broadly defined, makes room for the untamable aspects of spectacle. These categories and concepts will prove central to analyzing the particular interactions between moral cogni-tion and noncognitive excess that characterized the representations of the Orient in the historical melodrama and national drama.

2

Exotic Tragedy

The Orient on the
Ancien Régime Stage

FROM THE TIME IT WAS FIRST recognized as a genre, melodrama has been linked with tragedy. Napoleon, who had a great respect for classical forms of drama but little use for popular fare, called melodramas "tragédies pour femmes de chambre," tragedies for chambermaids (qtd. in Thomasseau, *Le Mélodrame sur les scènes parisiennes* 111). The emperor's opinion was shared by many of his contemporaries, particularly those who identified themselves as *hommes de lettres*. Those professionally involved with the secondary theaters, many of whom were very well educated, preferred to construe the designation of melodrama as "tragedy for the common people" in a more positive light, one that elevated the status of melodrama. Robert Heilbrun's *Tragedy and Melodrama* was the first full-length comparative study to place the two genres side by side on neutral ground, noting their formal and functional affiliations at the same time that he analyzed their dramaturgical distinctions. However, Peter Brooks maintains that melodrama can only be truly understood in its dissociation from tragedy. According to his very compelling argument,

The origins of melodrama can be accurately located within the context of the French Revolution and its aftermath. This is the epistemological moment which it illustrates and to which it contributes: the moment that symbolically, and really, marks the final liquidation of the traditional Sacred and its representative institutions (Church and Monarch), the shattering of the myth of Christendom, the dissolution of an organic and hierarchically cohesive society, and the invalidation of the literary forms—tragedy, comedy of manners—that depended on such a society. Melodrama does not simply represent a "fall" from tragedy, but a response to the loss of the tragic vision. (*Melodramatic Imagination* 15)

While the relationship of tragedies performed at the Comédie-Française to domestic melodramas performed at the Gaîté or Ambigu-Comique
remains open to discussion, the affinities between eighteenth-century
French classical or neoclassical tragedy and nineteenth-century historical
melodrama are less subject to debate. Both forms turned to European and
ancient history for their subject matter. The pressure to represent "local
color" accurately and impressively in sets and costumes was felt equally
in the Grands Théâtres and the secondary venues.[1] Interestingly, if not
surprisingly, melodramas portraying ancient civilizations bore the closest
linguistic resemblances to classical tragedy. Jean-Paul Davoine has traced
these intertextual connections in his article "L'Epithète mélodramatique."
Building on the distinction Jean-Marie Thomasseau makes in *Le Mélodrame sur les scènes parisiennes* between emotive and oratorical registers in
the language of melodrama, Davoine points out that the oratorical register
displays rhetorical traits characteristic of the language of classical tragedy.
Using passages from *Les Ruines de Babylone* to support his conclusions, he
observes:

> Of course, it may be that the overabundance of rhetorical figures can also be attrib-
> uted to the fact that we are in an Oriental setting and it is to be expected that Ori-
> ental speech will be more copiously embellished with the flowers of rhetoric. But,
> in order to assure this exotic tone, if that is what it is, the author has turned to the
> storehouse of the most stereotypical rhetorical devices of classical language. (184)

The linguistic connection between French classical tragedy and French
Orientalist melodrama is paralleled by correspondences in other areas as
well. While historical melodrama drew on the general repertory of Orientalist representations that were circulating in French culture, the theatrical
heritage remains especially relevant not only for establishing the genealogy of the Orient on stage but for clarifying the specificity of nineteenth-
century melodramatic representation. It should always be remembered
that tragedy and melodrama ought not to be exclusively thought of in
terms of chronological sequence but also recognized as coexisting theatrical forms. Even as melodrama asserted its dominance on the boulevards,
seventeenth- and eighteenth-century classical tragedies were being revived,
and—the loss of the tragic vision notwithstanding—new tragedies were
still doggedly being composed.

As far as the eighteenth century is concerned, the Orient as an imaginary but not fantastic construction was not likely to appear in the *drame
bourgeois* or the *comédie larmoyante*, the two forms of serious drama pecu-

liar to that century. As Diderot defined these genres, they were to address the domestic problems of middle-class life. While the Middle and Far East could very well figure in such works, it would invariably be in the context of business ventures that brought about either the financial ruin or the economic salvation of the family at the center of the drama. In these cases, it was the commercial enterprise rather than the foreign culture itself that was of interest to author and audience. It was therefore in the five acts of classical tragedy that the Orient as a fully developed imaginary construction appeared on the stages of eighteenth-century France.

Of the truly distinguished authors of tragedy, Voltaire especially enjoyed using exotic settings for his plays. During the course of his career he produced *Zaïre* (1732), *Alzire* (1736), *Mahomet* (1742), *L'Orphelin de la Chine* (1755), and *Tancrède* (1760), with locales ranging from Jerusalem and Mecca to Mongolia and Peru, with a medieval Syracuse threatened by Moorish invasion thrown in for variety. Each of these works represents not only a finely constructed tragedy but an illustration of the processes by which the exotic is integrated into an established dramatic form to create realities and establish meanings. Taken together, *Zaïre* and *Mahomet* exemplify the connections between Enlightenment philosophy, Orientalist discourse, and French classical tragedy and will therefore be analyzed in detail.

Zaïre

In October 1810, almost eighty years after it was first performed at the Comédie-Française, Voltaire's tragedy *Zaïre* was once again presented by the same company, now also known as the Théâtre Français or the Théâtre de l'Empereur. The play is set in the seraglio of Orosmane, the sultan of Jerusalem, at the time of the Crusades. He is about to wed Zaïre, who was abducted as a child from her Christian family when the Turkish forces captured Caesarea. Their attraction, even passion, is mutual. On the day of the marriage, Zaïre's former companion in captivity, Nérestan, returns from France. Captured, like Zaïre, as a child, Nérestan had recently been ransomed and then returned to France to raise an additional ransom to free ten Christian knights. The generous Orosmane instead offers to free a hundred Christians, on the condition that Zaïre and Lusignan, the last descendant of the French kings of Jerusalem, now elderly and ailing, not be included. At Zaïre's urging, however, Orosmane relents and Lusignan is released from prison. Lusignan expires before he can enjoy his freedom, but not before he discovers that Zaïre and Nérestan are in fact his own children, lost during the turmoil of the Turkish invasion. He obtains Zaïre's promise to abjure the Muslim faith and convert back to Christianity. Zaïre's surreptitious meetings with Nérestan to arrange for her secret baptism are misinterpreted by Orosmane as lovers' trysts. Flying into a jealous rage, the sultan stabs Zaïre to death. Upon learning the truth, he uses the same dagger to end his own life.

The 1810 production was far more warmly received than the 1732 premiere. This performance had encountered a singularly ungenerous parterre who were vociferous in expressing their displeasure over several hastily composed verses.[2] It was also suggested that the production suffered from some mediocre performances, perhaps because the players felt "dépaysés dans ce monde oriental et chrétien" (disoriented in this Oriental and Christian world ["Avertissement" to Zaïre 535]). Following some revisions by the author and improved interpretations by the actors, subsequent performances met with greater approval, and the play eventually closed as a great success. By the nineteenth century Zaïre had attained the status of one of the most respected works of the French classical repertory and was widely regarded as one of Voltaire's finest dramatic achievements. The standards by which the performance was judged in 1810 were in many ways consistent with those applied in the preceding century. One critic at least, however, introduced a set of criteria that exceeded more properly literary or theatrical considerations and are of central interest to this study. The critic who reviewed the performance for the Courrier de l'Europe on October 9, 1810, saw the work as yet another illustration of Voltaire's exceptional ability to portray characters from diverse cultures with truth and distinction:

A glory that belongs to Voltaire alone is the ability to vary his style in the most truthful manner according to the characters he is portraying; it is the ability to oppose foreign manners one to the other and to our own with astonishing skill; the brushes he uses to paint Zaïre, Tancrède, and Mahomet are not the same; it is impossible to indicate the distinctive traits of Turkish and French, Chinese and Tartar, Spanish and Mexican customs more naturally than he does in Zaïre or The Orphan of China or in Alzire.[3]

Zaïre is contrasted favorably in this respect with Racine's Bajazet (1672). Where Racine is criticized for affording only "des fadeurs à la française" (insipid renderings in the French fashion) when it comes to re-creating "la physionomie et le langage des orientaux" (the physiognomy and language of Orientals), Voltaire is praised for ensuring that each character "parle bien le langage qui lui est propre" (does indeed speak in language that is appropriate for him).[4]

One does not have to read far, however, to determine that the reviewer's perceptions of "les moeurs ottomanes" were not without bias and that his judgment regarding the relative merits of Racine and Voltaire as painters of cultures was not unproblematical. Cultural biases surface as he expresses his reservations regarding the depiction of the male lead, Orosmane, the sultan of Jerusalem: "It may be that Orosmane does not afford an entirely accurate portrayal of the Oriental character; but it may also be that he would be less appealing if he were truly Turkish; besides, he is so fine in his love, in his jealous transports, that too much would be lost if Voltaire had not softened the Muslim severity in depicting him."[5] As it stands, this comment implies that the "softening" of the Muslim character represented a lapse in the author's usual concern for authenticity. Quite to the contrary, however, this modification was a highly strategic and carefully justified move on Voltaire's part. Voltaire's purpose is explained by the dialogue on more than one occasion. Upon his entrance in act 1, scene 2, Orosmane at once sets himself apart from his "peers," here defined as other Muslim rulers:

OROSMANE: Les soudans qu'à genoux cet univers contemple,
Leurs usages, leurs droits, ne sont point mon exemple;
Je sais que notre loi, favorable aux plaisirs,
Ouvre un champ sans limite à nos vastes désirs;
Que je puis à mon gré, prodiguant mes tendresses,
Recevoir à mes pieds l'encens de mes maîtresses;
Et tranquille au sérail, dictant mes volontés,
Gouverner mon pays du sein des voluptés.

(1.2)[6]

Orosmane, then, refuses to indulge in the vitiating life of sensuality and luxury sanctioned for Muslim princes. In addition, he promises to observe a monogamous fidelity and vows that Zaïre will not be subjected to the constraints and abuses of the harem:

OROSMANE:
. . . Ne croyez pas non plus que mon honneur confie
La vertu d'une épouse à ces monstres d'Asie,
Du sérail des soudans gardes injurieux,

Et des plaisirs d'un maître esclaves odieux.
Je sais vous estimer autant que je vous aime,
Et sur votre vertu me fier à vous-même.

(1.2)[7]

In a subsequent scene (3.1), we are given to understand that Orosmane's atypical conduct and attitudes are not merely the product of individual temperament. As a demonstration of his sincerity, he allows Zaïre and Né-restan to meet alone one last time although this goes against traditional custom. He attributes his penchant for liberality to the fact that while he may have been raised in the Islamic faith, he was not truly an Oriental, having been born in that part of the Ottoman Empire that extended into the European continent:

 OROSMANE:
. . . Je ne suis point formé du sang asiatique:
Né parmi les rochers, au sein de la Taurique,
Des Scythes mes aïeux je garde la fierté,
Leurs moeurs, leurs passions, leur génerosité.[8]

This noble heritage, however, succumbs to the rival influences of Oriental culture when it appears to Orosmane that Zaïre has betrayed his trust. His jealousy drives him to embrace what he had previously rejected, the arbitrary and often cruel behavior of the unenlightened Oriental despot:

OROSMANE: . . .
Allons, que le sérail soit fermé pour jamais;
Que la terreur habite aux portes du palais;
Que tout ressente ici le frein de l'esclavage.
Des rois de l'Orient suivons l'antique usage.
On peut, pour son esclave oubliant sa fierté,
Laisser tomber sur elle un regard de bonté;
Mais il est trop honteux de craindre une maîtresse;
Aux moeurs de l'Occident laissons cette bassesse.
Ce sexe dangereux, qui veut tout asservir,
S'il règne dans l'Europe, ici doit obéir.

(3.7)[9]

Neither the nature and terms of the struggle between Oriental and Occidental values and behavior that were a central feature of Orosmane's character nor the vacillation between essentialist and performative models of cultural identity seem to have posed any problems in reception for eighteenth- and nineteenth-century audiences.[10] Although Voltaire had to pay the price for the imperfections of his poetry on opening night, his *Zaïre* was never criticized for having a farfetched plot or unconvincing characters. While the reviewer for the *Courrier de l'Europe* may have noted that Orosmane did not correspond to what was evidently considered common knowledge about "le caractère oriental," this departure apparently did not disturb the overall logic of the tragedy. To the twentieth-century cultural critic, however, it is readily apparent that a number of negotiations were being carried out in the person of this sultan of Jerusalem as well as in the larger narrative in which this representation was embedded. The terms of these negotiations were set as much by the conventions of classical French tragedy and the practices of the Comédie-Française as they were by the philosophy of the Enlightenment and the discourses and fictions of the Orient.

The relations between the programs of eighteenth-century philosophers, novelists, travel writers, and the like and contemporary constructions of the Orient have been examined in three illuminating full-length studies. In the earliest of these, *La Structure du sérail: La Fiction du despotisme asiatique dans l'occident classique* (1979), Alain Grosrichard traces the ancien régime conception of the Oriental despot to the confluence of otherwise divergent political interests and social trajectories. In his view, the substance and structure of this figure took form in the wake of the consolidation of an absolute power in the hands of a central monarch. Opposition from two groups—an increasingly disempowered nobility and a bourgeoisie still restrained in its exercise of power—converged with equal antagonism on the figure of the absolute ruler:

All the intellectual powers of France . . . nostalgic for the past or building toward the future, see in the *One* the instrument of an always fatal standardization, for the one because it means a leveling, for the other because it means servitude. In the eyes of the old nobility, the access of the bourgeoisie to positions of authority, the frenzy of ennoblements, intolerable since Colbert, perverted the royal function, which plays these lackeys in disguise against its most venerable allies, its blood brothers, and abolishes the true natural hierarchy in a specious uniformity. A bourgeoisie priding itself on being enlightened sees on the contrary the maintenance of privileges, and the structure of orders that support it, as the resources of an arbitrariness that affirms itself all the more insolently for feeling itself threatened. (7–8)

The extensive body of writing that these conflicting interests generated over several decades would culminate in the following entry (admittedly

derived from Montesquieu's *Esprit des lois* [1748]) under "Despotism" in
the 1771 edition of Trévoux's dictionary:

. . . form of government in which the sovereign is absolute master, has a limitless
authority, an arbitrary power, and who knows no rule but his will. Such is the government of Turkey, Mongolia, Japan, Persia, and almost all of Asia. The principle,
the character, and the evils brought about by despotism are adequately expounded
upon in the work of our best writers.[11] (Qtd. in Grosrichard 8)

Whereas Grosrichard limits his focus to the intellectual and geographical boundaries of France, Lisa Lowe covers wider ground in *Critical
Terrains: French and British Orientalisms* (1991). In addition to examining
the domestic facets of despotism, her study is equally concerned with the
ties between colonial enterprises and Orientalist representations, seeing
this relationship as an instance of "the persistent hegemonies that permit
western domination of non-Europeans and the Third World" (4). Her approach expands upon both Said's and Grosrichard's projects by emphasiz-
ing the always heterogeneous and often contradictory nature of Orientalism. In analyzing texts, Lowe is particularly interested in probing "those
junctures at which narratives of gendered, racial, national, and class differences complicate and interrupt the narrative of orientalism" as well as "the
points at which orientalism is refunctioned and rearticulated against itself"
(5). Lowe's readings resituate *Les Lettres persanes* in their original historical
context. She finds in Montesquieu's *Lettres persanes* not only the Persia described by Said in *Orientalism*—one that is constructed as the opposite of
French culture and which thereby allows French culture to be positively defined through that opposition—but also one that replicates the hierarchies
of the French social order to permit a critique of that order (55–60). More
specifically, the binary opposition of Persian tyranny versus French ratio-
nality is shown to be constantly interrupted by contemporary class and
gender narratives that were more interested in challenging French absolutism, aristocratic privilege, administrative abuses, and patriarchal structures
than they were in proclaiming French cultural superiority.

Julia V. Douthwaite's *Exotic Women: Literary Heroines and Cultural
Strategies in Ancien Régime France* (1992) shares many of the theoretical
bases and methodological assumptions of the previously cited works. What
sets her study apart is her thorough situation of the cultural narratives of exoticism in their institutional and material contexts as well as in a historical
and discursive framework. In addition, her strong feminist objective—"to
show how exotic female characters were used to question such key concepts
of Enlightenment thought as individual self-determination and rational

objectivity" (4)—leads to a critique of Enlightenment thought itself. Particularly relevant is her discussion of the contradiction between the cultural relativism espoused by philosophers and the essentialism presumed in their works. As Douthewaite demonstrates, even the best intentioned writers could not escape their historical positioning and cultural conditioning and invariably ended up substituting new essentialisms for old.

Even this most cursory summation of the observations and insights of these three writers provides sufficient guidelines to comprehend the genealogy and functions of Orosmane as an Orientalist creation. The despotic regimen that Orosmane first rejects then adopts is unequivocally that formulated by French thinkers of the late seventeenth and eighteenth centuries, following the centralization of monarchical power under Louis XIV. The sultan's alternation between Occidental and Oriental identities is neither capriciously motivated nor ideologically innocent. Orosmane proclaims his European origins and their legacy of superior *moeurs* when he is in control of himself and his environment, and so able to exercise wise and just governance over both private and public domains. But once he allows suspicion and passion to overcome reason and impair his judgment, he can only exercise the arbitrary and selfish power of the Oriental despot. The equivalencies posed between Europe, reason, and order on the one hand, and Asia, passion, and chaos on the other are integrated into the structure of classical tragedy in a manner that reinforces dominant discourses of Enlightenment philosophy: the consequences for allowing either the passions or the senses to dominate the rational faculties are inevitably disastrous for both the individual and the nation. As far as the tragedy of the individual is concerned, the agonies and eventual suicide of Orosmane speak for themselves.

The salutary benefits of reason and order for an entire nation or civilization are suggested in Orosmane's opening speech as he contrasts the lassitude of Muslim rulers with the aggressiveness of Christian forces:

OROSMANE: . . .
Mais la mollesse est douce, et sa suite est cruelle;
Je vois de Mahomet ces lâches successeurs,
Ces califes tremblants dans leurs tristes grandeurs,
Couchés sur les débris de l'autel et du trône,

. . . .

Je vois ces fiers chrétiens, de rapine altérés,
Des bords de l'Occident vers nos bords attirés;

(1.2)[12]

In this evocation of the internal and external dangers menacing the Islamic world, the colonialist aspect of Orientalist discourse makes its most conspicuous appearance in *Zaïre*. As Said has so convincingly demonstrated, the image of once great but now exhausted and dissolute Islamic civilizations would become a key element in the master narrative used to justify nineteenth-century colonization of the Middle East and North Africa by Europe. When pronounced on the stage of the Théâtre de l'Empereur in 1810, these lines would be very likely to call to mind the Napoleonic invasions into this region at the close of the eighteenth century.

In satisfying the conventions and codes of classical French tragedy and the network of practices associated with the Comédie-Française, Voltaire was not just working with an abstract set of requirements. He had to deal with leading actors who had certain expectations about the roles that they would be asked to play and with informed audiences who also came to the theater with demands to be satisfied. Voltaire himself was able to illustrate the ideal way for the actor to engage with his role and for the spectator to engage with the play. In demonstrating how the character of the long-imprisoned Christian leader Lusignan should be played, "[Voltaire] divested himself of his ordinary expression of countenance as easily as he would throw aside a mask, and he became Lusignan personified" (qtd. in Nagler 323). Voltaire also exhibited the ideal of the total absorption of the spectator as he coached the actor Lekain in the role of Genghis Khan in another of his great plays, *L'Orphelin de la Chine*. In a letter written on January 10, 1756, Lekain recalls, "All the passions I expressed were graven in turn on his features which showed how he had been moved and touched" (Lekain 382).

Of all the emotional responses to be evoked, one was privileged in the eighteenth century. To move the audience to tears was considered not just a theatrical accomplishment but a moral triumph (see Chapter 1). Key scenes in *Zaïre* were designed to evoke this pathos. The second act, devoted to the travails of the captured Christians and the recognition scene in which Lusignan rediscovers his long-lost son and daughter in Nérestan and Zaïre, was designed to produce a particularly moving effect on the audience. A record of the opening night reaction, based on Voltaire's own impressions, has been left by a fellow author of tragedies, Laharpe. Laharpe recounts that "the second act of *Zaïre*, the first time that it was performed, produced little effect, and even aroused some murmurs in the parterre while those in the loges cried; . . . but this moment of injustice was short-lived and, from the second performance, the play was highly praised" (qtd. in Voltaire, *Zaïre* 581, note 1).[13]

If the plight of the Christians was a central source of sentimental stimulus, the passionate love of Zaïre and Orosmane remained the source of the most powerful emotions of the tragedy. Orosmane, not Nérestan or Lusignan, represented the tragic hero. As such, it was vital that he should be able to attract the sympathy of the audience, allowing them to be "disarmed by emotion" as the spectators in the loges had been on opening night. The nineteenth-century review cited at the beginning of this chapter accurately identified the adjustments made to the eighteenth-century French model of the eminently unsympathetic Oriental despot in order to ensure that he would remain "intéressant"—that is, able to affect the audience emotionally as well as to sustain their interest in his actions. While this move was perceived as running counter to the prevailing trend toward ever greater historical accuracy and circumstantial verisimilitude, Voltaire's manipulations of the commonplaces regarding "le caractère oriental" made for a more effective dramatic work by adding layers to the characters' emotional and psychological conflicts.

In the eighteenth century the possibility of a sympathetic exchange between Christianity and Islam or between Occident and Orient was not confined to the realm of dramatic representation. Edward Said relates the use of Oriental motifs and elements in works such as Mozart's *Magic Flute* and *Abduction from the Seraglio* to the notion of historical sympathy advocated by historians such as Vico, Herder, and Hamann. They held that coherent cultures were bound together by a national idea, spirit, or genius that was accessible to outsiders through an "act of historical sympathy." It was presumed that by making a sympathetic effort at identification, "an eighteenth-century mind could breach the doctrinal walls erected between the West and Islam and see elements of kinship between himself and the Orient" (118). The playwright had a somewhat more complicated task than did the historian. In the theater, the barriers between Occident and Orient had to be breached to allow the audience to sympathize with characters like Orosmane at the same time that they had to be maintained to heighten dramatic tensions by creating insurmountable obstacles. In choosing between converting to Christianity or remaining a Muslim, Zaïre must also decide whether or not to place the bonds of lineage and her allegiance to her nation of origin above her love for Orosmane. The intensity of Zaïre's dilemma is founded on the irreconcilable differences and long-standing antagonism between the two faiths. If the tension generated by these differences were to have been relaxed, the structure of the tragedy would have collapsed.

Mahomet

Despite the frequent evocations of the harem in *Zaïre*, the narrative of class conflict was never engaged as it was in *Les Lettres persanes*. By being firmly embedded in the structure of classical tragedy, in the tragic narrative of *Zaïre*, the allegory of the harem had lost its political potency. In another of his major tragedies, *Mahomet* (1741),[14] Voltaire set about restoring the critical potency of Oriental allegory. Once again he counted on the resiliency of the barriers traditionally erected between the East and West, at the same time that he took advantage of the possibility of breaching them. The stakes were, by his own design, much higher than with *Zaïre*, and the result of his efforts was a controversy that temporarily forced the new play off the stage of the Comédie-Française. The grounds for the controversy are divulged by the title used in the 1743 edition of the work: *Le Fanatisme, ou Mahomet le Prophète*.

The plot of the tragedy contains the same ingredients of convoluted intrigue and passion found in *Zaïre*. The action takes place in Mecca around 630. Mahomet, portrayed as a worldly imposter who preys on the susceptibilities of the credulous to increase his own power and wealth, has established Medina as his base. Seeking to extend his domination to Mecca, he is resisted by the elderly Zopire, sherif of Mecca and the guardian of a young woman, Palmire. As a child Palmire had been abducted from her family, members of the unspecified "ancien religion" that had been supplanted by Islam. She was raised in Mahomet's camp and came to love a fellow captive, Séide. She had, however, also attracted the interest of Mahomet himself just before being rescued by Zopire's forces. Entering the city of Mecca under the pretense of conducting negotiations, Mahomet commissions Séide to assassinate Zopire, promising him Palmire in marriage. The murder is presented to Séide as an act of religious revenge. Séide carries out his "holy" mission, but before Zopire expires it is revealed that Séide and Palmire are in fact his son and daughter. Séide attempts to rally the citizens of Mecca against Mahomet, but falls victim to a slow-acting poison that had previously been administered by Mahomet's lieutenant Omar. Mahomet proclaims to the crowd that Séide's death was an act of divine intervention, which proved the righteousness of his own cause. Palmire, however, commits suicide, thus denying Mahomet a complete victory.

In the twists and turns of its plot, *Mahomet* has every appearance of following in the tradition of Corneille's *Polyeucte* or Racine's *Bajazet*—

the tradition of religious tragedy that had already moved Voltaire to write *Zaïre*. But as Voltaire had anticipated, had even hoped, *Mahomet* was not received as just another interesting tragedy of love and conversion. In a letter he sent to Frederick II of Prussia along with the first act of the play, he wrote: "I am therefore taking the liberty of sending you this first act of a tragedy that seems to me to be if not in a good style, at least in a new style. No one has ever put superstition and fanaticism on the stage" (Badir 79).[15] What many saw in *Mahomet*, however, was not an attack on superstition and fanaticism, but an assault on organized religion, accepted morality, and established government. At the end of April 1741, a trial run in Lille took place without incident; the tragedy was in fact enthusiastically received. Elsewhere, however, the word was put out that the play contained "horrors" and constituted a scandal. Jansenists in particular were offended by passages that seemed to attack the beliefs of their sect.[16] The concerted opposition would come when Voltaire proposed to have the work performed in Paris at the Comédie-Française.

The opposition now came from different quarters. The initial resistance, including rejection by the official censor, apparently had more to do with politics in the world of theater than in the world of religion or government. According to the editors' preface to the 1785 edition of the play, Crébillon refused to authorize the performance of *Mahomet* not because he was in league with those who wanted to suppress the play, but because he had been convinced that Voltaire's tragedy would surpass his own work. In order to obtain permission to have the play performed, Voltaire had to apply directly to Cardinal de Fleury, Louis XV's chief minister. In the cardinal's opinion, the play was written with appropriate circumspection, and all the dangers of the subject had been avoided with the greatest care (Badir 95). On August 9, 1742, the play opened to an unusually distinguished audience, which included the chief city magistrates and even cabinet ministers. The greater part of the assembly received the work with acclaim and apparently found nothing objectionable in it; but Voltaire's enemies had not conceded the battle and obtained the support of the high judicial court. A letter from the *procureur général* to the police administration presented a very different view of what was going on in the theater. Three eyewitnesses had reported that the play presented all manner of infamous, scandalous, antireligious, and impious acts. The work was called "une satire sanglante contre la religion chrétienne" (a bloody satire against the Christian religion), and the fanatical Mahomet was identified with Jesus Christ (see Hadidi 54–57). The enormity of the outrage was such that even the irreligious were moved to protest in "a universal revolt" (Badir 97). It was decided, with the reluctant approval of Cardinal de Fleury, to have the play removed from the stage to preempt any violent protests at future performances.

Voltaire was persuaded to withdraw his play voluntarily, but not without acrimony. In a letter dated August 22, Voltaire compared the campaign against *Mahomet* to that launched against Molière's *Tartuffe* in the previous century. He accused his opponents of incompetence as theater spectators:

Either because, due to the rapid flow of the performance, they were not able to follow the thread of the work, or because they had little experience of the theater, they were offended that Mahomet should have ordered a murder to be committed, and used religion to encourage the young man who was his instrument to become an assassin. It did not occur to these persons, outraged as they were, that the play presented this deed as the most horrible of all crimes, and that it is morally impossible to present it in any other light. ("Avis" to *Le Fanatisme* 98)[17]

In the case of *Tartuffe*, it was the king who brought deliverance. Voltaire sought his vindication from the pope himself. Voltaire proposed to dedicate the controversial play to Pope Benedict XIV. The pope, who was a great admirer of Voltaire's, accepted the honor. In his letter soliciting the pope's consent (August 17, 1745), Voltaire maintained that the work was an attack on the founder of "a false and barbarous religion" and posed the question: "A qui pourrais-je convenablement adresser la satire de la cruauté et des erreurs d'un faux prophète, qu'au vicaire et l'imitateur d'un Dieu de paix et de vérité?" (To whom could I properly address this satire of the cruelty and the errors of a false prophet, but to the vicar and imitator of a God of peace and truth? [*Oeuvres completes* 4:101]).

This gesture may have concluded the eighteenth-century dispute, but it just begins the most intriguing part of the twentieth-century discussion. There is ample evidence that Voltaire was not being entirely sincere when he claimed that his critique was directed solely against the person and practices of the founder of Islam. Two years before he applied to the pope for his literary benediction, Voltaire—not writing in his own name, however—asserted in the preface to a 1743 Amsterdam edition of the work that the play was intended to address the currents of religious fanaticism that had marred France's own history, leading, for instance, to the assassinations of Henri III and Henri IV. While Voltaire's strongest pleas for universal religious tolerance and his most pointed attacks on acts of fanaticism committed in the name of the Catholic Church would not appear until the 1760s, he had already questioned the authority of Catholic dogma by the time he produced *Mahomet*.[18] Furthermore, *Mahomet* was being performed just about twenty years after Montesquieu had established the precedent for using an Orientalized context to criticize French social, political, and cultural institutions. A contemporary spectator would have been invited to read in verses such as the following an evocation of bloody civil disorders and religious persecutions of recent European history:

ZOPIRE: [to Mahomet] Je rougis pour toi seul, pour toi dont l'artifice
A traîné ta patrie au bord du précipice;
Pour toi de qui la main sème ici les forfaits,
Et fait naître la guerre au milieu de la paix.
Ton nom seul parmi nous divise les familles,
Les époux, les parents, les mères et les filles;
Et la trève pour toi n'est qu'un moyen nouveau
Pour venir dans nos coeurs enfoncer le couteau.
La discorde civile est partout sur ta trace.

(2.5)[19]

It would seem, then, that Voltaire's accusers were not entirely unjustified in reading subversive elements in *Mahomet* (even if their particular actions were motivated as much by personal enmity as by religious conviction); nor were they the inept theatergoers he rather satirically portrayed. While they may have missed the finer points of Voltaire's argument, they at least knew better than to take *Mahomet* as just one more classical tragedy with an exotic setting. That setting, however, made it possible for Voltaire to offer an alternative, more acceptable interpretation of the play to his accusers. By focusing on the character of Mahomet as the perpetrator of various crimes against God and humanity, Voltaire gained the liberty to make a more powerful statement than he could otherwise have made in dramatizing his polemic against fanaticism in its Christian manifestations.

If as a philosopher Voltaire took advantage of the perception of Islam and the Orient as distinct from Christianity and France, as a dramatist he still counted on the possibility of sympathetic identification with the cast of Oriental characters to make *Mahomet* a theatrical success. However committed he may have been to the philosophical argument of his play, Voltaire was never indifferent to its qualities as a dramatic work. In his *Appel à toutes les nations: Des Divers Changements arrivés à l'art tragique* (1761), he describes the principal characters of *Mahomet* as he envisioned them:

[A] Seid who could be at once enthusiast and tender, fierce through fanaticism, humane by nature, who knew how to shudder and to weep; a Palmira animated, compassionate, terrified, trembling at the crime she is going to commit, who could feel horror, repentance, and despair at the moment the crime is committed; . . . a father, who should acknowledge his two children in his two murderers, who should embrace them shedding tears with his blood; who should mix his tears with those of his children, who should rise to clasp them in his arms. (Qtd. in Nagler 297)

Mahomet far more than *Zaïre* follows in the tradition of *Les Lettres persanes* not only in its use of the Orient to criticize aspects of contemporary French society but in its participation in a precolonial Orientalist discourse that would eventually be used to support the French invasion and colonization of the Middle East and North Africa. Voltaire himself was sensitive to the fact that his works were not being played in total isolation from the realities of the Islamic world, and that the content of *Mahomet* would be a tremendous affront to members of that faith. One of the reasons Voltaire did not press for an earlier date for the Paris opening was the presence of the Turkish ambassador in the capital. In indicating his willingness to delay the performances until after the ambassador's departure, he observed that "in truth, it would not be courteous to denigrate the Prophet while entertaining the ambassador and to mock his church in our theatres" (Badir 94).[20]

The particular form that Voltaire's denigration of the Prophet took can be traced to the fifteenth century. Magdy Badir's archaeological investigation of representations of Muhammad in Christian Europe finds that prior to the twelfth century, Muhammad was generally seen as the incarnation of evil and identified—whether in theological discourses or chansons de geste—as the leader of an idolatrous pagan sect or as a heretic. As the Christian and Muslim worlds drew closer together in the twelfth through fourteenth centuries, more favorable views of Muhammad surfaced. In various chansons de geste it is suggested that he was a prophet of Christ or even a prelate of the Roman Catholic Church (see Badir 25–34). With the rise of the mercantile classes in fifteenth-century Europe, however, accounts of Muhammad's life took a new approach to the denunciation of the "false prophet" by essentially portraying him as a "marchand parvenu," to use Badir's phrase (35). Over the next three hundred years, various histories of the Islamic religion would continue to promote this narrative of social, political, and economic opportunism on the part of its founder. Intellectual, theological, and artistic sources could therefore have been cited to provide authoritative justification for transforming Muhammad into the Tartuffe of the eighteenth century. Voltaire, however, was astute enough to acknowledge that his portrayal of Mahomet was based more on common preconceptions than on actual fact. He openly acknowledged that he had tampered with history to make both his argument and his play more effective, and he made no apologies for substituting a preconceived model for more fully and faithfully developed renderings: "A preconceived notion suffices for a painter or a poet. Where would Virgil and Homer be if someone had quibbled with them over the facts? A falsehood that produces a good situation in the theatre, is preferable in that case to all the archives in the Universe" (Badir 78).[21] Unlike his admirer who reviewed the 1810 production of *Zaïre* for the *Courrier de l'Europe*, Voltaire was ready to admit that what he was presenting in his Oriental plays was not a fiction that referred to a truth, but a fiction that referred to other fictions. This was an observation that would apply equally well to the nineteenth-century melodramas and military epics that would follow the Orientalist tragedies of the eighteenth century. In the case of the nationalistic dramas, however, it was an observation that would be made rarely.

3

Exotic Boundaries

Reading the Censors

The Bureau of Censorship

Of the various institutions shaping nineteenth-century boulevard theater as a system of communication, the Commission des censeurs exerted the most overt and coercive force.[1] The integration of the theater censors into the central administrative apparatus under Napoleon I reflected a shift in emphasis from repressive censorship exercised by the police in the theaters to preventive censorship applied to the play-texts themselves. This gesture, in turn, represented official acknowledgment of the theater's capacity to serve as a site for expressing political contentiousness, thereby contributing to the shaping of public opinion and the formation of political subjects.

Contemporary perceptions of the manner in which theater operated as a political and social institution are indicated by the administrative offices in which its overseers were housed. Most notable is the consistent linking of theatrical activity with print journalism. Shuffled about among various ministries through the early years of the Restoration, the Bureau des Théâtres, charged with the reading of play manuscripts submitted for approval prior to the first performance, was designated the *troisième bureau* of the *Division littéraire* in 1816. Significantly, this division of the ministry of the Police générale was also charged with the surveillance of newspapers and periodicals. Throughout the nineteenth century strict censorship and other official controls of the theaters and the press would for the most part be imposed or lifted in tandem, even as other forms of expression such as the novel would be more leniently regarded. The administrative linking of the theater with newspapers and periodicals continued after the reorganization of 1819, when both were assigned to the newly formed *quatrième bureau* of the office regulating printing presses and booksellers. Finally, in

1829, the commission charged with the examination of dramatic works was placed under the direction of the office of "Sciences, Lettres, Beaux-Arts, Journaux et Théâtres," where it remained until the close of the nineteenth century.

While the general function and procedures of the censors may have remained fairly constant, their socioprofessional origination, perceptions of their status, and the focus of their proscriptive energies shifted over the years. During the First Empire, appointments were made largely to reward loyalty to the ruling regime. In 1800, as first consul, Napoleon had placed the theaters of the nation—both state-subsidized and independent institutions—under the jurisdiction of his younger brother, Lucien Bonaparte, then Minister of the Interior. Those appointed to act as the actual examiners—usually numbering five at any given time—were drawn from the ranks of literary authors, journalists, and/or politicians. Their primary concern was to suppress unfavorable allusions to the imperial regime and any commentary on domestic and foreign policy. Many of those appointed under the First Empire remained in office following the Restoration in 1815 and, to quote Odile Krakovitch, "demonstrated the same zeal in the defense of royalist ideals that they had applied to supporting Bonapartist and imperialist views" (*Hugo Censuré* 32). Assuming a high degree of individual responsibility, these men considered themselves as much adjudicators of literary quality as guardians of public morality and order. Continuing in the tradition of the First Empire, all those appointed as censors under the Restoration were considered "men of letters," and a few were even members of the Académie française.

This profile of the censors changed markedly after the proclamation of the Monarchie de Juillet (July Monarchy) in 1830. In accordance with the liberal principles proclaimed upon the establishment of Louis-Philippe's "bourgeois monarchy," all censorship was officially abolished. Almost immediately, however, the disadvantages to the government of this tolerance became evident, and in 1835 preventive surveillance of the theaters was reinstituted. Under the new structuring of the Bureau of Censorship, however, the authority and prestige of individual censors were curtailed as they all became subject to directives received from above. Censors were in effect reduced to the status of bureaucratic functionaries.

From 1835 to 1848 the directives issued to the censors instructed them to focus their attention on a number of areas or motifs. Some, notably those relating to morals and religion, were inherited from previous regimes; others, primarily those relating to political and socioeconomic matters, were particular to the circumstances of the July Monarchy. As broadly categorized by Krakovitch in *Hugo Censuré*, the censors' activities were chiefly concerned with the defense of the royal person in particular and royalty in general; the suppression of plays showing any political or military conspiracies, assassinations, revolts, or revolutions (particularly the most recent ones of 1789 and 1830); the defense of the political and electoral, including all officially constituted bodies charged with the maintenance of public order or national security (police, judicial and penal systems, national guard, army, etc.); the defense of various institutions on which the social order was constructed, such as the banks of the stock exchange and the official or "legitimate" press; the avoidance of extreme oppositions between the rich and the poor; the regulation of representations of actuality (ranging from an assortment of *fait divers* to international politics) and living persons; and, finally, the control of the Napoleonic legend.

The censors' labors, however, proved ineffectual as the events leading to the overthrow of the July Monarchy and the establishment of first the Second Republic and then the Second Empire would demonstrate. Within two weeks of the outbreak of revolution in the streets of Paris on February 22, 1848, censorship was once again abolished. And once again this state of affairs would prove to be only temporary. As early as July 17, 1848, the Assemblée Nationale appointed inspectors for the theaters of the capital. On August 1, 1850, provisional measures for a system of censorship were passed. The final organization of the bureaus of censorship for both the theater and the press were set by laws passed first on July 31, 1850, and then on December 31, 1852, a few weeks after Louis Napoléon had converted his position from that of president to emperor. Once reestablished, the new Office of Censorship exercised a far more repressive control than that of the commission that had been dismantled. The central concerns of the new censors are stated in the following directives handed down to the newly appointed censors. The order of presentation reflects the shifts in priorities occasioned by the changing domestic situation:

The examining commission must mainly combat the continual tendencies of authors to seek dramatic situations and effects:

    1) in the antagonism between lower and upper classes *where the latter are invariably sacrificed*;

    2) in attacks against the principle of authority; against religion, the family, the courts, the army; in a word, against the institutions on which society is founded;

    3) finally, in the more or less bold depiction of the depraved morals of loose

women and the life of disorder that is presented to our youth in colors that are all the more dangerous for being attractive. (Krakovitch, *Hugo Censuré* 224–25)[2]

The instructions closed by stressing that it was essential "to completely remove from the theaters all scenes marked by a *revolutionary spirit* as well as all manner of struggle between parties, on the grounds that *the theater must be a place of relaxation and distraction and not an open arena for political passions*" (*Hugo Censuré* 225).

Napoleon III's moves to depoliticize the theatrical terrain would profit from the errors of his predecessors, which had contributed to his own accession to power. He realized that it was not enough to attempt to control texts and representations: the very physical and economic structure of the secondary theaters as an institution would have to be radically altered. This restructuring was overseen by Georges Eugène Haussmann (see Chapter 1). In its first phase, it led to the rearticulation and redefinition of the internal and external spaces of the existing theaters: for example, separate numbered seats, with correspondingly higher ticket prices, replaced the benches of the pit; and the outdoor shows and other forms of street entertainment were banned from the Boulevard du Temple. No longer able to afford the price of admission to the theater buildings, and deprived of the former free entertainment of the streets, the working classes had little reason to frequent the district. Thanks to the enforced and "voluntary" exclusion of the lower socioeconomic strata of society, the boulevard theaters now became the cultural province of an almost exclusively bourgeois public. Furthermore, the new, comfortable, and isolating conditions of viewing, of reception, discouraged any fractious displays from the more contentious members of even this clientele. As the repertories of the theaters changed to accommodate this more or less homogeneous public, the representation of controversial concerns disappeared, to be replaced by treatments of common preoccupations.

In accordance with Bourdieu's model of social dynamics, this reorganization may also be seen as part of the inevitable reshaping of cultural institutions required to maintain their congruence with the realigned field of tensions between the working classes and the bourgeoisie. The theaters of the "Boulevard du Crime" had taken shape as cultural institutions during and immediately following the Revolution, when there was a genuine contest for power between the lower and middle classes and even an intermittent overlapping of their interests. Over the succeeding decades of the nineteenth century, an ever increasing divergence in interests between the two groups, and the attendant desire of the bourgeoisie to distinguish itself as the dominant class, legislated the formation of separate sites of public diversion. This move would in turn contribute to the widening gap between the experiences and practices of the working classes and the bourgeoisie as a critical area of shared cultural competency was eliminated or at least significantly reduced in scope.

Protocols of Spectatorship

For as long as the different segments of nineteenth-century French society did share the theater as a cultural institution, they were practitioners of common protocols for viewing and creating meaning. These protocols can be reconstructed to varying degrees from a variety of sources. Censorship reports remain among the most revealing documents in this regard. Given the circumstances under which they were produced, these reports reflect not merely narrow professional readings, but a history of audience response and current modes of spectatorship.

A valuable supplement to the original reports is to be found in the two-part study of the history of French censorship, *L'Histoire de la censure théâtrale en France* (1862) and *La Censure dramatique et le théâtre* (1871). Written by Victor Hallays-Dabot, head of the Bureau of Censorship under the Second Empire and the early years of the Third Republic, this highly partisan work was composed to demonstrate the benefits theatrical censorship offered to society and to illustrate the particularly enlightened approach to censorship taken under the author's own administration. While this agenda renders the study suspect for many purposes, it makes it invaluable as primary testimony regarding the mentality of the nineteenth-century censors. The two texts are of further value because they quote extensively from many *procès-verbaux* and other police records that were subsequently lost in a fire that destroyed a significant portion of the police archives in 1871. Finally, Hallays-Dabot's descriptions of the general climate of the theaters and of disturbances in the theaters, however biased, were nevertheless drawn from firsthand experience and accounts.

Hallays-Dabot opens his study with a pointed description of the interrelationship of theater, politics, and society as it was conceived of in the mid-nineteenth century. While the conviction that the three are actively and intimately linked can be traced to the ancient Greeks—Hallays-Dabot himself cites Plato—the sense of immediacy and urgency that characterizes these paragraphs can be dated as postrevolutionary, as is the dialectical relationship between the (ideological) state apparatus and cultural production that he outlines:

The theater is a kind of intimate history of a people; it reproduces the physiognomy of an era, it reveals its moral temper, it echoes whatever rumors are afloat, it transmits the caprices of fashion, [and] finally, it comments on, often even explains political movements. Of course, it would be a puerile exaggeration to place the *Marriage of Figaro* among the causes of the Revolution . . . ; but who can refuse to see in these works, and even more so in the feverish success with which they were greeted, a faithful reflection of the progress of ideas, the state of mind, the aspirations, and the bold deeds of the various classes of society?

In continuous contact with men, with the passions, the incidents of the present moment, the theater is inevitably drawn into giving full rein to its first impulsive and provocative urges. The day when plays either offended the public conscience by portraying loose morals, or ruffled governments with overly acerbic satires and personalities, the authorities intervened and put an end to these excesses. At that time, there emerged between the powers and the writer a struggle—a struggle rich in lessons. If one knows the sacrifices imposed upon, as well as the freedoms granted, the writer, will not both the banned play and the approved scene reveal the public mentality and the mentality of the government on the day of the ban, at the moment of authorization? It is from this particular point of view that we want to consider the history of the theater. (*L'Histoire* v–vi)[3]

At the same time that this passage situates Hallays-Dabot as a mid-nineteenth-century reader of politically implicated texts, it reveals remarkably current assumptions regarding critical reading practices. The historically and institutionally contextualized approach to the reading of cultural texts suggested here is essentially that which would be adopted by members of the twentieth-century Annales school as part of their methodology for researching *l'histoire des mentalités*. Modifications and refinements of this methodology (introduced by Marxist literary critics, French sociocultural historians, and Anglo-American New Historians) do not challenge its fundamental assumptions regarding the process of textual production expressed here. Even the emphasis on the reliability of replication of patterns of thought is not as contestable as it might be in other forms of imaginary representation. As already suggested, and as will be discussed further, the specific circumstances surrounding theatrical production and performance in the nineteenth century made it one of the more overtly mediated forms of representation, closer in many respects to journalism than to fiction.

Hallays-Dabot proves to be equally astute in his assessment of conditions of reception as key elements in the production of meaning, anticipating the perspective of twentieth-century cultural critics, semioticians, and reception theorists. The following statement provides a vivid account of the circuit of communication that made nineteenth-century theater a unique and powerful disseminator of ideas and images, distinct in its effects from print media:

It is not the same with drama as it is with a book. The latter is read in the quiet of the home; the ideas it propagates, the paradoxes it advances, the pictures it presents influence the mind of the reader only as far as his imagination and individual opinions will take him. The ordinary laws and tribunals will always have the time to perform their duties effectively.

The dramatic work emerges with a suddenness that requires another form of action. Watch the absorbed masses as a performance unfolds before their eyes, study the faces that mirror all the passions of the drama with bated breath, listen to the outbursts of approbation, the conclusion to an unforeseen logic, the irrevocable judgments that escape from a thousand mouths to fly from the salon to the workshop, from the cafe to the cabaret, and you will understand with what energetic power the theater takes hold of the popular imagination, what seed, bad or good, it plants in the mind. (*L'Histoire* viii–ix)[4]

At the same time that it affirms the importance of the pragmatics of reception, this passage reinforces the contention that the broad and powerful impact of theater as a representational medium was derived from its ability to manipulate the cultural competencies acquired by the theater-going public as a whole. This power was *not* an outcome of the unsophisticated sensibilities of uneducated and unrefined spectators—allegedly spontaneous, sensual, and emotional, and therefore easily exploited.[5] This view, once dominant in scholarship concerned with popular theater, has been resilient enough to surface even in the work of scholars who recognize that a wide range of social classes made up the regular viewing public of the boulevard theaters. Krakovitch, for instance, has persisted in designating the least socioeconomically privileged members of society as the target audience of boulevard theater—an audience that was poorly educated, ill-informed, and, consequently, deeply impressionable: "The theater was addressed, it must be remembered, to a population more than one third of which was illiterate. Even among the most liberal writers, rare were those who dared claim total freedom for the theater in the face of the influence it could exercise over a public for which it was the unique source of information and formation" (*Hugo Censuré* 27). But, this appraisal is contradicted by Hallays-Dabot's commentary—written well into the nineteenth century in 1862—which makes no distinction whatsoever between the modes of reception of the cultural elite, the bourgeoisie, and the working classes. Opinions are described as circulating freely "du salon à l'atelier" (from the salon to the workshop). The very terms of the comparison, the measuring of the impact of a drama against that of a book, places not only literate, but even educated audience members among the attentive masses and the breathless faces evoked by Hallays-Dabot.

Challenges to the concept of rigid boundaries between the literate and the illiterate, the upper and the lower classes, and stage and print cultures are supported by recent research conducted by Daniel Roche and Jean Hébrard, among others. They have found that the rates for functional literacy in the adult male population of Paris in the late eighteenth and early nineteenth centuries were higher than originally estimated. Nor were the functionally illiterate confined to the lowest strata of society; they were as likely to be found among the petite bourgeoisie as among the laborers and artisans.

The frequent assertion that the theater served as the primary, if not the sole, source of information for the populace until the introduction of the mass illustrated press under the Second Empire has also been shown to be inaccurate. Françoise Parent has determined that it was precisely the Revolution of 1789 that introduced new practices of reading and with it new circuits of information to which all segments of the population had access:

[D]uring a time of revolution, under the pressure of compelling social demand, it becomes possible to formulate the question [of the reader-reading relationship] in a new way. Situating the reader-reading relationship requires that the problem of the popular audience be addressed at the outset, and that the actual boundaries of the world of ancien régime readers be redefined by deemphasizing the reality of an as yet high rate of illiteracy; it must be acknowledged that the revolutionary event and the [public's] desire to keep informed about that event or to participate in it brought about a lowering in the level of skill required to decode the writings that recorded the event, as each "citizen" became a "potential reader." (606)

The flood of newspapers, pamphlets, and leaflets produced during the Revolution and the postrevolutionary period were read and discussed in the street, in political clubs and societies, and in the armies. The increasing access to printed material accorded the lower strata of the populace was, as Jean Hébrard writes, "not only an obvious, easily verifiable phenomenon, but it was, moreover, immediately designated as an event—awaited or feared—by a wide variety of apparatuses or representations that maintain[ed] an incessant discourse around it" (471).

The documents produced by the censors must be seen as part of this "incessant discourse," along with the writings of literary and theater critics, civic administrators, and others who could be categorized as fearing or resisting the access of the lower classes to positions of power, means of production, and apparatuses of representation. The historically specific and politically motivated nature of these documents was frequently overlooked when they were used as the basis for models of nineteenth-century popular theaters that regarded them as purveyors of crudely formulated mass entertainment and potential sites for underclass disruptions. In a similarly uncritical move, scholars more sympathetically disposed toward the working classes were led to stress the bourgeoisie's control over the forms and content of theatrical fare and posit the attendant indoctrination of the working-class portion of the audience. Ironically, these scholars were undermining their own project by ignoring the fact that such evaluations formed part of a larger discourse designed to justify the exclusion of the working classes from positions of power.

When the evidence from the censors is considered with due regard for the socioprofessional biases of the authors, there is strong support for the contention that, at least for the period between 1789 and the 1860s, the relationship of different groups to the theater as a social, political, and cultural institution is most profitably examined as a function of a given group's proximity to or removal from various forms of power. It is in fact illuminating to cast the dynamics governing these relations in terms of the interplay of strategies and tactics suggested by Michel de Certeau. The history of eighteenth- and nineteenth-century popular theater could very well be written as an account of the strategies of empowered groups—manifested in the exercise of censorship and in the presence of the police—being continually countered by tactics that took the form of "applications" and "allusions."

These tactics exploited the double order of communication that characterizes theatrical activity to unique advantage. This double situation of communication, or enunciation, has been described most concisely by Anne Ubersfeld: "What is seen in every performance is a double situation of communication: (a) the theatrical or more precisely the scenic situation in which the transmitters are the author and the practitioners (directors, actors, etc.) and (b) the represented [or diegetic] situation, which is constructed among the characters" (*Lire* 229). Both the allusion and application made highly aggressive use of the external or scenic circuit of theatrical communication at the same time that they totally disrupted the

diegetic or fictional circuit. Strictly speaking, allusions were veiled references to topical issues or conditions, deliberately inserted into the dramatic
text by the author with the full expectation that the audience would appreciate the intended analogies. Contemporary performance practices also
made it possible for the manager-director or actors to introduce allusions
into the performance text. Making "applications," on the other hand, was
the province of members of the audience. In its earliest manifestations in
the late eighteenth century, it would seem that this prerogative was primarily exercised by rambunctious young men in the pit "seizing on a line
or a couplet in a well-known play and drawing attention, by shouts and
clapping, to its applicability to some current crisis" (Hemmings, *Theatre
and State* 123). While these interventions were originally perceived as acts
of impertinence, the stakes became higher and participation more general-
ized just before, during, and after the Revolution of 1789.

While F. W. J. Hemmings and Hallays-Dabot ascribe somewhat different degrees of consciousness to those availing themselves of the opportunity to express otherwise suppressed or proscribed opinions, they agree
that it was the collective nature of the experience that encouraged this license. Hemmings describes "the theater auditorium [as] the ideal arena for
the anonymous expression of subversive opinion, delivered in conditions
that assured virtual impunity" (*Theatre and State* 123). In addition to the
promise of anonymity, Hallays-Dabot blamed the dynamics of a crowd
mentality that induced spectators to react and behave in ways they ordi-
narily would not:

Anonymous courage, or rather cowardice, is such a powerful force! . . . A malicious, even scathing, allusion will not shock timid spirits, when, lost in the crowd,
they have the pleasure, and not the risks, of demonstration. The most daring and
misguided social theories will exalt a people who, caught up in the emotion of the
drama, will no longer be able to discern the perfidy of the declamations and pictures being presented to them. (*L'Histoire* viii–ix) [6]

Allusions and applications may have first served the needs and interests of those opposed to absolute monarchy, but as circumstances changed,
it became the republicans who called for censorship of the theaters, seeing
in the theater a potential arena for the demonstration of royalist sympathies
and a rallying place for members of the aristocracy. In 1791, for example, at
the performance of a play satirizing one of the most notorious antiroyalist
works of the time, "[t]he aristocrats applauded, the republicans whistled"
and "the ever increasing disorder degenerated into a general mêlée at the

fifth performance" (Hallays-Dabot, *L'Histoire* 168). During the volatile period surrounding the trial of Louis XVI, efforts were made first to shut down all theaters, then to seek the voluntary cooperation of theater directors in avoiding potentially inflammatory plays. The official decree noted that "émigrés, aristocrats abound in Paris; it is important not to furnish them with a place of gathering" (qtd. in Hallays-Dabot, *L'Histoire* 177). No social group, therefore, was unskilled in the protocols of spectatorship needed to decipher allusions or to make applications; nor was any party exempt from being provoked into exercising those competencies. As could be predicted from Roger Chartier's findings in the field of print culture, there was clear evidence of fluid circulation of genres, ideas, and practices among the various groups, as well as "intricate cultural mixtures of discipline and invention, reutilizations and innovations, models imposed . . . and freedoms preserved" (*Cultural Uses* 4).

The continuing social and political instability of the next century would preserve the environment that fostered, even necessitated, the use of allusion and applications as channels for political expression.[7] Increasingly, the material submitted to the censors for the expurgation of suspect plots, passages, or characters included plays dealing with non-European subject matter. The documents generated during the process of review not only reveal the nature and extent of censorial control as it relates to representations of non-Western societies in general and the Orient in particular, but offer evidence of the structures of thought and perception applied to these subjects as well.

Exotic Havens

Of the hundreds of plays submitted annually to the censors, a relatively small number were refused outright and returned to the author.[8] For the most part, plays were approved provided certain passages were suppressed or rewritten and other features revised. Chief among the strategies believed to be effective in neutralizing potentially inflammatory or otherwise undesirable effects was the simple removal of the action from the realm of history, and thus presumably from actuality. This could be accomplished in a variety of ways.

Often it was not considered necessary to remove a play entirely from the realm of history to fiction if a change of setting in time or place would suffice. During the Restoration a one-act *mimodrame, La Vivandière* (1824), generated several reports before a compromise solution was arrived at. The censors disagreed as to whether or not this *tableau militaire* of General Kléber's victories in Egypt would have the undesirable effect of arousing Bonapartist enthusiasm. Lemontey, known to be the most moderate and reasonable of the censors, was of the opinion that the audience could be counted on to distinguish one French general from another:

> The action takes place in the French army in Egypt when Kléber had been made the commander in chief. The name of Kléber evokes no favorable memories for Bonaparte. The glory of this famous expedition belongs to France. His Majesty has adopted it in continuing to have its history published at his own expense. I therefore see no need to deprive the theater of these picturesque images. (F 21–991) [9]

A dissenting view came from Alisan de Chazet, notorious for his severe judgments and his hypersensitivity to allusions, whether verbal or visual:

> The action takes place in Egypt during the Kléber era, and I believe that Bonaparte's wars have been talked about enough for such a subject to be laid to rest. If the author can set the scene in another country, and in another time, his work can be performed. Until then, I have the honor to propose to your excellency that the performance of the play be postponed. (F 21–991) [10]

The author's accommodating response to Chazet's objections provides interesting insights into one popular playwright's approach to the creative process (an approach that was not unique) and attests to the censors' role as cultural producer:

> When I laid out the plot of the *mimodrame* entitled *La Vivandière*, I was not in the least thinking about the setting or the period of the scene. . . . I was only seeking a dramatic exploit with the potential for creating a theatrical effect. . . . If the scene was set in Egypt, under the command of General Kléber, it was only to vary the costumes and the enjoyment of the spectators. Several *mimodrames* whose action takes place in Spain have recently been performed. I therefore could not set the action in that country.
>
> If it is impossible to preserve Egypt, I consent with all my heart that the scene should take place in Bohemia under Chevert, at the time of the Battle of Fontenoy, or during the Seven Years War. I rely entirely upon your judgment, as to which of the three periods to choose. (F 21–991) [11]

There was no objection to Bohemia.

But alterations in time and place were not always deemed sufficient to remove the potential for allusions and applications. Often only removal to the realm of the purely fictional or, even better, the fantastic would suffice.

An opinion written about a three-act *mélo-féerie* based on the popular fairy tale *Peau d'âne* or *Donkeyskin* reflects the general perception that the realm of the fantastic automatically offered a sanctuary secure from the intrusion of contemporary social, political, or religious concerns. In this *féerie*, the princess Peau d'âne is condemned to be burned as a witch by the Spanish Inquisition. Such an incident would have been highly objectionable in a drama or melodrama, but apparently was rendered benign in this context. The Inquisition could be accepted as an innocent "dramatic device, without allusion, without reflection, without veracity as to locale [*la vérité locale*]" (F 21–976).[12]

The absence of a verifiable or recognizable locale raises an issue particularly relevant to the study of the representation of non-European regions. The benefits of the indeterminate locality of *Peau d'âne*, the *dépaysement* of fantasy, were similarly attributed to exotic cultures. The early nineteenth-century censors apparently were convinced that the combined effects of the exotic and the fantastic afforded a doubly secure safeguard against undesirable influences. In reporting on a three-act melodrama, *L'Ayeule* (1825), the censor concluded that since the scene was set in Poland, where neither the customs nor the costumes resembled those of France, "the common people, who make up its spectators, only witness *a curious spectacle belonging to a world that is not theirs*" (my emphasis). Furthermore, the appearance of the eponymous ancestor as a ghost "would further remove the French public and cast a purely fantastic tint over the entire work" (F 21–976).[13]

As suggested here, the coupling of the exotic and the fantastic offered a particularly happy solution to troublesome allusions.[14] As early as 1812 the case of *Pauliska, ou la Vengeance d'un bon coeur*, a pantomime in three acts, offered an exemplary illustration of this logic in action as it applied to the Middle East. The censors' initial report of June 13 expressed reservations regarding possible allusions to the pending invasion of Russia. By the end of July, however, the author had arrived at the happy solution of transforming *Pauliska* into *Zoraïde et Zuliska, ou le Bien pour le mal* in order to contain any undesirable proliferation of meaning. His solution met with the approbation of the censors who now freely gave their consent: "The author has just eliminated the grounds for [our earlier] decision . . . by transposing the action and the characters of the play to the land of the thousand and one nights. It is now merely a question of a sultan, some janissaries, and some desert Arabs" (F 21–976).[15] Another ten years and, as the censors' review of Pixerécourt's *Ali Baba, ou les Quarante Voleurs* reveals, the distancing effect of a fabulous Oriental setting could be taken for granted: "There is no need to mention that these thieves of the barbarous countries of Asia have nothing in common with the evildoers of civilized countries, and that their appearance in the theater does not at all produce the same effect" (F 21–976).[16]

When taken as a body, the pronouncements of the censors such as those cited above indicate that, however the "exotic" might have been used in common parlance, as far as theatrical representation was concerned the frontiers of exoticism were traced over the dividing line between industrialized and nonindustrialized societies. It would seem that, in the estimation of the censors, the absence of a homologous social and cultural frame of reference triggered a shift in the mode of audience reception to that of witnessing a curiosity; this mode precluded the possibility of any effective transaction from stage to reality, a transaction considered a key property of dramas and melodramas. It is this incongruity of social and religious institutional structures, even when shaped by generic conventions, that is credited with establishing a different mode of reception for *Les Natchez, ou la Tribu de Serpens*, a prose melodrama in three acts written in 1827. The alien frame of reference was perceived to contextualize murders performed on stage in a manner that removed the potential for harmful influence: "The setting is a country whose inhabitants are savages to whom our morals and our religion are foreign, who don't have the same horror as we do of murder and suicide. The example of what may happen on the shores of the Mississippi is not contagious for the inhabitants of the banks of the Seine" (F 21–976).[17]

The presence or absence of homologous institutions as the critical differentiating factor, as opposed to nationality, ethnicity, or race itself, is indicated by instances where parallels or "identification" across racial lines in a nineteenth-century sense were recognized as possibilities. This was the case in the 1850s when Harriet Beecher Stowe's *Uncle Tom's Cabin* was adapted for the French stage. The censors required certain modifications, the nature of which can be deduced from what is clearly a follow-up report:

One consideration that did not seem unimportant to us is that the authors took the precaution of making Harris, that odious master who mistreats the Negroes, a mulatto, formerly a slave himself.

We think that this drama can be authorized, in consideration of the changes that have been made and which above all had as their goal *to make any assimilation between the Negro slaves and European workers disappear*. (F 21–974; my emphasis)[18]

The censors' fear of any inflammatory identification between the oppression of African-American slaves and that of European workers was

conditioned by the atmosphere of political and social instability left by
the violent Revolution of 1848 that resulted in the overthrow of the bourgeois July Monarchy by the working-class parties. These immediate political considerations overrode any differences in race that might otherwise be
expected to bar such identification. The critical role of extratextual social,
political, and intellectual context in predisposing an audience to make such
cross-cultural references is further illustrated by the censors' response in
1859 to *Atar-Gull*, a melodrama in three acts and six tableaux:

This melodrama, taken from a novel of Eugene Sue as the brochure reports, was
performed in 1832, when there was no censorship, and when the socialist ideas that
came out into the open in 1848 existed only in embryonic form in some dangerous
minds and in the works of certain authors.

Since 1850 the drama of *Atar-Gull* has been maintained on the list of banned
plays, and we are being consulted today as to whether there is cause to keep it on
this list or, on the contrary, to authorize its performance.

After a conscientious examination, without prejudice, it seems to us that *the
cruelties of the colonists, followed by the atrocious and almost legitimate revenge of the
Negroes poorly disguises the antagonism between the owners and the workers, between
the rich and the poor.*

The step taken by the administration to ban the play was evidently the result of
fears of the same nature and we think that there are grounds for maintaining it.
(F 21–974; my emphasis) [19]

At this particular juncture in history, race or color in themselves evidently were not critical factors in determining whether or not a theater
audience would identify their condition or situation (but not yet themselves) with a character or group of characters. This state of affairs cannot
be attributed to the fact that racially based controversy and antagonism
had not yet entered the field of theatrical representation. As early as 1806,
the following acrimonious views appeared in the review of a melodrama
entitled *Zamor, ou les Deux Fils*:

A Negro being the hero of this play, the intentions of the poet are a little behind
the times. One could, twenty years ago, heartily praise the virtues of Negroes, all
the more to criticize the whites; for at that time it was a question of submitting the
whites to the blacks, by having the latter enjoy the great benefits of liberty, equality,
and fraternity. One could also rejoice over the patriarchal and almost celestial customs of the peasants, for it was necessary to drive out their lords and despoil the
property owners. Today, blacks, peasants, and the urban masses have given us a
clear picture of their perfection, and St. Domingue is sufficient to attest to what
we can expect from the unchained multitude that can have no other interest than
to cut the throats of their former masters in order to take their place.[20]

However derogatory and ideologically interested this early comparison might be, it is notable for eluding the essentialist arguments of difference that had already begun to appear in authoritative discourses and would create an unbridgeable gap between European and African by the end of the century. Instead, any atemporal opposition of European to African is subordinated to a historically specific association between the French Revolution of 1789 and the Haitian revolt of 1791 and a correlation of the two groups based on their socioeconomic function.

This comparison of the positions occupied by black slaves and French peasants and laborers at the bottom of their respective social hierarchies and their demonstrated willingness to overturn a repressive order through violence could continue to prevail over abstract categories of race and color as long as certain categories of experience remained active. In order for domestic organization and situation to predominate over racial divisions, contact between the French population and other races needed to remain restricted. While such contact increased significantly over the nineteenth century, it was confined to overseas contexts and limited to distinct occupational categories. Such general contacts as there were within French borders were in fact often theatrical, with "exhibitions" of people who were not of European origin, or performances by actors, usually from the Americas. At the same time the uniform cross-casting across the full range of roles in all types of dramatic theater accustomed audiences to seeing French actors, trained in the French tradition of acting, playing non-European parts that had often been written to evoke "interest" (de l'intérêt) in their situation—the prime factor in eliciting spectator engagement in boulevard drama. This is the situation that would prevail until changing historical circumstances provided a more immediate and compelling context than that of domestic revolution and altered narrative structures precluded sympathetic relations between French spectator and non-Western character.

4

Oriental Escapades

Les Ruines de Babylone, or Positioning the European Spectator

Audience and Author

In the edition of Guilbert de Pixerécourt's *Théâtre choisi* published between 1841 and 1843,[1] his admiring editor wrote, "Vous êtes le créateur d'un genre. . . . C'est vous, mon ami, qui avez fondé les règles de ce genre qu'on essaierait en vain aujourd'hui d'exclure de nos habitudes théâtrales" (You are the creator of a genre. . . . It is you, my friend, who have established the rules of this genre which we would try in vain to exclude from our theatrical practices today [Ducray-Duminil 3]). While twentieth-century genre theorists, not to mention many nineteenth-century critics, would be quick to take exception to the exclusive credit accorded Pixerécourt,[2] no one has ever contested his standing as one of the most successful and highly regarded producers of melodrama in all its varieties. As always where cultural production is concerned, this success was in large part due to Pixerécourt's ability to take his target audience into partnership even as he used his text to produce and position that audience. As Ubersfeld has noted:

The spectator is coproducer of the performance at two critical moments: at the outset and at the finish. One could say that it is not *the same* spectator at the outset and at the finish, in the planning and in the reception, and the distance separating spectator A foreseen by the transmitters and spectator B who attends the performance measures the unpredictability of the reception. At the outset, the spectator is present in the spectacle to the extent that the various transmitters (writer, director, designer, actor) take into account the universe of reference of the spectator, or rather his universes: that of his experience as well as that of his culture. (*Ecole* 304)

Like many of his fellow dramatists, Pixerécourt had a vision of key segments of his target audience that was not entirely complimentary.

Whatever general appeal his works might hold, in his view, they were required to establish a particular relationship with the less well-educated spectator. For Pixerécourt and many other—although by no means all—melodramatists, behind the aesthetic principles governing the genre lay a self-proclaimed moral and social mission they considered inseparable from the practice of their craft.

Melodrama, . . . when sound morals are its compass, especially when nothing happens that is not within the grasp of the intelligence of the working and manufacturing class, can only be useful, even politic, and help to keep this same class on the right road of those moral qualities so necessary to the tranquillity of every family and of society as a whole. (Qtd. in Krakovitch, *Hugo Censuré* 34–35)[3]

Such positions were often articulated in defense of the genre, which was subject to frequent attacks as a purveyor of moral degeneration and a school for crime. Most recent studies of melodrama, led by Peter Brooks's analysis, would agree that such fears were not well founded. In fact, as John McCormick notes, the morality promoted by melodrama "was fundamentally conservative, advocating the preservation of the status quo rather than social revolution" (157–58). For those authors who were not motivated by purely commercial considerations, the formulation and application of aesthetic principles were allied with an acute and highly interested understanding of the theatergoing practices and public of the time.

In Pixerécourt's case, insights into the complex interaction of experience, practice, and belief are offered by various forms of documentation. A selection of autobiographical pieces, treatises, and essays inserted in the volumes of his *Théâtre choisi* constitutes Pixerécourt's own discursive constructions of the relationship between his life experiences and his work. What emerges is an account of an aesthetic philosophy that stemmed from a clear sociopolitical positioning and was rooted in the momentous historical events of the time.[4] The "Souvenirs du jeune âge," which appeared in the first volume of the collection, focus on the writer's highly disciplined, even rigid, upbringing, which included a strong emphasis on religious instruction. In his "Souvenirs de la Révolution," prepared for the second volume, Pixerécourt constructs a narrative that stresses the traumatic impact of his personal experiences of the French Revolution.

Born in 1773 to a family of the provincial military nobility, Pixerécourt first witnessed violence directly related to the revolutionary movement in 1790 when he was studying law in Nancy. In September of that year he and his father were confronted on their own lands by peasants armed with scythes, pitchforks, and even some swords. The incident provoked the

family's flight from their estate. Pixerécourt's recall of his reactions to this
attack was vivid and his retrospective analysis remained unequivocal:

> It was very natural that I should be angry with these peasants with whom I had
> constantly lived on familiar terms; besides, my mother was so charitable, so atten-
> tive to all of them, that it was only fair to assume that they were devoted to us. The
> dreadful disappointment of this expectation upset me terribly; from that moment
> on, I conceived a strong aversion to them, and the revolution horrified me. ("Sou-
> venirs" viii) [5]

The outcome of the Revolution brought a particular source of distress to the Pixerécourt family. According to Pixerécourt, for seven years
prior to the outbreak of the Revolution, his father had been working to
have all feudal and seigneurial rights restored to lands he had recently pur-
chased, and to have his estate elevated to the status of a marquisate.[6] The
termination of these hopes as a result of the overthrow of the monarchy
apparently made a deep impression on Pixerécourt, who in his memoirs
alludes to "l'événement cruel qui venait frapper mon père" (the cruel event
that befell my father) and remarks that "il ne lui restait plus de Pixerécourt
que le nom" (there remained to him nothing of Pixerécourt but the name
["Souvenirs" viii]). Pixerécourt himself spent the most turbulent years of
the Revolution in exile with his family and many other nobles in Coblence,
where he enlisted in *l'armée des Princes*. When, under the Directory, Pixerécourt returned to Paris, it was, according to his "Dernières Réflexions de
l'auteur sur le mélodrame," "with religious and providential notions, . . .
and with moral sentiments that [he] embarked upon the thorny path of a
career in the theater" (493).[7] It should come as no surprise that with views
so firmly dedicated to supporting the existing order, Pixerécourt's relationship with the censors was an extremely harmonious one, marred only by a
single exception that will be discussed below.

Generic Practices

If the institutional context defined the general protocols of spectatorship
to be applied in the viewing of a performance, it was left to the individual
work to determine the spectator's mode of entry into the fiction of a particular performance and his or her subsequent positioning. This entry and
positioning took place within the set of possibilities offered by current generic practices — both on the page and on the stage. Of Pixerécourt's many

works based on historical subject matter and set in locations that qualified as exotic, *Les Ruines de Babylone, ou le Massacre des Barmecides* presents
itself as the most appropriate choice for identifying and analyzing several
of these practices and conventions. The "Tableau Chronologique" inserted
in the first volume of Pixerécourt's *Théâtre choisi* reports that of his fifty-
nine melodramas, *Les Ruines de Babylone* ranked sixth in total number of
performances. First performed on October 30, 1810, at the Théâtre de la
Gaîté, the play ran for 318 performances in Paris and another 594 in the
provinces, and was subsequently translated into several languages for performance and publication abroad. When analyzed at the textual level, *Les
Ruines de Babylone* offers one of the clearest illustrations of the possibilities
afforded different segments of the public for the selective interpretation of
narrative lines and emphases, and of the role of institutional and generic
context in producing meaning. Finally, this play demonstrates many of the
most common procedures used in boulevard melodrama to adapt and construct the visual and discursive configurations that constituted the Orient
of the early nineteenth century.

Revising the Narrative

The material that served as the armature for the characters and narrative of *Les Ruines de Babylone* was originally recorded in Arabic historical
annals (comprised of both chronicles and commentaries) and a courtly literature dealing with the personages and events of the Abbasid dynasty,
which ruled the Muslim Empire from A.D. 750 to 1258. The historical figures on which the central characters of the melodrama are based are Harun
al-Rashid, who ruled as the fourth caliph from 786 to 809, and Ja'far b.
Yahya, his wazir or chief minister, and a member of the powerful Barma-
kid family, which held administrative control of the empire during the first
part of Harun's reign. The Barmakids' position and influence came to an
abrupt end in 803 when the leading members of the family were arrested,
and Ja'far, who had been the caliph's chief adviser and his closest companion, was summarily executed; his corpse was dismembered and displayed
on the bridges of Baghdad for three years before finally being removed and
burned. Various causes have been assigned to Ja'far's execution and the fall
of his family. Pixerécourt selected the most romantic among them as the
thesis for his play. The nineteenth-century French interpretation of this explanation was summarized by Colnet in the October 31, 1810, edition of
the *Gazette de France*:

Everyone is familiar with the troublesome decree that the caliph Haroun-al-Raschid imposed on the valiant Giafar the Barmecide, his vizir, and the foundation of his throne, upon marrying him to his sister Abassa. Giafar only obtained the signal honor of alliance with the family of the Abassides by swearing on the Koran that he would treat the princess as his sister and never claim the rights of a husband. The promise was a rash one and difficult to keep with a young, beautiful, and witty woman; accordingly, it was promptly broken. The caliph was informed and Giafar and more than forty Barmecides were sacrificed as part of his revenge; the unfortunate Abassa was spared only to live out her life in humiliation and misery.[8]

These sad events had already inspired Laharpe to compose a tragedy around them many years earlier. Laharpe's tragedy, however, while well received enough, earned only eleven performances. Although this was considered a thoroughly respectable number of performances for a new tragedy, it was of a totally different order than the overwhelming success of Pixerécourt's melodrama. This gap to a large extent was generic rather than particular and can be traced to the fundamental differences in the relationship between representation and reality delineated for each dramatic form. The result of following the conventions associated with each form was, in Colnet's words, that "[t]he one . . . remained scrupulously faithful to the truth of history, while the other, making full use of the privileges of his art, . . . concerned himself only with composing a story filled with interest."[9] In effect, the authors of melodrama had greater license to negotiate a balance between the historical and the legendary on the one hand and the theatrical on the other. This negotiation was accomplished with due consideration for preserving a sufficient degree of verisimilitude to allow the affective engagement of the spectators in the dramatic action. "Verisimilitude" must be understood not as the result of a transparent coordination of sign and referent but as a theatrical effect. This was already recognized in Pixerécourt's time. As Geoffroy observed in the *Journal des Débats*, Pixerécourt's script was "rich in pathetic situations and in marvelous incidents, without, however, exceeding the boundaries of *poetic and theatrical probability*" ("Notice" 9; my emphasis).[10]

In his version of the fall of the Barmakids, Pixerécourt mitigated the harshness of the original outcome by replacing it with the conciliatory resolution of melodrama. He followed the generally accepted lines of the historical legend for the action that preceded the opening of the play, but once the curtain had been raised little remained of the original tale. He did, however, take the precaution of changing the name of the heroine from Abassa to Zaïda to deprive any malicious wits in the parterre of the opportunity to disrupt the performance with the pun "A bas ça" or "Down with it." Pixérécourt's interpretation supplied a hidden refuge in a forest near the palace, where Giafar and Zaïda's child was being secretly raised. This refuge is discovered by the head eunuch, Isouf, the active villain in the piece. In the second act, guided by Isouf, Haroun surprises the little family in their blissful retreat. As Geoffroy observes, "Anyone other than the proud Haroun would have been touched by this sight; never was there a more pardonable offense, if a despot knew how to pardon."[11] Instead, the furious caliph orders the death of Giafar, his son, and the entire Barmecide family. His sister is driven out of the palace to wander in the wilderness. With the help of his loyal friend Raymond, Giafar manages to flee with their son. The third act is situated amid the ruins of Babylon, currently occupied by a band of Bedouin Arabs. Not surprisingly, all the major characters soon manage to converge on this spot. Isouf comes to offer the Bedouins money to assassinate Giafar and his son, but Raymond makes a more attractive counteroffer for them to protect these innocent beings. The unfortunate Zaïda, overcome with exhaustion, and perishing from hunger, arrives to seek refuge among the ruins. A young man, hearing her lamentations, emerges from a nearby fortress. He attempts to console her and offers her food and shelter. It turns out that this young man, named Hassan, is the caliph's own son; his father had him raised in this isolated fortress to protect him from the temptations and corruptions of the court. When Haroun arrives to visit his son, Hassan implores him to forgive his sister. The caliph is finally moved to do so, but then he is suddenly attacked by the Bedouins. On the verge of succumbing to their blows, Haroun is rescued by Giafar, who, it so happens, is a friend of the Arab chieftain, having once saved his life. The story concludes happily: "With this stroke of generosity, [Giafar] disarms the monarch's vengeance" (Geoffroy, "Notice" 8–11).[12]

Despite the drastic alterations to the generally accepted historical account, it was not the narrative revisions to history or legend that provoked Pixérécourt's critics, but a notation in the program stating that "[l]'action se passe en 796, à Bagdad et dans les ruines de Babylone, qui n'en sont éloignées que de trois à quatre milles" (The action takes place in 796, in Baghdad and in the ruins of Babylon, which are only three or four miles distant).[13] As some critics took great pains to point out in their reviews of the premiere, Babylon was in fact situated on the banks of the Euphrates and so was actually quite far from Baghdad, which was built on the Tigris; it was therefore highly inaccurate to place the ruins of Babylon in the vicinity of Baghdad. Countering what he called "une chicane géographique" (geographical quibbling) instigated by those who were envious of Pixerécourt's success, Geoffroy defended the dramatist by noting: "Several writers, who have reason to be held to higher standards of accuracy than an author of melodramas, have made the same mistake and their opinion, although inaccurate, is enough to excuse M. de Pixeré-court" ("Notice" 7).[14] He further pointed out that the ruins of the ancient city of Seleucie, which had been known as the second Babylon, were in-deed located on the west bank of the Tigris not far from Baghdad. The final and greatest justification for Pixerécourt's choice of title and setting, how-ever, lay in the authorization cited by so many other authors of historical and national plays: the demands of a form designed to entertain for profit. Geoffroy was not alone in thinking that Pixerécourt "did well to consult euphony over geography," rejecting the dry and obscure Seleucie in favor of the sonorous and evocative Babylone ("Notice" 7–8).

The Spectator's Entrance

The importance of the spectator's phased entry into the diegetic world of a dramatic representation has been recognized by practitioners and theorists alike. It is during this process that the general theater spectator is consti-tuted as the spectator of a particular genre and of a particular work. At the most fundamental level, the successful engagement of a spectator requires his or her acceptance of the imaginary status of the work. Once this en-gagement has been established, as Roger Odin has observed with regard to cinematic representations,

[N]othing can seriously interfere with our enjoyment of the fiction: neither those elements which, when compared to the logic of the ordinary world, ought to ap-pear blatantly incoherent to us; nor those "unbelievable phenomena" that all films, even the most realistic, must necessarily contain: . . . the passing from one plane to another, the presence of music . . . ; nor the depiction of the most fantastic, the most unlikely, the most burlesque, or the most tragic events. ("Entrée" 205)

This general statement must, of course, be further modulated to apply to different genres. For example, in nineteenth-century boulevard theater, the *féerie*, with its focus on the supernatural and the fantastic, required that the spectator grant the broadest range to the imaginary. In the case of *Les Ruines de Babylone*, expectations surrounding a work advertised as a historical melodrama set in the Orient would condition the spectator to accept the unfamiliar as well as the unlikely or improbable—the latter two demands being made to varying degrees on audiences for all forms of melodrama. As compared to domestic melodramas, the limits of willing acceptance for the Oriental melodrama would be extended toward the impossible and therefore the unreal by an audience largely familiar with the tales of the *Thousand and One Nights*. A wide cross section of the French population became acquainted with these stories in the late eighteenth and early nineteenth centuries as the first translations and popular editions of the work became available. The imaginary and material association of stories involving historical figures and tales featuring magic carpets and genies which existed between the covers of the same volumes would have pushed the mode of reception toward the unreal. The commonly known stories about Harun al-Rashid and his court therefore conjured up a realm of legend and fantasy rather than one of social, political, and geographical realities. The extent of the audience's acquaintance is suggested by Geoffroy: "[I]t is even something of an advantage for the author who has put [these characters] on the stage; his actors are already known to the young and the old; there is no child who does not tremble at the name of the commander of believers and of his prime minister" ("Notice" 7).[15] This preexisting association would act to condition the spectators' mode of entry into the fiction of the performance even before the curtain was raised.

This connection was promoted on stage by the design of sets and costumes that could have served an Oriental melodrama or a *féerie* equally well. Once the curtain went up on *Les Ruines de Babylone*, the initial contextualization that was provided by the evocative title and audience familiarity with the *Thousand and One Nights* cycle was consciously and continuously reinforced by the design of the sets and costumes. These aimed at reproducing the images of material opulence and sensual elegance that had come to be closely associated with the Orient. Rojare, writing in the *Petites Affiches*, noted, "The management has lavished on this play everything that Asiatic luxury has to offer that is most brilliant and elaborate; this goes for the costumes as well as for the sets" (October 31, 1810).[16] This attention and expense was well justified, not only from the point of view of increased revenues, but in terms of the semiotic effectiveness of all that was to follow.

Not only did the sets and costumes provide the visual stimulation and sensory novelty considered essential to melodrama, they were also powerful agents in establishing and maintaining an essentially nonrealistic mode of reception for the duration of the performance. Geoffroy's commentary implicitly acknowledges their role in effecting a removal from actuality:

"The sets, the costumes, everything possesses a freshness, a brilliance that leaves nothing to be desired, and *that makes the spectators forget what country they are in*" ("Notice" 12; my emphasis).[17] The effect of this *dépaysement* was not simply geographical nor even merely temporal. An attendant social and political removal of the kind discussed in the preceding chapter will become evident, along with the mechanisms by which it was achieved, as the text of the play and its reception are analyzed.

While no visual representations of the sets have survived, the descriptions contained in the stage directions are detailed enough to furnish a clear idea of the sets and opening tableaux that served as a visual context for the staged events. The transportation into an unfamiliar milieu began as soon as the curtain rose:

The set depicts the interior of the harem gardens. At left, Zaïda's apartments, with one casement window overlooking the garden. At right, a kiosk, very simple in appearance. In the background, an elaborate grillwork. Upon opening the Venetian shutters with which it is equipped, one can see the Tigris which laps against the walls of the palace and the covered bridge that spans the river. The opposite bank offers a pleasant countryside dotted with pretty dwellings. (*Ruines* 21) [18]

The opening action set in this framework is the preparation for the festivities that will greet Giafar upon his triumphal return. Slaves are decking the set with flowers arranged in vases and in garlands. The foreign architecture and countryside signal a cultural disorientation, delivering the removal in space promised by the title. The introduction of the harem with its slaves, a social institution without any European equivalent, specifically bars any transfer from fictional representation to real world facilitated by structural homologies of the type feared in *Uncle Tom's Cabin* or *Atar-Gull* (see Chapter 2). What the harem did have, on the other hand, were innumerable imaginary referents in French theater: outside of tragedy, a form with a relatively limited following in the early nineteenth century, the harem was invariably the site of comic imbroglios or amorous intrigues. Far from promoting any connections with the European political or social situation, it convincingly discouraged, perhaps definitively precluded, any such association. Indeed, the ornate openwork of the architecture, the lavish floral decorations, the "campagne riante" and its "jolies habitations" create a carefree atmosphere of lightness and gaiety—the characteristic prelude to a comedy or fantasy.

While the dramatic stakes have risen by the beginning of the second act, the set does not reflect any escalation in tensions:

The set depicts a pretty round or octagonal pavilion in a pleasant forest. There are trees to be seen on either side of the pavilion, as well as through the doors and casement windows. The latter are decorated with blinds consisting of painted trellises. This structure must be very elegant and most of all very light. It occupies the entire width of the stage. (*Ruines* 53) [19]

Completing the picture of this idyllic retreat is the appearance of a young child, Naïr, the son of Giafar and Zaïda. He emerges from a secret entrance concealed by a marble tile and runs about the stage gathering flowers. This depiction of childhood innocence in an idyllic setting was that typically evoked in domestic melodrama to heighten the sense of invasive disorder brought on by the malignance of the hero's enemies. The sets, however, would continue to act as a constant reminder of the exotic circumstances of these injustices and of their origin in tales of fantasy and legend.

The decor of the third act is in some ways radically different from those of the first two acts. Its function, however, ultimately remains the same. For this final act,

The set depicts a portion of the ruins of Babylon, which extends toward the Tigris. At right, at the depth of the second and third wings, are the walls of a fortified castle, with a small concealed door that opens onto the stage. Very close to the forestage, on the same side, is a hut covered with palm branches. (*Ruines* 79) [20]

As the act opens, this set is populated by an encampment of Bedouins replete with "packs, camels, slaves, and draperies thrown over palm branches, etc." [21] The "etc.," primarily addressed to the set designers, suggests the high degree of codification that visual representations of the desert-dwelling Arabs had attained by 1810. The desolate aspect of the set performs the dramatic function of doubling the course of the narrative and shaping affective responses. At the same time, it continues to foreground the factors of difference. The signs of Oriental luxury, opulence, and fantasy are here merely replaced by those of the grandeur of ancient Mesopotamian history and civilization and those of the nomadic life of desert tribes. From curtain rise to curtain fall, the aggressive exoticism of the stage decoration held the spectators at a constant remove from the structured and structuring practices of their everyday existence. Once established, this mode of reception would account for certain liberties or a license that probably otherwise would have met with official censure beforehand and invited oppositional responses from different segments of the audience. Even before the actual presentation to outside readers and spectators, the fabulous context and exotic setting would prepare a mode of conception that, as we shall see, would allow Pixerécourt to compose scenes that might otherwise run counter to his own sense of social order and his self-proclaimed doctrines of artistic purpose and responsibility.

Differentiating Reception

Even as the sets, costumes, and subject matter cooperated to create a common recreational experience of disorientation and dislocation for all spectators, other elements permitted or even encouraged variations in audience reception. Not surprisingly, the major variations in reception corresponded to broad social divisions. Accounts of the opening night confirm that all segments of society were represented among the audiences drawn to *Les Ruines de Babylone*. Beaumont, reporting on the event for the *Journal de Soir*, declared,

Never, perhaps, did "Iphigénie en Aulide immolée" or the *Misanthrope* or *Tartuffe* see so massive a crowd make its way to their opening performances as did yesterday's melodrama. All the loges were reserved without exception; the Boulevard was congested by the immense number of spectators or would-be spectators; and finally, the barriers that some prudent foresight had set up in anticipation of their impatience were overturned. This is what we saw yesterday to our great risk and peril. (October 31, 1810) [22]

It would seem that the crowds were not disappointed, and there was a collective appreciation of the high production values of the melodrama. In the *Gazette de France*, Colnet gave due credit to those who had joined the author and actors in creating a new masterpiece for the boulevard stage, noting that "[n]ever, perhaps, have such fresh sets, such rich costumes, such gracious ballets been seen in Boulevard theater. The tailor, the choreographer, [and] the set designer have vied in imagination and talent, and each of them deserves to be crowned" (October 31, 1810). [23]

Not all elements of the play or production, however, were designed in a manner to produce uniform experiences of enjoyment. One character in particular, Raymond, was constructed in such a way as to elicit different modes of identification from various segments of the audience. These variations would be the result of the selective recognition or decoding of messages being transmitted along the internal and external circuits of communication. It would seem that there was both conscious and unconscious encoding on Pixerécourt's part. The distinctive features of this character can be identified partly as the residue of generic conventions and partly as a product of invention for this particular occasion.

Raymond can best be described as a character of strangely but significantly indeterminate status. According to the list of characters in the published edition of the play, his salient characteristics are that he is "français" and the "ami secret de Giafar." Going into further detail, Geoffroy writes: "The author has given the outlaws as their guardian angel a Frenchman named Raymond, all of whose sallies delight the caliph: this young man, full of wit, gaiety, and courage, is devoted to the interests of Giafar, follows him everywhere, and delivers him from the greatest dangers" ("Notice" 10).[24] From the outset, contemporary commentators regarded Raymond as a readily identifiable stock character of melodrama, the comic figure, drawn from original models in comedy and the closely allied genre of the *féerie* or *mélo-féerie*. Colnet was struck mainly by the comic function of the character: "[T]he author has drawn from his brain a French comedian, clever and possessed of great presence of mind and courage."[25] For Jean-Marie Thomasseau, looking back from a distance of 160 years and presenting an overview of classical French melodrama, Raymond was clearly identifiable as one of the stock figures associated specifically with historical melodrama: *le bouffon*. The features and function of this character (the fool, buffoon, jester, or clown) were closely intertwined with those of another permanent resident of the genre: the tyrant. Thomasseau outlines their relationship in the chapter of his study on melodrama devoted to the cataloging of "Les Personnages." The tyrant-fool pairing, which the Haroun-Raymond duo in *Les Ruines de Babylone* seems to exemplify, is discussed in the section on "Le Personnage du traître," under the subheading "Les Types généraux dans le mélodrame historique":

These [tyrants] are above all omnipotent podestas, who are very proud of their all-powerful status. The characteristic traits by which they achieved popular recognition are arbitrariness and cruelty. A tyrant is necessarily somewhat stupid and very bloodthirsty. They strike terror into the hearts of their subjects.

Nothing can, nothing must, be allowed to resist them. If anyone ever opposes their will, they unleash a boundless fury. Only certain favorites, a fool or an innocent, are entitled to say what they really think of their master. And the master, charmed by the straightforwardness of the fool, casually allows some liberties to pass. The fool restores to the tyrant the lucidity that his anger had banished. We find in the character of Haroun, in *Les Ruines de Babylone*, an excellent example of the tyrant king, and the little couplet to the credit of the fool is not missing. (224–25)

The strength of the precedent for identifying Raymond as a comic figure with a critical supporting function is made clear by Thomasseau: "This obligatory intervention of the comic, absent in the earliest forms of melodrama . . . was slowly codified until little by little it became an indispensable convention, demanded both by the requirements of the genre and by public taste" (295). Pixerécourt's own commitment to this requirement has been documented, and there is every indication that he conceived of Raymond as the comic interest of the piece. He was convinced that the relatively poor reception (61 performances in Paris and 163 in the provinces) of his earlier historical melodrama, *Les Maures d'Espagne* (1804), could be traced to the very fact that it lacked any comic leavening. In a retrospective assessment he wrote: "Undoubtedly, the fault [lay] in the style of the play, which [was] completely serious, whereas all my other dramas are mixed with gaiety" (*Maures* 15).[26] In *Les Ruines de Babylone* the figure of Raymond was designed to remedy this deficiency.

The supporting aspect of Raymond's role as "l'ami de Giafar" also had ample precedent in melodrama. Generally, the type of relationship that existed between the central heroic figure and a devoted subordinate was that of master and servant. These servants were, in Thomasseau's words, "entirely devoted to the interests of their master, and even ready, if called upon, to sacrifice their lives for them"; the servant's attitude toward his master was "made up entirely of deference and genuine affection" (105–6). This ready classification, however, begins to seem premature if all the details of the characterization are carefully considered. Despite the fact that the character of Raymond was certainly conceived of according to the aesthetic or dramatic principles of the fully formalized genre, certain aspects of his speech and behavior seem to violate critical moral and political tenets—tenets that were central to the development of the form and to Pixerécourt's own perceptions of his function as a dramatic author.

Raymond's transgressions of the bounds of generic conventions, which would have relegated him as a comic and auxiliary figure to a secondary and subordinate status, begin very early in the play. They are evident at the levels of both dramatic and linguistic structuring. The nature and extent of Raymond's overturning of the hierarchical order of melodrama is brought out when excerpts from the dialogue are analyzed in the light of Anne Ubersfeld's approach to the mode of functioning of dramatic dialogue. She observes that "the mode of exchange is already a sign that makes possible the construction of meaning, and is itself a bearer of meaning" (*Lire* 256–57). She stresses the fact that "[t]he basis of dialogue is the

relationship of power between the characters, this formulation being understood in its broadest sense: [since] the relationship of love can also be a
relationship of domination, to desire is thus to be a supplicant in a position of 'inferiority' with regard to he who is in possession of the object of
desire" (*Lire* 257). Ubersfeld's model of theatrical dialogue is founded on a
semio-pragmatic approach to the production of meaning in conversational
exchange. The key premise as far as the analysis of theatrical dialogue is
concerned is the following:

A theatrical dialogue therefore has a double layered content; it delivers two types
of messages; the same system of (linguistic) signs has a twofold content:
    a. the content itself of the utterances of the discourse;
    b. the information concerning the conditions of production of these utterances.
    To forget this second layer of information, because it is less apparent, amounts
to mutilating the meaning of the utterances themselves. . . . Theatrical dialogue is
created on the basis of a presupposition that governs it: that one of the interlocu-
tors, for example, has the capacity to dictate the law of dialogue. Let us go further;
the first message of the dialogue of the theater is precisely the verbal relationship
and the presuppositions that govern it. (*Lire* 257–58)

    A reading of the dialogue according to Ubersfeld's model reveals that
Raymond's position in conversation with his "master" is actually always
at least that of an adviser and in many cases exceeds that of a subordinate
in any capacity. Raymond, having served in the role of Giafar's "eyes and
ears" during the grand vizir's absence, apprises him of the current situation
in the caliph's court. It soon becomes clear that Raymond's role is not limited to that of messenger and facilitator, but extends to that of adviser and
even more. These more assertive aspects of his role emerge clearly in the
following exchange. (It should be noted that throughout the play, Giafar
uses the forms of *tu* in addressing Raymond, while Raymond always responds with *vous*.)

RAYMOND: Where is your son?
GIAFAR: In his refuge.
RAYMOND: Is it impenetrable?
GIAFAR: To all eyes.
RAYMOND: May you be right!
GIAFAR: What is the cause of this uneasiness? Have you come to tell me of
some misfortune?
RAYMOND: No. But I fear everything from the plots of your enemy. I don't

know what secret foreboding tells me that the departure of Haroun is only a ploy to find out more about your moves. Be doubly on your guard, my Lord, or you are lost.

(2.4)[27]

Raymond's role is not restricted to gathering information from sources inaccessible to Giafar; he goes much further by assessing this information, forming his own conclusions, and then presenting his recommendations in the imperative mood to his benefactor and superior. By the end of this fragment of dialogue, Giafar will once again assume the dominant role, in terms of his language and authoritative gesture. He takes charge of the situation and the conversation, but not before he has been shown as sharing the right to take the initiative in both speech and action.

The fact that Raymond's cautions are intended and heard as prescriptions and are not mere outcries of concern is assured by the context in which they are presented. They follow immediately upon an exchange in which Raymond is shown to possess the right to initiate and direct the dialogue. But even earlier, from the very beginning, in fact, Raymond is depicted as the instigator of the action. The curtain rises on a scene of great activity as preparations for a festival to honor Giafar are being made. Raymond is clearly at the center of this action. The stage directions note that "Raymond directs everything. His recommendations and his activity impart great animation to this tableau" (1.1).[28] When introduced to the audience, then, Raymond is presented in a position of dominance both in the diegetic universe—the universe of the fiction—and in the theatrical universe of the Théâtre de la Gaîté.

The circumstances of his first encounter with Giafar reinforce this impression of dominance and control. Giafar makes his first appearance surreptitiously, disguised as a slave. Raymond's reaction, his assumption that the mysterious figure is a supplicant in need of a favor, are indicative of his position of power in this milieu. While Giafar reveals his identity as soon as Raymond has dismissed the other slaves and the scene of recognition cited above takes place, it is not before Raymond has been established as a central and authoritative figure. From the moment of his unmasking, Giafar will share center stage with Raymond, but even with the backing of all the attributes of the traditional hero of historical melodrama—-as loving husband and father, loyal subject and valiant conqueror—he will never be able to reclaim it entirely for himself. Contrary to Geoffroy's perception, throughout the course of the play Raymond never "follows" Giafar around. He *seeks out* Giafar on his own initiative at critical moments; he is in fact sought out by Giafar; and, most importantly, in the final act he takes it upon himself to act in the place of Giafar. On this occasion, by rescuing Giafar's son Naïr from execution, he performs the role properly occupied by the father. Raymond's status as a surrogate rather than an assistant is reinforced by an implicit comparison to a parallel rescue of Naïr by his father.

An ostensible explanation for Raymond's dramatic centrality, theatrical visibility, and linguistic authority is in fact inserted into the text. In act 1, scene 5, we learn of the events accounting for Raymond's devotion to Giafar and the circumstances of his emigration to Baghdad:

RAYMOND: . . . I owe a great deal to Giafar: during this minister's stay at the court of Charlemagne, I had occasion to experience the goodness of his heart. My family was oppressed; he restored to them all their assets at one and the same time, their honor and their fortune. I attached myself to him, and I left France to follow him to Baghdad. He considered me as a second self and confided his innermost thoughts to me.[29]

The implication is clear: Raymond came from a family of some, however vague and indeterminate, social and financial standing. This solution, however, does not hold up when the theatrical conventions of the period are considered. Up to this time, except for a brief period during and immediately following the Revolution, it was inconceivable that in a licensed theater a member of the aristocracy or even the haute bourgeoisie should be cast in a predominantly comic role. Not only does Raymond sing vaudevillian couplets, but he accompanies the musical refrain of this song by dancing "d'une manière bouffonne" for the amusement of the caliph and the audience. Furthermore, as all reviews and subsequent discussions up to the present demonstrate, the ostensible facts of Raymond's background do not seem to have registered as significant information. This is not surprising, as no effort was made to foreground this information in subsequent scenes.[30] Raymond's origins quickly fade into the background. Instead, it becomes clear that the authorization for his transgressions of hierarchy derives not from his social status but from his national origin.

The fact that Raymond is "français" was singled out by Pixerécourt as the primary identifying feature of the character in the cast listing. Audiences were never allowed to forget that Raymond was a Frenchman. At one time or another, Raymond is referred to as "ce Français" by his adversaries and by those with whom he is allied. Isouf, his evil counterpart, is particularly given to making asides along the lines of "Ce Français peut m'être utile! essayons de le séduire, sauf à le perdre ensuite" (This Frenchman may be useful to me! Let's try to seduce him, only to bring about his downfall afterward [1.5]). In the opposite camp, it is Zaïda who is prone to exclaim things like "Ce Français est charmant" (1.11) or to observe that his wit or perceptiveness is "digne d'un Français" (worthy of a Frenchman [1.10]). As for external appreciations, Colnet's description of Raymond as "un comique français plein d'adresse, de présence d'esprit et de courage" has already been cited. Even more emphatic on this point is Geoffroy's evaluation of the character as written and performed. Once again the qualities of being "plein d'esprit, de gaîté et de courage" (full of wit, gaiety, and courage) are connected to the fact that this is, as Colnet pointed out, "*un Français* nommé Raymond" (my emphasis). Furthermore, this implied ascription is made explicit on the theatrical plane as Geoffroy vaunts the same "French" qualities in praising the actor's performance: "This role is played by Tautin, with a vivaciousness, a finesse, and a playfulness worthy of the French nation" ("Notice" 10).[31]

All of the attributes and qualities mentioned above would have contributed to the entire audience's (or at least to its French members) appreciation of Raymond as a theatrical character. The source of his high appeal—apart from the comic effectiveness with which the part was written and played—has already been traced to the complicity he establishes with the audience from the outset; this complicity, as noted, relied in part on the presupposition of a common French identity and benefited from the repeated assertion of that identity. In these respects, the appeal to all segments of the audience could be assumed to be equal in magnitude and common in nature. I would argue, however, that the character of Raymond also possessed a more selective appeal. Scene 7 of act 2 consists of a monologue by Raymond which includes the following lines:

RAYMOND: . . . Let us be on our guard; let us redouble in guile and activity; let us not forget that the wicked are not in the least discouraged by reversals: they unceasingly find, in the desire to do harm, the courage and resolve necessary to form new plans. *It is therefore fair that those who are forced to obey should be more ingenious than the one who is in command.*

(My emphasis) [32]

Taken in their immediate context, Raymond's comments refer to the binary opposition of good versus evil established by the conventions of melodrama. But, by this time, the action of the play has established his position of enunciation as that of a speaker who does not participate in officially organized forms of power.

Taken in the context of the play as a whole, the closing line of the speech sums up the mode of operation by which disempowered members of society are able to exercise some degree of control or creative direction within the limitations of a situation structured from above. Here Michel de Certeau's model of opposing strategies of control and tactics of resistance, which has already proved useful in explicating the phenomenon of applications and allusions (see Chapter 2), can be applied to understanding the audience-performance relationship generated by the figure of Raymond. As de Certeau has described the tactic, it is "a calculated action determined by the absence of a proper locus" (37). Therefore,

[The tactic] does not . . . have the options of planning general strategy and viewing the adversary as a whole within a distinct, visible, and objectifiable space. It operates in isolated actions, blow by blow. It takes advantage of "opportunities" and depends on them. . . . What it wins it cannot keep. This nowhere gives a tactic mobility, to be sure, but a mobility that must accept the chance offerings of the moment, and seize on the wing the possibilities that offer themselves at any given moment. (*Practice* 37)

Interested audience members may or may not have seized upon this particular remark and interpreted it out of context in the manner of an allusion. But all along they could not have helped but recognize and identify with the underlying *logic* of Raymond's behavior with an appreciation known only to those who have lived their everyday lives according to that logic. Raymond's social status may have remained obscure, but the origins of his mode of operating were not. While many members of the audience enjoyed the ubiquitous character as a purely theatrical creation, others were afforded the opportunity to witness the staging of their own deterritorialized mode of operation.

Occident and Orient

The representation of the Orient in *Les Ruines de Babylone* was subject not only to the institutional forces and generic considerations that shaped the melodrama as a whole, but to the pressures of continually evolving Orientalist discourses as well. The very choice of subject matter engaged the play in contrasts between Occident and Orient that were quite literally medieval. Harun al-Rashid's contemporaneity with Charlemagne seems to have provided an open invitation for a comparison of the two rulers. This invitation was accepted by both Geoffroy and Dusaulchoy. Their remarks offer direct evidence of the conceptual and perceptual frontier that would increasingly separate the Occident, more specifically France, and the Orient in both authoritative discourses and the popular imagination. Each makes the comparison betwen the two rulers with a slightly different focus, but to the same end: to proclaim the superiority of the French monarch over the Oriental despot.

In his review of *Les Ruines de Babylone*, Dusaulchoy compares the two figures as individuals. In the following passage the definite articles in the terms "le monarque français" and "le despote oriental" are employed to specify rather than to generalize. The relative merits of two men and not those of two systems of government are under discussion:

Haroun-al-Raschid was the fifth caliph of the race of the Abassides. He has been compared to Charlemagne; but how great was the superiority of the French monarch over the oriental despot! In all the great things that Haroun did, one always saw nearby his vizir Giafar the Barmecide, born of a family at all times known for its generosity; this minster shared the glory of his master, anticipated all the mistakes he might make, and taught him excellent lessons. Now, it would be difficult to name Charlemagne's minister. . . . [33]

It is interesting to note that the absence of prominent ministers at Charlemagne's court is cited as an indication of his greatness as a ruler. The mythologies surrounding the Oriental ruler, however, caused a similar absence to be interpreted as evidence of absolutist, despotic control.

Geoffroy's unfavorable comparison of the two emperors is more damaging. He comes much closer than Dusaulchoy to situating the comparison on a more global level and directly opposing the Occident to the Orient. He still stops short, however, of suggesting that there is some inherent superiority of one civilization over the other. The form of government exercised is held responsible for the excesses of the rulers and their arbitrary use of power:

Haroun-al-Raschid was the contemporary, but not the rival of Charlemagne. The illustrious Western emperor was always as wise a monarch as he was a courageous one; the caliph of the Orient was too often a senseless despot: to some acts of justice and generosity, he added too great a number of bizarre, extravagant, and cruel actions, the sad destiny of oriental princes, who can do whatever they want: it rarely occurs to them to want what is reasonable. ("Notice" 8) [34]

Here, although the exercise of absolute power is being denounced, the possibility of generosity and wisdom in Asian government and governors is still admitted. This view left room for the stock roles of the *bons* and the *méchants* of melodrama to be distributed over a non-Western cast. Authoritative models of despotic government, notably those produced by Enlightenment philosophers, were readily subordinated or simply entirely sacrificed to dramatic exigencies. This accommodation was essential since the lack of virtue, honor, and ambition considered endemic to despotic states was entirely incompatible with the conventions of a dramatic form that required the opposition of good and evil within a single community.

Pixerécourt's actual treatment of Haroun offers a striking example of the adaptation of a culturally coded figure to a set of generic requirements, themselves shaped to a considerable extent by political concerns. All the qualities most commonly identified with the Oriental despot are enumerated in the course of three acts of *Les Ruines de Babylone*. The despotic prince's propensity for making arbitrary decisions and behaving erratically are in fact central to the action of the play. The pertinent features of the caliph are summed up in a speech by Giafar:

Who better than I knows this arrogant despot, so astonishing by the inconceivable mixture of the best and the worst of qualities. I know that this prince, justly renowned in the Orient for his bravery, his liberality, and the good deeds with which he has showered his peoples, has shown himself to be capricious, ungrateful, even cruel; that he sacrifices, without scruple and without regret, the most sacred rights of gratitude and humanity to his unfounded suspicions and to the eccentricity of his tastes.

(1.3)[35]

Conspicuously absent here, however, is any suggestion, such as that made by Geoffroy, that a system of absolute governance might produce despotic behavior. The other characters similarly reduce Haroun's conduct in all areas public and private to the level of personal idiosyncrasy. For example, Raymond describes Haroun's behavior as "une suite naturelle de la bizarrerie de son caractère" (a natural outcome of the eccentricity of his character). The most plausible reason for insisting that Haroun's arbitrary exercise of power be seen as the consequence of individual quirks or character defects is the same that lay behind Pixerécourt's decision to transfer all blame for the Barmecide's troubles to Haroun's first wife, Almaïde. In Pixerécourt's adaptation of the story, an intensely jealous and vengeful Almaïde, the rejected lover of Giafar, is the one to suggest the marriage

between Haroun's sister and the vizir in the first place. In introducing
Isouf, Geoffroy added the point of information that "he serves the sultana
Almaïde's hatred for the vizir, who disdained her favors" Notice" 10).[36]

Given the conservative ideological orientation of so many melodramatists and critics and the tight control of the censors, it seems certain that
such moves were incorporated into the form in response to the injunc-
tion to place questions of unjust government firmly in the realm of the
personal. This move was an extremely familiar one by 1810, after a decade
under Napoleonic rule. So familiar was it, in fact, that it seems to have become almost a structural reflex on the part of Pixerécourt. The obsession
with suppressing any depiction of the defiance or overthrow of legitimate
ultimate authority, even when this figure was the head of an enemy state
(see Chapter 2); the concern to avoid presenting the justified criticism of
any such figure; and the desire to dissociate heads of state from the possibility of a fundamentally evil nature—with significant modifications in
the case of the Oriental despot, which will be discussed shortly—all have
been amply attested to in the censorship reports of the time. The device of
placing final responsibility for malicious acts and conspiracies on traitor-
ous subordinates, jealous spouses, or rejected lovers, was, as just seen in
the case of Almaïde, routinely used.

The neutralization of issues regarding just rule and the appropriate
exercise of power by relating them to purely personal motives based on
ambition or the desire for revenge or material gain was equally commonplace. In this case, however, the point—much like Raymond's genealogy—
often seems to be driven so far into the background as to be forgotten
by the characters. After the initial revelation by Isouf of the true perpetrator of the persecution of Giafar and Zaïda in act 1, scene 5, the fact is
alluded to on a couple of occasions, but Almaïde's existence is superfluous
as far the advancement of the narrative is concerned. Her role is made all
the more inconspicuous by the fact that Almaïde never appears on stage
and the critical final scene of resolution is carried out without any further
mention of her role as instigator. In the final scene and tableau, Haroun
is charged with full responsibility for all the injustices and persecutions as
though Almaïde had never existed, and the resolution is enacted around
him. But neither Almaïde's existence nor her absence was a cause for criticism, dissatisfaction, or even comment as far as the reviewers or audience
were concerned. It seems likely that her actual presence was eliminated in
the interests of dramatic focus and economy, while the token attribution
of blame was observed as a matter of form in a traditional concession to
the sensibilities of the censors.

The dictum to neutralize any challenge to the order or legitimacy of government receives its most assertive expression in the final scene and closing tableau of *Les Ruines de Babylone*. In the next-to-last scene, Haroun, who has already indicated his willingness to revoke his death sentence upon the Barmecide race, is attacked by Aboulcasem—chief of the Bedouins, ally of Giafar, and *not* one of Haroun's subjects—and soon disarmed. The impending fatal blow—implied but not specifically indicated by the stage directions—is averted by the precipitous entry of Giafar, which opens the final scene. In the dialogue of this scene, the revised balance of power will be reflected in language itself: here for the first time Giafar addresses Haroun as *tu*. Giafar first calls Haroun's attention to the hopelessness of his situation.

GIAFAR: . . . You can see, Haroun, your situation offers no hope of salvation; your guards are devoted to me; the Bedouins are your enemies; here you are alone in the midst of the most fearsome dangers, and you no longer even have to defend you, the support of your crown, your most ardent friend, Giafar.[37]

Calling for a vocal demonstration of loyalty and unquestioning obedience from the assembled company—a loyalty that is solemnly sworn in the name of the same Mahomet whose name was taken in vain by Raymond in the opening scene—Giafar then pronounces his judgment on the caliph:

GIAFAR: (*With energy.*) Very well then, follow me. (*He raises his scimitar. The soldiers and the Bedouins do as much.*) Everyone bow down before your legitimate sovereign. (*All set down their weapons and prostrate themselves before the caliph. Slaves and Bedouins run in and fill the ruins.*)
HAROUN: Ah! Giafar! . . . how unjust I have been, and how noble is your vengeance! (*He raises him and reaches out his arms. Giafar runs into them.*) Zaïda, Naïr, Hassan, Raymond, come all of you into my arms.
GIAFAR: Oh my master! (*The curtain falls.*)[38]

To complete the discussion of the relationship between the representation of Oriental despotism and domestic political concerns, there is a final point regarding the reception of *Les Ruines de Babylone* that must be raised. Or rather, once again, it is the very lack of discernible reaction on a certain point that calls for comment. Pixerécourt's views on the unstable nature and latent violence of *le peuple* and his ideas regarding the role of theater in keeping those forces in check are not to be equated with a rejection of political opposition across the board. On the contrary, he advocated the criticism of and opposition to a repressive regime if it was carried out by "responsible" and educated citizens.

Seven years earlier Pixerécourt himself was thought to have engaged in the more subtle forms of criticism connected with the theater. The incident involved *Tékéli, ou le Siége de Montgatz*, his most popular historical drama, first performed on December 29, 1803, at the Ambigu-Comique. This play recounted the adventures of a deposed Hungarian ruler named Tékéli, who eventually is restored to his throne. It appeared in an atmosphere of political instability created by a recent series of royalist plots. Certain scenes concerning the sheltering of a political fugitive were thought to present suspiciously close analogies to an actual recent event, even though the play had been in performance for a month before the occurrence of the incident in question. These resemblances, however, appeared in conjunction with remarks more or less blatantly directed at the emperor. One monologue exhorted:

Oh you privileged beings, whom chance, birth, or talent has placed at the head of nations; always show yourself to be just and good to the peoples who are subject to you: through generous deeds wisely apportioned, know how to win the hearts of those who surround you; in the midst of your glory, perhaps a reversal awaits you, you will find a friend in each of those whom you have made happy.

(1.2)[39]

In scene 6 of the same act, another character offered the observation: "Fame magnifies objects and often makes the very great reputation of a general, at the expense of one or another of his officers or even his soldiers, who has contributed, more than he, to his successes" (qtd. in Thomasseau 122).[40] Rumors of the provocative content of the melodrama had apparently circulated and prompted the attendance of Murat and Duroc, two government officials, at the forty-eighth performance. The fact that the objectionable passages were uttered by the actors playing the naïfs of the cast failed to distract the government agents. On their recommendation, the play was closed as of the following evening. Some compromise was evidently reached, as the play eventually ran for 904 performances in Paris alone, and no subsequent play of Pixerécourt's encountered any objections from the censors.

Les Ruines de Babylone, however, contains lines that could easily have been interpreted as containing a renewal of anti-Bonapartist criticism on Pixérécourt's part. This critique takes the form of a rider attached to the traditional advocation of submission to legitimate authority. Giafar's speech to the defeated Haroun holds the caliph himself responsible for the disaffection and rebellion of his subjects through his abuse of absolute power:

GIAFAR: . . . You forced [Giafar] to desert your cause, both through your injustice and your cruelties. Recognize finally how dangerous it is to abandon oneself to the impetuosity of passions. He who governs a great people owes them great examples. If, suppressing a blind rage, you had heeded only the voice of justice, by keeping a wife and son for he who had just saved your states, you would not, in a single day, have tarnished your glory, outraged friendship, gone against nature, and compromised the supreme rank.

(3.15)[41]

In 1810, to all outward appearances, Napoleon was still at the height of his power in France and Europe. The borders of the Napoleonic Empire had reached what would be their outer limits the year before, and in April 1810 he had married his second wife, Marie-Louise of Austria, who soon became pregnant with an heir (born in March 1811). This promise of a dynasty, however, took place against the growing resentment of the bourgeoisie at Napoleon's absolute control over all aspects of public life. Expressions of such resentment were consistently being stifled by an efficient administrative system that included surveillance by censors, police, and courts over the press, theater, and political activity. (Once Napoleon had been deposed, many writers would openly proclaim the resentment and hostility they had felt during the last years of the Empire.) In February 1810 Napoleon created a directorship of the press, which shortly thereafter shut down 97 out of 157 printing presses in Paris; compelled booksellers to apply for licenses and submit to an oath; and greatly restricted the activities of reading rooms and lending libraries.

While there was a period of relative relaxation in dramatic censorship around mid-decade, 1809 saw a renewed intensity of surveillance following some unfortunately timed productions of plays that involved divorces prompted by the lack of an heir (Welschinger 239ff). A letter dated February 8, 1810, from Napoleon to the superintendant of theaters, Rémusat, stated: "Vous ne devez mettre aucune nouvelle pièce à l'étude sans mon consentement" (You must not undertake any new play without my consent

[Welschinger 240]). While the emperor himself was primarily concerned with the official theaters, it seems highly unlikely that those charged with the surveillance of the secondary theaters could have been uninfluenced by this demand for renewed vigilance.

Given these conditions of increasing internal discontent and a recently stimulated body of censors, it might seem surprising, first, that Giafar's speech should have been allowed to remain intact in the first place, and second, that no members of the audience availed themselves of this opportunity to voice their political sympathies. Even though the implied criticism is more firmly embedded in the fictional narrative than it was in *Tékéli*, where the offending monologues were not always convincingly motivated by the action, the censors had proved themselves ready and able to ferret out far more obscure allusions. Furthermore, this particular passage aside, the fundamental premise of the play condemned an absolute ruler in a context that in many respects corresponded more closely to the position of Napoleon than did the situation in *Tékéli*.

Undoubtedly a number of factors contributed to the general consensus that, in the case of *Les Ruines de Babylone*, exhortations regarding the responsible exercise of absolute power should remain relegated to the internal circuit of communication. But the evidence gathered from the censors' reports and critical reviews regarding plays on non-Western subjects indicate one overriding reason for this response or lack thereof. In particular, the difference in response to *Tékéli* as opposed to *Les Ruines de Babylone* bears a striking resemblance to the documented case of *Pauliska*, which was presented in 1812, only two years after *Les Ruines de Babylone*. It will be recalled (see Chapter 2) that the censors felt certain that the removal of the action from Russia to "le pais des mille et une nuits"—with the accompanying change of title to *Zoraïde and Zuliska* and the transformation of the characters into "un Sultan, des janissaires, d'Arabes du désert"—would safely preclude any allusions or applications to contemporary political and military events. In the case of *Les Ruines de Babylone*, the immediate association with the fantasy of the *Mille et une nuits* removed the play's contents so thoroughly from the realm of actuality that any transfer from the diegetic to the real world was blocked. As mentioned above, this distancing was reinforced and reimpressed upon the public each time the curtain rose on a new act to reveal sets designed to create a world of marvelous lightness and exotic opulence, or a desert wilderness far removed from any European landscape. As for the critical representation of the omnipotent ruler, the configurations of the Oriental despot had been so securely codified and so well established as a theatrical and fictional presence over the seventeenth and eighteenth centuries that not only would the character of Haroun fail to elicit any comparison with Napoleon but, as we have seen, he actually served as a reminder of the infinite superiority of French absolutism. The line of otherness was indelibly drawn between the Orient and the Occident as far as any application to political and social realities were concerned.

This line dividing East and West, however, did not yet interfere with the great latitude that existed with regard to fictional Oriental characters. As mentioned earlier, the entire repertory of melodramatic roles and a complete hierarchy of power could be distributed over an Oriental cast, and the audience would experience the satisfyingly full range of emotional stimulation that was the province of melodrama. As Salgue of the *Journal des Arts* remarked: "Pretty ballets, fresh settings, these are for the eyes; but the heart and the spirit must also be engaged, and the prodigious crowds that make their way to the increased number of performances of this work offer ample proof that the author has not neglected any means to please and to move."[42] In short, all testimony indicates that audience responses to *Les Ruines de Babylone* were in the end regulated primarily by generic considerations and competencies.

The extent to which generic conventions dictated the mode of reception of *Les Ruines de Babylone* is reflected in the juxtaposition of radically opposed treatments of the Islamic religion that occur in the one play. The initial tone is set by the highly irreverent, even sacrilegious nature of Raymond's opening number:

Je ris tout bas de votre Mahomet;
Que le Prophète ici me le pardonne!
Mais aux plaisirs que sa loi vous promet,
Moi, je préfère un baiser qu'on me donne.

Aux vrais croyants, dans son livre divin,
Après leur mort, il promet l'ambroisie.
Ah! sans attendre un bonheur incertain,
Transportons-nous d'avance en l'autre vie.

Ah! si j'étais maître de ce séjour,
Du vrai bonheur trouvant la route sûre,
Je bannirais Mahomet de ma cour,
Pour y fixer à jamais Epicure.[43]

Figure 5. The inebriated Muslim. Alcide Tousey in the role of Dogard. Frontispiece for *Lekain à Draguignan*, by MM. de Forges and Paul Vermond (1839). *Magasin Théâtral*, vol. 24. The New York Public Library; Astor, Lenox and Tilden Foundations.

This number had ample precedent in treatments of the Orient in the comedies and vaudevilles of the first decade of the nineteenth century. The inebriated Muslim, for instance, was a familiar source of comedy on the boulevard stage (Figure 5).

What is curious in the case of *Les Ruines de Babylone*, however, is that this opening mockery of Islam, which recurs at regular intervals, in no way prevented the Islamic faith from functioning as the requisite signifier of the virtue, integrity, and moral stature of the principal characters. Jean-Marie Thomasseau has emphasized both the indispensable nature of a providential presence in melodrama and the readiness with which other faiths or sects could be substituted for a Christian model:

> One must not suppose however that this God being beseeched is more Catholic than Protestant or Hindu. A remarkable discretion always allows some ambiguity to linger as to the religion practiced by honest folk. Whether they are Tartars, Moldavians, Spaniards, Hungarians, Genevans, or French, they always invoke the same God who never fails to answer them. . . . A great religious tolerance reigns in the universe of melodrama. What does it matter whether one prays to Buddha, a totem, or Allah, so long as one has a religious soul. (95–96)

Accordingly, in the most touching moments of maternal, paternal, or general familial distress, under the duress of unjust persecution, and in the utterance of most solemn oaths, "le Dieu des Croyants," "la protection du Prophète," and so on, could be invoked to full dramatic effect. Even Raymond, who, as the only non-Muslim in the cast, is the sole perpetrator of the jests belittling the Islamic religion in comic scenes, bears a respectful demeanor before expressions of piety on the part of Giafar and Zaïda in the dramatic scenes. It is not that Raymond abruptly alters his attitude at specific, isolated moments. The variations occur on a scene-by-scene basis marked by shifts in the very style or level of his language: the rhetoric Raymond employs ranges from the elevated or noble style of melodrama in its tragic mode to the familiar style of its comic manifestations. The only requirement for stylistic consistency seems to have been that the integrity of a scene be maintained.

The confidence with which Pixérécourt could count on deriving essentially contradictory comic and dramatic effects from the same source—features of the Islamic religion—attests to the high degree of competence of the public of the Gaîté. Familiar with the conglomerate nature of melodrama and comfortable with the lack of classical stylistic coherence, they would automatically shift into the appropriate mode of reception scene by scene. Individual figures—here, the evocation of Muhammad—fulfilled the function assigned them by their immediate context, which included the style or mode of the scene. Spectators found no incongruity and experienced no difficulty in alternating between modes of representation through the course of a single play.

In the decades to come, as will be seen in the next section, the opportunities for mixed reception and the option of "full-cast distribution" regardless of the designated origin of the characters would gradually be eliminated from the dramatic repertory and only the more limited and interested possibilities presented in the national or military dramas would remain. In these works virtue was invariably housed in the French camp or settlements, while the opposing forces of evil, injustice, oppression, lawlessness, and the like became identified with the racial attributes of Arabs and the religious tenets of Islam. Similarly, the prioritization of dramatic form over authoritative discourse would become not only less frequent where the Orient was concerned, but unnecessary as the new forms of national drama and military epic incorporated the very structures of political, intellectual, scientific, and military discourses.

PART II

DRAMATIC CAMPAIGNS

It would be some time before re-creations of historic moments and re-enactments of memorable military engagements in the Middle East would supersede the exoticism of historical melodramas as the primary form for structuring popular theatrical representations of the region. But as an increasingly large segment of the French population began to have actual contact with the Middle East and North Africa either as invaders, travelers, or settlers, the delicate balance between fantasy and verisimilitude that was crucial for the success of Orientalized melodramas was irremediably upset. This loss of equilibrium was precipitated not only by the new scale of involvement but also by the increasing regularity and efficiency with which reports from these regions were disseminated to an everbroadening public. These reports, couched in the language of administrative, scientific, and journalistic discourses of Orientalism, betrayed attitudes inconsistent with the anodyne portrayals and sympathetic positionings characteristic of historical melodrama. Evolving relations called for new representative paradigms, the generation of which would be anything but spontaneous.

The problems attendant upon any representation of reality have been eloquently laid out by Hayden White. In "The Value of Narrativity in the Representation of Reality," he notes: "Narrative becomes a *problem* only when we wish to give to *real* events the *form* of a story. It is because real events do not offer themselves as stories that their narrativization is so difficult" (8). He characterizes "narration and narrativity as the instruments by which the conflicting claims of the imaginary and the real are mediated, arbitrated, or resolved in a discourse" (8). Although White is concerned with historiography rather than with dramaturgy, his observations are equally appropriate for considering the reconstitution of historical events for the stage.

Anne Ubersfeld has in fact already posed the problem of this negotiation for theater in general in her discussion of the concept of *l'effet du réel* (the reality effect) discussed at greater length in Chapter 1:

According to a stubborn illusion, the task of *referentialization* (the manufacturing of a context) involves relating the story to something real, constructing a socio-historical reality on stage. In fact, the situation is more complicated: the theatrical manifestation never refers to something real, but to a discourse on the real; never to history, but to an idea of history. (*Ecole* 259)

As always, it ultimately remains for the spectator to construct the relationship between the fiction and his or her own experience. Ubersfeld insists on the ideological function inherent in the process of referentialization, activated as producers seek to control audience reactions by blocking or directing the possible connections to be made. As we have already seen, attempts on the part of various authorities to forestall certain connections were regularly thwarted. As we shall also see, in the case of the national drama, equally concerted attempts to compel favorable spectator responses toward government policies and actions or specific social values and conduct could just as easily prove ineffective. Whether the official intention was to suppress or to promote an agenda by allowing the audience as little interpretive license as possible, the very act of putting the spectacle before an audience was always in itself an open invitation to commentary, both vociferous and demonstrative.

Military spectacles and national dramas were by definition designed to sustain regimes, parties, or individuals currently in power. These aims, in order to be realized, required that the events be presented in a narrative and visual framework that was as engaging and appealing as it was ideologically motivated. From the outset, it was apparently taken for granted that even the most recent events could not be represented in the theater without being subjected to some "artistic" shaping or transformation. This shaping ranged from what was described as a simple "dramatization" of the incidents as they were recorded to increasingly elaborate and aggressive fictionalizing of the established chronicle. Establishing the limits of acceptable revision presented a field for formal experimentation, as the tensions between "the desire for the imaginary" and "the imperatives of the real, the actual" were resolved (White 8).

Fortunately, the negotiations surrounding this territory took place not just on stage but in the records of the censors and, even more prominently, on the pages of the daily papers of Paris, where they may still be traced. Read in conjunction with the texts of the plays, these documents reveal a process whereby the generic conventions of melodrama, already ideologically invested in the manner described in Part I, was overlain with the clear-cut dualities attendant upon military conflicts. When these conflicts involved adversaries in the Middle East or North Africa, we shall see that a third set of dualities—those opposing the Occident and the Orient—were readily mapped onto the preexisting structures.

5

National Images

From *La Bataille d'Aboukir* to *Bonaparte en Egypte*, or The Evolution of National Drama

. . . But pardon, gentles all,
The flat unraised spirits that have dared
On this unworthy scaffold to bring forth
So great an object: can this cockpit hold
The vasty fields of France? or may we cram
Within this wooden O the very casques
That did afright the air at Agincourt?
O, pardon! since a crooked figure may
Attest in a little place a million;
And let us, ciphers to this great accompt,
On your imaginary forces work.
Suppose within the girdle of these walls
Are now confined two mighty monarchies,
Whose high upreared and abutting fronts
The perilous narrow ocean parts asunder:
Piece out our imperfections with your thoughts;
Into a thousand parts divide one man,
And make imaginary puissance;
Think when we talk of horses, that you see them
Printing their proud hoofs i' the receiving earth;
For 'tis your thoughts that now must deck our kings. . . .

   —Shakespeare, Prologue to *Henry V* (1599)

The staging of battles in our theaters is a rather difficult undertaking. Their restricted dimensions do not permit the maneuvering of many troops. Armies of from 20 to 30 men at the most cover this small space, engage in combat, take towns by assault, and win victories; but these means, feeble as they are, often produce considerable effect when they are well handled and combined with skill. Then art acts as a supplement to numbers, and the spectator, already inclined to create an illusion for himself, transforms his eyes into multipliers, and represents to himself, instead of several men who file along, entire armies on maneuver.[1]

—Review of *La Bataille d'Aboukir*,
published in *Le Courrier de l'Europe*,
September 9, 1808

National Images and Scenarios

The practice of celebrating and commemorating significant military victories through theatrical re-creation is a long-standing one in European history. A genre recognized since the Middle Ages, such productions became extremely elaborate during the Renaissance when court pageants and festivals presented highly allegorized and intricately choreographed versions of recent battles. At the same time, as the epigraph from *Henry V* (1599) indicates, conventions for staging such events in fictionalized and narrativized forms were also being established. As Hassan El-Nouty has observed, the move from the choreographing of festivals to the staging of battle scenes entailed significant shifts in form and function. In the latter case, "[t]he desire to amaze was subordinated to the primary concern to *galvanize*. The original ceremony had changed in nature: the stylized feudal war of the tournament was replaced by the national war symbolized—which is a way of stylizing—by an exemplary action or moment" (29).

Both the allegorizing and fictionalizing traditions would be continued into the nineteenth century in France. At first glance, it would seem that in the two hundred or so years separating *Henry V* and *La Bataille d'Aboukir* little had changed with regard to the representation of great military engagements on stage. The problems of scale, stature, and reception faced by Shakespeare and MM. Cuvelier and Augustin, the authors of *La Bataille d'Aboukir*, sound remarkably similar. The spectator was still called upon to be complicitous in creating and sustaining the dramatic illusion—one that must always fall far short of the actuality. The task was further complicated by the fact that the re-creation had to be matched against the chronicles of history and, in the latter case, the exigencies of memory. But even as many of the issues surrounding the staging of epic struggles remained unchanged, significant alterations in the relationship between event and representation had taken place.

These alterations were in large part prompted by the need to fill the "vacuum in collective cultural orientation"—to use John Tomlinson's paraphrase of Benedict Anderson (83)—that occurred in the years following the French Revolution. Military spectacle and national drama, operating as part of a greater network of cultural constructions made possible by advances in technology, were recognized as effective means for fostering a collective cultural imagining that would define or redefine a cohesive national identity. At the same time, the insertion of these works into an industrialized culture in which the bourgeoisie were consolidating their position of dominance would bring significant alterations in modes of representation, presentation, and reception. The most notable of all these modifications were the result of an articulation of the traditional requirements for grandeur, scale, and national glorification with the conventions of pictorial realism and narrative logic that had begun to take shape in the eighteenth century and that would dominate cultural production in the nineteenth century. Reenactments—characterized by Bill Nichols as "imaginary events tightly based on historical fact" (21)—rather than the symbolic transformations that had characterized the allegorical festivals and pageants of previous centuries would become the defining process of representation as military pantomimes, historical tableaux, and hippodramas became the dominant genres used for the staging of reality (Figure 6).

Given the vital social, political, and cultural renegotiations taking place in the late eighteenth century, it is not coincidental that the parameters that would define the relationship between political interests and public performance for the nineteenth century were set during and immediately following the French Revolution of 1789.[2] As with all forms of public theater, these parameters were in large measure coercively established by the decrees of officially appointed censors. Perhaps most striking among the developments in revolutionary-era theater was the immediacy with which current events were dramatized in what was accepted as a realistic mode. Within weeks of their occurrence, major events found their way to the stage. Victor Hallays-Dabot's account recalls the wealth of material presented by the precipitous pace of the times: "The Revolution triumphs in all the theaters. Everything is a pretext for a popular play, Mirabeau's death as well as the king's flight. This unfortunate attempt of Louis XVI was a piece of good luck for patriotic authors" (*L'Histoire* 163).[3]

It was, however, very quickly determined that such a profusion of

Nouveau théâtre de l'Hippodrome. — Représentation du *Siege de Silistrie.*

Figure 6. Outdoor performance of the military drama *Le Siege de Silistrie* at the new Paris Hippodrome (1854). *L'Illustration, Journal Universel*, September 16, 1854.

politically explicit material posed dangers to the public order. The censors expressed the following opinion: "Despite the freedom of the theaters that has been decreed . . . it must however have limits, and the most harmful consequences may arise if what has already caused such discontent is again presented on stage" (Hallays-Dabot, *L'Histoire* 163).[4] So suspicious were those in power of the effects that the representation of actuality, whether in the recent or the distant past, could have on volatile popular emotions, that at times of political instability, most notably during the Hundred Days, all *pièces d'occasion* were banned.

While plays depicting recent or ongoing events were the prime cause for concern, works claiming to portray a more distant history also came under close scrutiny. Under the protocols of censorial reading, which mirrored the protocols of public spectatorship, the relationship of the material to the political climate of the moment was as meaningful as the topic itself. Partisanship in itself was not the sole factor that would determine whether a sensitive play would be authorized or banned. As F. W. J. Hemmings has observed:

It is clear that the censorship, while always ready to pounce on plays covertly ridiculing the abuses and foibles of the current regime, did not necessarily put the stamp of approval on works attacking the critics of the established order. The guiding principle to which the censorship worked was apparently to make sure that audiences should on no occasion become overexcited or be given any opportunity to manifest political partisanship of one sort or another. (*Theatre and State* 47)

While those in power urged the censors to be vigilant, they nevertheless promoted staged representations of incidents drawn from the history of France or of relatively recent military campaigns, for they recognized their potential to perform a useful patriotic function. This was only practical given the unstable conditions that complicated attempts to construct a sense of nation over the next century.[5] As various antagonistic classes and factions vied for ascendancy in the new national order, each in turn supported the judicious use of the theaters to foster "national" sentiment. Such productions were perhaps least controversial when the country was waging a war that had a broad base of support. The regime in power hoped that if the war was proceeding successfully, such performances would augment its the prestige; if the war was not going well, the regime hoped that performances would help revive declining morale. In 1814, as foreign armies advanced toward Paris, Hallays-Dabot recalls:

The theater has recorded the changes in public mood in Paris during these painful times. The cry of alarm resounded on every stage. Similar crises that the country had to overcome were sought in history: Philippe Auguste, St. Louis, Charles Martel, Bayard, [and] Jeanne Hachette came out of their tombs to recount with what national elan one chases the foreigner from the soil of the fatherland.[6] (*L'Histoire* 232)

As might be expected, no matter what their dramatic potential, events that did not show France in general and the French armed forces in particular to best advantage were summarily condemned. Forty-seven years after the 1814 invasion by the Allies, an ambitious project entitled *L'Invasion*, which recalled those "painful times" in five acts and fourteen tableaux, met with strong opposition, an opposition intensified by dynastic interests. The censors noted:

Despite the signal revenge that France has [since] exacted, despite the glorious place among nations that the Emperor Napoleon III has reconquered for her, we think that under the Napoleonic dynasty, the profoundly distressing and humiliating spectacle of the calamities for which a partisan spirit has reproached the First Empire and presented as the cause of its downfall cannot be put before the eyes of the public. (F 21–975)[7]

Censors considered it part of their mission to safeguard the national reputation by setting standards for the presentation of incidents and figures that were regarded as part of the national patrimony. Events were to be depicted with appropriate dignity, scenic richness, and even dramatic skill. The "sept scènes equestres en trois actions" of *Tanneguy du Châtel*, which portrayed the disastrous reign of King Charles VI (1380–1422) during which the greater part of France was ceded to England, was rejected not so much because of the depressing subject, but for the perceived inability of the Cirque Olympique to represent the material in a sufficiently elevated fashion. Characterizing the performers of the Cirque as "mountebanks," the censors noted that "[t]o expose on the stage, without compromising the royal dignity, the masquerade and madness of Charles VI, would take an art and a talent that is not to be found at the Cirque Olympique" (F 21–991).[8]

It was not only internal perceptions of national image that were of concern. Plays that incorporated historical events were carefully reviewed for the effect they might have on international relations. With more than a touch of chauvinism, Hallays-Dabot conveys the delicacy of such situations:

Our theater occupies, since the middle of the eighteenth century, such a high place in Europe, it has acquired such great influence, that foreign nations always have their eye on the performances of Paris, and ambassadors give their active attention to everything that may concern their native land. Before 1789, the banning of more than one play, as we have seen, was imposed by diplomatic susceptibilities. It would be the same under the Empire, the Restoration, and the July government (*L'Histoire* 227).[9]

The efforts of censors acting on behalf of the government to protect favorable diplomatic relations were constantly pitted against the desire of entrepreneurs to take advantage of public interest generated by developments abroad. Such a conflict of interest arose in 1822 at a time when Greece was in revolt against Ottoman rule. British, Russian, and French involvement would eventually help Greece gain independence in 1829, but the French government was not ready to make such a commitment in 1822.

When the management at the Panorama-Dramatique sought to present a three-act melodrama entitled *Ali, Pacha de Janina*, the request provoked consternation among the censors, who felt that the subject offered inevitable comparisons with the circumstances of the ongoing war between the Greeks and the Turks. Rather than venture onto this embattled ground, the censor declared: "Here ends the competency of the dramatic Censorship, and it falls to the lights of the superior authorities to decide if such a subject, purged of all the passages that I propose be suppressed, can, without any political disadvantages, be transferred to the theater" (F21–993).[10]

Because of the constant presence of foreign diplomats in the capital, it was especially important that the *current* state of international relations be respected. Such a situation is well documented in the case of Anglo-French relations. In 1854, with the outbreak of the Crimean War, it was deemed desirable that the public should be reminded to overlook centuries of hostile relations between France and England and to think instead of the fresh alliance between the two nations; at the same time antagonism toward the new enemy, Russia, was to be intensified. A five-act drama entitled *Anglais et français, ou la Prise de Bomarsund* performed precisely these functions. The censors noted with satisfaction:

> Throughout the entire course of this drama, despite a constant difference in humor and mutual teasing, the Englishman and the Frenchman do not cease to act with the most complete accord.
>
> The Russians are depicted in this work in the most odious terms. They crush the invaded territory without mercy and commit the greatest atrocities.

There was, nevertheless, concern that the authors had not properly respected the royal person of the czar. Persuaded that "it is harmful to hand over as fodder for the popular passions the sovereign majesty, even in the person of an enemy," the censors suppressed from the work "everything that could refer to the Emperor Nicholas in a troublesome manner" (F21–974).[11] Thus even in the midst of their concern for maintaining proper international relations, the censors' attention was not in the least diverted from their responsibility for simultaneously preserving domestic order by shielding the person of an absolute sovereign from public criticism.

Napoleon and the Theater

The development of military spectacle and drama in the nineteenth century cannot be considered apart from the influence of Napoleon and the

campaigns of *la Grande Armée*.[12] These campaigns were directly responsible for the resurgence of a number of forms of military spectacle and
performances. Tableaux and pantomimes celebrating the victories of the
French forces were presented to Parisian audiences beginning in 1797. Such
productions gained permanent venues when the Franconis, who had specialized in equestrian entertainment since the French Revolution, moved
indoors to the Cirque Olympique in 1807.[13] A second site was reserved
for such works when the Théâtre de la Porte-Saint-Martin, offering too
much competition for the imperial Académie de Musique, was instructed
to restrict its repertory to four nondramatic genres and to reopen under
the name of Salle des Jeux Gymniques. Two of the four genres, the *tableau historique* and the *évolution militaire*, were dedicated to the promotion
of national honor and imperial prestige. The directive from the minister of
the interior delimited these categories in the following manner:

> *Les tableaux historiques*, in the manner of Servandoni. In these tableaux, the sets
> must be the principal part. Each tableau may present one deed, one great event.
> *Les évolutions militaires*. This spectacle will consist of marches, assaults, and contests
> of infantry or cavalry. (Qtd. in Albert 233) [14]

They were also permitted to present prologues necessary to explicate the
main performances. While this switch was by no means voluntary, the
management proved very adept in its new mission. By 1810, the "civic zeal"
they had demonstrated in retracing "two or three epochs of glory for the
French name" was praised in the pages of *Le Courrier de l'Europe* and consistently rewarded by "the presence of persons of the highest rank and the
applause of all good citizens" (no. 1058, May 16, 1810).[15]

   The majority of tableaux and pantomimes, particularly the earlier
ones, combined allegorical and realistic approaches to the representation
of their subject matter. The prestige of allegorization, derived from its association with European dynasties of the previous three hundred years,
was borrowed to legitimize Napoleon's succession to the heritage of absolute rule. The reenactments of highlights of actual campaigns (as detailed
as performance conditions permitted), on the other hand, performed their
function by activating sentiments generated by the memory of the events
themselves. Spectators were invited to draw correspondences not only
with their own experiences but also with information that had been published or circulated as common knowledge. The forging of these correspondences relied in large measure on establishing what Bill Nichols has
identified as the "indexical bond to the historical world," a bonding con-

stitutive of all representations of reality.[16] In the military tableau or drama, visual citations from widely disseminated engravings or prominently displayed paintings of events—especially plentiful since military genre painting was undergoing a parallel development[17]—were a key means of fashioning this bonding. These citations took the form of climactic tableaux and *tableaux vivants*, both expressly designed to reproduce the composition of two-dimensional visual renderings.[18]

The application of these principles of representation can be seen in *L'Homme du Destin*, produced for the Jeux Gymniques in September 1810. The work was categorized as "tableaux historiques et allégoriques à grand spectacle" and opened with a prologue depicting a convocation of the Greco-Roman gods. The gods had assembled to create the eponymous "Man of Destiny" who would possess the combined attributes of Achilles, Trajan, and Charlemagne. Needless to say, their creation was Napoleon Bonaparte. Following the prologue, the curtains parted to reveal a fleet at sea carrying the "Hero of France" and his troops across the Mediterranean toward victory in Egypt. The pantomime was divided into several *actions*, each of which recounted a major battle and featured an incident that lent itself particularly well to theatrical effect. The first episode, for example, took full advantage of the picturesque opportunities offered by the Battle of the Pyramids and concluded with a celestial vision that announced to Napoleon that France had need of him. The episode featuring the Second Italian Campaign was similarly highlighted by the crossing of the Alps at the spectacular Great St. Bernard Pass, a moment that had already been glorified in a series of paintings by Jacques-Louis David.

Among the most noticeable qualities separating *L'Homme du destin* and similar tableaux and pantomimes from their Renaissance and Baroque predecessors was the realistic ideal that directed the scenic design and construction and motivated the use of machinery. The *Courrier* reviewer praised the backdrop of the *première action* for its faithful reproduction of geographical and architectural detail, in particular calling attention to the great accuracy with which the arid ground and the immense pyramids of Egypt were painted, and extolling the impressive rendering of the monuments and artistic masterpieces of Italy. It would seem, however, that in the earlier memorializing pieces, the realistic style of the scenery and the faithfulness of the reenactment did not reflect substantial changes in the essentially presentational mode of reception as determined by the allegorical framework. The response to *Les Français en Pologne* (1808) could be considered typical for a form that, in the enforced absence of narrative due

to licensing restrictions, privileged visual impressions over intellectual recall: "This is only a quick sketch but one in which a great deal of movement
prevails. Besides, it is pleasing to have before one's eyes, even in miniature, the image of the combats, and when they recall the constancy and
the glory of the heroes who with their exploits immortalized the plains of
Saxony and of Poland, they acquire a new degree of interest" (*Le Courrier
de l'Europe*, no. 290, March 15, 1808).[19]

Such fictional elements as there were in military tableaux and in many
of the earlier pantomimes did not compete with the commemorative function of the spectacle. In pieces like *L'Homme du destin*, it was fully expected,
as the *Courrier* critic said, that the subject be "embellished with all that fiction could offer that was dramatic and imposing to the imagination,"[20] but
it remained for individual memory and the prestige previously attached to
the events in question to engage the spectator rather than an absorption in
situation, plot, or character.

Following a period of repression under the Restoration, when it was
considered undesirable to stir up Bonapartist sentiments, the military pantomime gained a renewed popularity with the advent of the July Monarchy
in 1830, as the Orléanist monarchy of Louis-Philippe sought to place itself
in a direct line of descent from the French Revolution and the Napoleonic
era. This revival was of course intensifed under the Second Empire beginning in 1851. Critical reviews of Fabrice Labrousse's *Bonaparte en Egypte*
(1851) (Figure 7), one of the first productions to celebrate the restoration
of the Napoleonic dynasty, reflect the extent to which certain aspects and
functions of the *drame militaire à grand spectacle* had been modified. As in
the more condensed ancestors of the Second Empire *mimodrame*, the main
theatrical contribution to creating audience enthusiasm relied on the perceptual and sensory stimulation brought about by the re-creation of the
sights, sound, and even smells of battle. The relative balance of literary,
psychological, and spectacular elements can be inferred from the testimony
of T. Sauvage of *Le Moniteur universel*:

M. Labrousse for one has no literary pretensions: on horseback at the Cirque, he
serenely wages his little battle without concerning himself with style or originality.
Neither do we have anything to say about his works, which would require a great
tactical general for a critic. We must restrict ourselves to acknowledging the noisi-
est, most astonishing success that has been known since powder was first burned
in the theater. Magnificent sets magnificently framing magnificent maneuvers, and
one comes out deafened by the cannon and the applause, blinded by the fire and

CHAQUE PIÈCE, 20 CENTIMES.
623ᵉ ET 624ᵉ LIVRAISONS.

THÉÂTRE CONTEMPORAIN ILLUSTRÉ

MICHEL LÉVY FRÈRES, ÉDITEURS,
RUE VIVIENNE, 2 BIS.

BONAPARTE EN ÉGYPTE

PIÈCE MILITAIRE EN CINQ ACTES ET DIX-HUIT TABLEAUX

PAR

M. FABRICE LABROUSSE

MISE EN SCÈNE DE M. ALBERT. — MUSIQUE DE M. FESSY. — DÉCORS DE MM. WAGNER, DEVOIR, CHÉRET ET DUFLOCQ

REPRÉSENTÉE POUR LA PREMIÈRE FOIS, A PARIS, SUR LE THÉÂTRE NATIONAL (ANCIEN CIRQUE), LE 25 DÉCEMBRE 1851.

Figure 7. Title illustration for *Bonaparte en Égypte*, by Fabrice Labrousse (1851). *Théâtre Contemporain Illustré*, ser. 125 (1869). The New York Public Library; Astor, Lenox and Tilden Foundations.

the smoke, and perfumed with gunpowder like a veteran of the Old Guard. A performance is worth a campaign. (No. 364, December 30, 1851)[21]

The spectacular excess described here was enhanced by the unique design of the third Cirque Olympique (or the Théâtre National as it was called at the time), which integrated a traditional proscenium stage with the arena traditionally used for equestrian displays (see Figure 2). Midcentury machinery made it possible to extend the forestage out into the open space of the arena at the same time that two mechanically operated

ramps were put into place to bring the stage action out into the open
ring where it was surrounded by the audience. The relationship of the real
and the imaginary that predominated in traditionally designed boulevard
theaters like the Porte-Saint-Martin, the Ambigu-Comique, and the Gaîté
was altered by this special configuration of theatrical space. Without the
proscenium and footlights to separate the audience from the action, the assault on the senses was rendered as direct and immediate as possible. While
fictional elements, as we shall see in the next chapter, were essential to the
popular success of military and national dramas, the power of sensation
and spectacle in generating excitement cannot be overestimated. The noise
and commotion were magnified by the sheer scale of the productions. In
Enter Foot and Horse (23–24), A. H. Saxon describes a typical grand entry
of the French infantry, cavalry, and artillery that preceded climactic battle
scenes. As many as five or six hundred extras were said to have been used;
the illusion of even greater numbers was created by having the actors march
through the arena only to circle around backstage for a change of costume
and a second entry as a member of another regiment. The procession of
the French troops was followed by the appearance of the enemy forces on
the stage. The charge of the French army was therefore invariably from the
disadvantaged lower position, making their inevitable victory all the more
glorious.

The most significant difference between the First Empire productions
and their Second Empire reincarnations was in the rationale for the multiplication of episodes. This proliferation—*Bonaparte en Égypte* is described
as a "mimodrame militaire en 19 actes"—was no longer governed mainly
by the technical and aesthetic demands of set changes required by varied
locales. Now not only were the sites of key conflicts to be shown, but non-
military aspects of the French expedition into Egypt were to be stressed as
well. The new organization proceeded as much from the concern to display the participation of French scientific, intellectual, and even cultural
institutions in the occupation and colonization of Egypt as it did from
the obligation to follow the chronology of actual troop movements. The
reconfiguring of the legend of the new emperor's uncle served a broader
strategy for projecting the Bonapartist state as "a neutral agent of the
national interest above political and social rivalries" (Jenkins 67). The reconfiguration was made possible by the fact that the Napoleonic era was
now perceived as history rather than as an ongoing actuality. Consigned
to this more distant realm, the Napoleonic myth no longer existed pri-

marily for the posthumous benefit of the "Héros de France" himself, but was readily subordinated to the interests of subsequent regimes.

Whether in early or mid-century, the military tableaux and panto-mimes were patronized by a core audience drawn from "*amateurs de gloire et de fumée*," as one critic put it. The loyalty of these spectators, initially mainly veterans of *la Grande Armée*, supported a cadre of writers who specialized in the genre. Auguste Lireux's comments on *Bonaparte en Egypte* attest at the same time to the loyalty of the spectator and the security of the writer, although one assumes neither of these shared the weariness evinced by the critic:

We saw or saw once again *Bonaparte en Egypte*—the same horses, the same soldiers, the same gunshots that for a hundred performances have been attracting the amateurs of glory and smoke. . . .

. . . M. Labrousse's *mimodrame* fulfills all the requirements of the genre. How could it be otherwise? The author for his part has done every campaign of Napoleon at least twice; he should not be at a loss to begin them all over again. (*Le Constitutionnel*, December 30, 1851)[22]

The loyal core audience and long-standing appeal that military spectacle enjoyed would be expanded several times over by full fictionalization. The process of settling upon narrative structures to house these new fictions would occupy the better part of the century and will be documented fully in the next chapter. Chapter 7 will go on to examine the privileged relationship that existed between historical reenactment and print journalism, especially as that relationship had a bearing on representations of military campaigns in the Middle East and North Africa. Of all the public discourses dealing with military affairs, the journalistic reporting of expeditions and campaigns bore the closest relationship to theatrical representation.[23] The flow of influence between print and stage, however, would be far from unidirectional: if dramatic authors did indeed rely heavily, even exclusively, on dispatches and commentaries published in the daily papers for their plot outlines and composition of scenes, journalists just as consistently organized their reportage in terms of dramatic scenarios. Both mediums, in fact, achieved their greatest effectiveness as forms of communication by inviting the emotional engagement of readers through a personalized perspective and sensational presentation.

6

Fictions of War
Reading the Critics

THE DEVELOPMENT OF FULLY FICTIONALIZED and narrativized national dramas has been documented in a way that would not have been possible before the advent of journalistic criticism as a recognized profession.[1] The reviews produced by this new category of writer have long been consulted for detailed summaries of many more plays than have survived as complete scripts, for descriptions of the physical elements of production and performance, and as indicators of public reception. Their prime value for this study, however, has been as a record of the genesis of dramatic structures used to reorganize reality into fiction—structures that remain operative to the present day. Despite the critics' claims to impartiality and objectivity, which were quick to surface, they were no more free of institutional constraints than were their fellow "critics" working for the Bureau of Censorship. It is therefore both prudent and enlightening to examine the institutionalized practices that defined their activities and to get a sense of the ideological positionings, both political and aesthetic, that characterized members of this corps of professional theatergoers.

Theater, Press, and Politics

By the 1830s the major *quotidiens* or daily newspapers such as *Le Moniteur universel*, *Le Constitutionnel*, and *La Gazette de France* had begun to print regular and extensive coverage of the theaters in every issue. This coverage included daily listings of the programs of the state-subsidized Grands Théâtres and all the major boulevard theaters; announcements and reviews of new productions; and occasional articles on theater administration, organization, legislation, and like topics. These reviews are of particular interest as they were often noticeably colored by the liberal or conservative views of the papers in which they appeared, views that must be taken into account when reading these writings as historical documents. Under periods of strict censorship of the press, in fact, when direct discussion of politics was rigidly controlled if not suppressed, it was often in the pages reserved for literature, theater, and the arts that such political opinions surfaced. Maurice Descotes describes this phenomenon under the First Empire:

Strictly regulated as to the topics of news reports and political commentary, the press could no longer reflect changing opinions on subjects relating to the progress of the state. Hence the debate of ideas, inevitable in a country that remained profoundly divided, would carry over into neutral, even frivolous domains—and news of the theater was one of these. This news would be commented on first and foremost (even if this is not apparent to the modern reader) in terms of the positions of the editor, the [political] leanings represented by that newspaper. (*Histoire* 186)

While the newspapers and periodicals that had no official party affiliation and devoted their coverage exclusively or primarily to the theater usually did not have a formally stated editorial position on political affairs, this is not to say that they did not express political convictions and social interests. Nor did these publications remain aloof from current events, whether they concerned politics at home or diplomatic and military affairs abroad. At times of such crisis or preoccupation, the editors either suspended publication or turned their pages over entirely to the discussion of unfolding events. As the Napoleonic armies advanced into Prussia, for instance, under the banner of the October 28, 1806, issue of *Le Courrier des Spectacles*, the editors proclaimed that the campaign offered "such a fine spectacle" in itself that they felt obliged to suspend all news concerning the theaters in order to present to their readers only "the scenes of bravery and heroism that have enabled our armies to add new laurels to those which have crowned them for so many years."[2] It was, in fact, this compelling interest in national concerns on the part of both the *Courrier*'s editors and apparently their actual and potential subscribers that led to the transformation of *Le Courrier des Spectacles* into *Le Courrier de l'Europe*. Not content with the regular but limited coverage of national news introduced in March 1797, the *Courrier*'s editors proposed more drastic changes in the publication's format and objectives. On May 31, 1807, MM. Clément, Legouvé, and Vigée and the other "littérateurs distingués" responsible for *Le Courrier des Spectacles* over the previous eleven years announced that henceforth the publication would undertake to specialize in both politics and literature. It was their fervent conviction that if "[they] could combine literary merit with that of the most inclusive and up-to-date politics (the object of such great interest at the moment) [their] subscribers would have nothing left to desire."[3]

Ten years later similar attestation as to the precedence that political and national events should take over theatrical happenings is found in the *Journal de Commerce, de Politique et de Littérature*. Following the national elections in which representatives to the Chambre des Députés were chosen in twenty-four departments, the drama critic of the newspaper explained that his recent neglect of the "dramatic novelties" of the last few days was prompted by a sense of civic responsibility—his own and that of his readers:

> It seemed to me that at a time when a part of our nation was being called upon to exercise the most precious and most legitimate of its prerogatives, it was important not to distract the readers of this newspaper, dedicated as it is to the defense of the rights of the people and of constitutional liberties, from their noble concerns. What attraction could discussions, arguments, [and] judgments made regarding actors or new plays hold for our subscribers, while the most imposing of spectacles lay before our eyes, absorbing all minds, commanding everyone's attention? (September 29, 1817)[4]

This preoccupation with politics, and an attendant neglect of the theaters, was not restricted to the print media. Taking some literary license, it must be assumed, the critic concludes his brief discourse by noting that because everyone in Paris from financiers to artists to young ladies was caught up in the sweep of the political drama, it was only fitting that "the theaters should find themselves abandoned, or serving as places of assembly, where one hoped to learn the names of some of the newly elected."[5]

Theater reviews also provide innumerable accounts of instances in which the participation of theaters in national events was not limited to their usefulness as a place of public assembly. Reviews dating from the Napoleonic era in particular offer vivid descriptions of the simultaneous celebrations held inside and outside the boulevard theaters, occasioned first by the victories of *la Grande Armée*, and then by the emperor's final defeat. The August 6, 1807, edition of *Le Courrier de l'Europe* describes the evidence of national rejoicing displayed on the facade, in the auditorium, and on the stage of the Ambigu-Comique when the French victory over the Russians at Friedland led Czar Alexander I to agree to a ceasefire:

For several days all Paris has been resounding with songs of joy; everyone is celebrating the return of peace, everyone is rushing to express their gratitude to the hero who has restored it to us. In our theaters, there are only hymns in honor of the conqueror and pacifier of Europe. The Ambigu has also sought to distinguish itself on this memorable occasion with expressions of its zeal and its devotion. The façade of the theater yesterday was illuminated in an ingenious manner. The crowd that presses each day upon the boulevards stopped to contemplate the august image of the emperor in a transparent temple magnificently illuminated. The interior was occupied with a multitude of the curious, anxious to mix their applause with the open and naive expressions of gratitude and admiration of which the actors were the interpreters.[6]

Just over seven years later, similar rejoicing would again be manifested, this time, however, upon the downfall of Napoleon and the restoration of the Bourbon monarchy. An ecstatic report by the drama critic of the *Journal de Paris*, A. Martainville, makes it clear that public opinion found expression in response not only to various *pièces de circonstance* composed for the celebration, but also to allusions latent in previously written works:

Every evening our theaters resound with such lively and unanimous acclamations and applause that one would think that the numerous foreigners mingling among us have been pleased to forget their native land for an instant to strive with enthusiasm alongside the French in the expression of their love for this august prince, this *Bourbon* whose name brings back such sweet memories, whose virtues and goodness promise such happiness. Everywhere, more or less direct allusions are greeted with transport: the new plays follow one upon the other, the old are rejuvenated, and there is not a day that Melpomene, Thalia, Euterpe, Polyhymnia, and even the mad Momus do not pay tribute to the best of kings. (August 6, 1807)[7]

Critical Tastes

While momentous political events brought out overt statements of political position in newspapers, views deriving from the socioprofessional origination of the critics consistently overflowed into the theater reviews themselves, despite the detached impartiality professed by certain writers. As in the case of the censors, the failure to recognize or remember that this supposed position of neutrality is in fact historically and professionally localized led many modern critics to accept as objective statements what are in fact subjective formulations. Instead of too readily accepting the assessments of the theater critics at face value, we must keep in mind Pierre Bourdieu's comments on this particular brand of professional criticism:

"By refusing to recognize any other relationship between the producer and his public than either cynical calculation or pure disinterestedness, writers and artists give themselves a convenient device for seeing themselves as disinterested, while exposing their adversaries as motivated by the lust for success at any price" (*Distinction* 240).

While Bourdieu is speaking in terms of twentieth-century models, by the early nineteenth century a carefully cultivated detached professionalism was already held to be the chief mark of distinction of a group that identified itself as "*hommes de lettres.*" The publishers of *Le Courrier des Spectacles* reiterated their commitment to this approach to dramatic criticism and reaffirmed its social value even as they broadened the scope of their newspaper to treat political and economic concerns directly. The last issue published under the above title carried the following declaration:

Strangers to all passions, we have expressed our opinion with openness, decency, and liberty. We believed that the first concern of the man of letters, when he is giving an account of a work, is to *examine its merit independently of personal considerations.* We imagined that far from maintaining the fire of dissension, with bitter and passionate censure, far from stirring up factions and forever setting them against one another, the most noble and sacred of our responsibilities was to maintain the bonds of concord and peace among all men, with whom the happiness of society and of states resides. (May 31, 1807; my emphasis) [8]

But an actual reading of the articles and reviews published during the eleven-year existence of *Le Courrier des Spectacles* reveals that the operative category of "tous les hommes" as used by the "littérateurs distingués" in the exercise of their most noble and sacred duty was not as inclusive as it might have been. The public esteem they sought would also seem to have been confined to a more limited circle than their formulation would suggest. Foremost among the excluded groups, whether actually present in the theater or represented on the stage, were those blamed for having disturbed the public order and peace. As the review of *Zamor, ou les Deux Fils* quoted at the end of Chapter 2 revealed, this was certainly the case with French peasants and black slaves. In other instances, the basis for exclusion cannot be as readily ascribed to class-based interests.

The bourgeoisie too finds itself outside "les liens de la concorde et de la paix," certainly not because of any fostering of violence and disorder, but ostensibly because of their failure to exhibit the appropriate tastes in their choice of cultural fare. Although this principle of distinction is absent from the 1807 notice, it is explicitly stated in a piece written in 1797. This

earlier notice was similarly designed to reassure the *Courrier*'s readers that
an expansion undertaken to include news of national interest would in no
way compromise the impartiality of the theatrical reviews:

We will still show the same candor, the same impartiality in our examinations. Our
critique, of the plays as well as the actors, will continue to be dictated by our love
for the art of the theater, and the desire to see it resist bad taste, and to bring it
back, if possible, to that of the great men who guaranteed French superiority in
this genre over all other nations of the world. (May 5, 1797) [9]

Subsequent pieces would elaborate upon the grave consequences of a failure to resist the tide of "bad taste." In June 1797 an essay entitled "Nouvelles observations sur les causes de la décadence du théâtre" (New observations on the causes of the decline of the theater) pinpoints "bad taste" as
the dominant underlying cause of this degeneration, outstripping even the
introduction of dubious genres such as the drama and melodrama:

We have already attributed the decadence of dramatic art to several causes. We have
ascribed it to the birth and success of the genre known as drama, which, in presenting a seductive appeal to authors with its facility, turns them away from the lengthy
and in-depth study of the ancients, which alone, seconded by genius, can produce
a tragic author, and from the meditation that true comedy requires. We have recognized this indulgence, which is born of bad taste and tends to perpetuate it, as
being highly contrary to dramatic art.
    It is plain to see that it is bad taste alone that is at the root of all other causes.
This is even more noticeable in the preference that the public seems to display for
mediocre, and even bad, works, over the masterpieces of the art. (June 24, 1797) [10]

    Such abysmal forecasts could be considered prophetic if "dramatic
art" is narrowly restricted to the written texts alone; on the other hand,
there can be no question that *theater* taken in its full performance context flourished over the next several decades until film began to take over
the functions of popular entertainment. So apt would the nineteenth-
century forms prove to be for an urban, industrialized society that even as
the medium changed, many of the generic conventions of representation
would remain intact well into the twentieth century. Among the most resilient aspects of these forms would be the narrative structure developed to
support the military or national drama. In the case of these spectacles, the
critical reviews can be called upon not so much to rectify skewed assumptions as to fill a vacuum with the account they provide of the formalized
representation and fictionalization of national events. When one reads the
sometimes heated opinions offered regarding various authors' strategies

for embellishing the historical chronicle, the occasional instrusions of critical condescension may be safely bracketed.

The Representation of Actuality

Controversies over the appropriate blends of fact and fiction began along with the century when the premiere of *Kléber, ou les Moeurs orientales* at the Théâtre de la Cité was rather poorly received. The core of the problem is exposed by the action of the final moments of the play. Following Kléber's triumph in Egypt, one of the Mameluke leaders promises his daughter in marriage to the Turk who will assassinate the French general. At the moment when Kléber is about to grant the Mameluke in question a pardon for the Turks who attacked him, an aspiring son-in-law springs out of his hiding place and kills Kléber. In the opinion of the reviewer writing in the September 28, 1800, issue of *Le Courrier des Spectacles*, the failure of the production was in no small part due to the haste with which it had been mounted. But of even graver consequence were the facts that "the author wanted to plot out a historical event himself, he departed from faithfulness to the reports, and the event itself is still too recent for one to alter the truth of history to that extent."[11]

On this point, a double standard apparently applied to historical dramas portraying the distant past as opposed to those that represented recent occurrences. Despite the considerable liberties taken by the author, one M. Hubert, in his treatment of the occupation under Charles VII, the play was extremely successful. This latitude met with the disapproval of *Le Courrier de l'Europe*'s critic, who also took the opportunity to deplore what had apparently become a noticeable trend:

The advantages and disadvantages of historical novels have often been discussed, but our novelists have found a good number of imitators: vaudevilles, songs, melodramas—everything is historical now, and one should not be surprised that henceforth historical tales and fables should be composed. In the meantime, here is a melodrama the subject of which, while drawn from the history of France, is an almost fabulous concept, given the details with which it is loaded down and the romantic incidents that follow one after another. (July 12, 1809)[12]

The writer seemed to know that his objections would meet with well-rehearsed answers. While remaining resistant to the unchecked fictionalization of history, he was forced in the end to admit that the unqualified success of the final product provided the crowning argument in favor of a boulevard author's "embellishment" of the raw data of historical "facts":

[S]hould the author be reproached, he will answer that he had to embellish a historical fact with all the charms of fiction; that a theatrical play is not a history lesson; that if some serious authors allow themselves to alter [history] in works performed on the first stage of the capital, the same liberty can well be excused at the Théâtre de la Gaîté, to which one brings fewer pretensions; finally he will answer with the brilliant success he has achieved.

Nevertheless, unwilling to concede everything, the critic concluded by maintaining that in this particular case, "the author could, however, without compromising the grand effects of melodrama, have borrowed more from history." [13]

This debate regarding the treatment of history on the stage went back at least to July 1806, when an article entitled "Suivre l'Histoire, violer l'histoire" (Following history, violating history) was published in what was still *Le Courrier des Spectacles.* The author of the article presented what seems to have been the operative concept of history for the "hommes de lettres" on the *Courrier* staff: "The goal of history is . . . to establish facts and to fix opinions, supported by proof and authoritative sources. When an event is not questioned, when one has not gathered the testimony that attests to its occurrence, when writers disagree among themselves, when they refrain from rendering a judgment, there is no more history, there is only doubt" (July 11, 1806).[14]

The *Courrier* critics' vigilance regarding matters of historical accuracy seems to have been the common attitude among those of their calling. On October 17, 1811, "R.," the newly installed principal critic of *Le Journal de Paris*, began his tenure with "Quelques réflexions sur les feuilletons de spectacles." In identifying what he saw as the chief duties of anyone writing an article on dramatic art, he included the responsibility "to seek out the historical origins of subjects that have been transposed to the stage; to judge to what extent the poet has been faithful to or departed from truthful portrayals of characters and the accuracy of facts; [and] to blame or justify any liberties he has taken." [15]

As already seen, the departures from historical fact that the critics were most likely to condemn were those that contradicted events with which large numbers of the public would be personally familiar, either through actual experience or through variously disseminated accounts. And, as will be seen, critical displeasure continued to be matched by audience dissatisfaction with the more blatant distortions of what was known or generally believed to have taken place.

One of the more farfetched attempts to recast historical events in terms of established generic conventions was executed by one Colonel Grosbert. His *"opéra-mélodrame"* entitled *La Bataille des Pyramides*, first performed at the Théâtre de la Porte-Saint-Martin on April 18, 1803, had not profited from the example of *Kléber, ou les Moeurs orientales*. Even making allowances for the limited talent or inadequate craftsmanship of a man whose primary occupation was not that of dramatic author (apart from his military career, the colonel was author of a geographical and ethnographic study of Egypt and a lengthy treatise on theater design, *De l'Exécution dramatique considérée dans ses rapports avec le matériel de la Salle et de la Scène*), there seems to have been a fundamental problem with the basic premises of Grosbert's enterprise. In retrospect, it would be easy to say that the production's failings were announced by the play's subtitle. The full billing of this *opéra-mélodrame* was *La Bataille des Pyramides, ou Zanoubé et Floricourt*. As might be expected, the intermingling of stock characters and amorous intrigues typical of eighteenth-century opera with figures and episodes drawn from one of the most celebrated battles of the Egyptian campaign was even more poorly received than *Kléber*'s comparatively mild modifications of history. F. J. B. P. G*** of *Le Courrier des Spectacles* found the intentions behind *La Bataille des Pyramides* laudable, but could praise little else:

One of the events that brought the greatest distinction to the French in Egypt and to the hero who always led them to victory was the Battle of the Pyramids. To paint this celebrated action before our eyes, an experienced brush worthy of retracing it was needed. The Frenchman desires nothing more than to honor by his suffrage the memory of victories, the brilliance of which reflects on everyone; but when the artist is far beneath his subject, while fully applauding his intention, one mercilessly rejects his painting, or more accurately, his caricature. This is what happened yesterday at this premiere. There can be nothing colder, more ridiculous, more improbable than the amorous intrigue linked to the plot of this work. (April 19, 1803) [16]

His lack of enthusiasm was apparently fully shared by the other spectators in attendance; as the performance progressed to the accompaniment of yawns, whistles, and laughter, "enfin même les amis de l'auteur, ont reconnu la nullité de cette conception" (eventually even the friends of the author recognized the nullity of the conception). The spectators' responses on the second evening confirmed that it was indeed the dramatic action that disturbed or displeased, while purely visual and spectacular elements were greatly appreciated. On this occasion, readers of *Le Courrier* were told, the intensity of the negative reaction had diminished significantly; but then so had the number of spectators in attendance (April 20, 1803).

Despite such inauspicious starts, successful narrativization and fictionalization would eventually establish military drama on its own terms. One of the essential elements required for the effective negotiation of the imaginary and the real for the stage is indicated by various critiques of Cuvelier's *La Mort de Kléber, ou les Français en Egypte*. This piece was performed at the Cirque Olympique in 1819, almost nineteen years after the panning of *Kléber, ou les Moeurs orientales*. *La Mort de Kléber* itself did not incorporate a fictional narrative. As the reviewer for *Le Camp Volant* put it, "[I]l n'y a dans cette pièce qu'une action militaire" ([T]here is nothing to this play but a military action). Nevertheless, it would seem that the work attracted an audience and interest that exceeded those of the ordinary *action militaire*. *Le Camp Volant*'s review continues by noting that "since the Franconis have associated the immortal Kléber with their works, all Paris is taking part; and far from diminishing, the interest increases from one battle to the next" (February 13, 1819).[17] Indeed, the play would continue to be performed in repertory through the fall of that year, providing additional confirmation that the play had reached beyond the core audience of the Cirque. *Le Camp Volant*'s critic attributed this unusual success to the national interest of the events portrayed; the personal prestige of the central figure, Kléber (who was then being strongly promoted as a national hero to recall the glories of the First Empire without the danger of stirring up Bonapartist sentiment); and the play's high production values. But it remained for a rival critic at *Le Journal de Commerce* to point out the critical factor—the possibility of emotional engagement—without which military history re-created for the stage could attract only a restricted group of *amateurs*. This writer was sensitive to the fact that the Cirque Olympique, in resurrecting the "painful image" of the heroic and illustrious Kléber's "cruel and premature death," had offered to the public "a tender and curious spectacle" that gave them the opportunity "to mingle tears with their applause" (January 9, 1819).[18]

Even without a fully developed fictional narrative and characterizations, this pantomime was apparently able to present and evoke a wider emotional range than the usual commemorative or celebratory military spectacle. And even though *Le Camp Volant*'s critic came to different conclusions regarding the emotional impact generated by *La Mort de Kléber*, in effect he acknowledged that such qualities had come to be expected of a good drama based on contemporary events. Lauding Cuvelier for his patriotic sentiments and national ambitions, he suggested that on this occasion the work had produced a mediocre effect only because the author had failed "to link an engaging action to the interest inspired by the main character and to give to his death a more dramatic aspect" (January 10, 1819).[19] In other words, in this instance Cuvelier had not satisfied the fundamental condition for allowing fiction to coexist with actuality. In the almost twenty years separating *La Mort de Kléber* from *Kléber, ou les Moeurs orientales*, it had been recognized that the fictional action could be linked to actual occurrences only as an adjacent action. There could be no substitution of the fictional for the actual, nor could imaginary, almost always purely personal, motivations replace political, economic, or strategic causes. Contemporary figures and recent events could be embellished by being given "un aspect plus dramatique," but only to the extent that this embellishment did not contradict commonly accepted or known facts, or, just as importantly, the *logic* that experience and observation had proved to govern the activity in question.

By the time a revitalized military drama appeared under Napoleon III, it is clear that these principles were widely acknowledged and that certain elements had become formulaic. Elementary dramatization had evolved into elaborations of plot and subplot that required five acts, numerous tableaux, and innumerable scenes to develop. In his review of one of the finest Second Empire spectacles, *La Guerre en Orient*, the critic of *Le Moniteur universel*, Edouard Thierry, presented a catalogue of what had become the proven ingredients for creating an emotionally provocative national drama:

All the elements are there: an aging blind father who has only one grandson remaining and who gives him to France; the young man who is in love and who fears destiny because he loves; the young woman, happy to be loved, who fears for her happiness and for that of another. But next to them are the soldier who has become a sergeant, who has already paid for his cross with his sweat and asks only to pay for it still more; the commander who makes a fraternal appointment on the battlefield with the officer serving under him; the bad worker whom the flag teaches the meaning of honor; the idle and ruined gentleman who wants to make himself a gentleman again with his courage; everywhere the feeling of the nobility of arms, of the excellence of discipline in ennobling, renewing, and fortifying souls; the experience of manly joy, and, as a conclusion, the festival of departure, the colors displayed, the solemn march of the regiments, to the cries of Long live the Emperor and Long live France! (July 18, 1854)[20]

What's more, all of the above appeared in the opening episode depicting the recruitment and departure of the French troops destined for the eastern front.

While the basic guidelines for joining fiction and reality had attained the status of a generic convention by the middle of the century, new issues surrounding the narrativizing of actuality would arise under the Second Empire. The nature of the new controversy is suggested by Thierry in the opening lines of his report on *La Guerre en Orient*: "*La Guerre en Orient*, so be it; the title is a happy one, but it is only a title and the beginning of a drama the fairest scenes of which are as yet in God's hands."[21] In other words, the authors specializing in this genre had started to compose scenarios based on events that had only begun to unfold and had yet to reach a resolution. A review by Thierry of *Constantinople*, which along with *La Guerre en Orient* exemplified the mature five-act military drama, reflects the extent to which this practice was perceived as a radical departure and suggests some of the reasons for this innovation. In the first place, by the 1850s there had been a significant reduction in the time lapse separating an action in the field and its representation on the stage. Using *Constantinople* as his point of departure, Thierry comments on the Cirque repertory in general:

It is not the poem of the past that is being organized into a spectacle, it is the military bulletin, it is last month's gazette, it is the tale of the current war, of this campaign of the Danube, where Russia seems to provoke the world and where Turkey forms the avant-garde of civilization, to the applause of an astonished Europe. The play follows the various phases of the struggle that is being waged. (April 17–18, 1854)[22]

The closing of this gap was in part a consequence of the acceleration in communication made possible by the telegraph.[23] The theater sought to keep pace with the news made available through other media. Thierry remarked, "The Cirque is prepared to reproduce the telegraphic dispatch, the official communiqué every evening."[24] But, as already suggested, it was prepared to do even more: it was even "ready . . . to sing the Te Deum with our soldiers and publicize victories that are as yet in the hands of the armies. This is a new and singular enterprise, where timeliness can substitute for many things and where the immediacy of execution must be counted as a merit."[25] For the first time, and for what would be a relatively short period, the production capabilities of the theater and its unique positioning between the realms of reality and the imaginary were used not only to commemorate and to report, but to project victory in a vivid manner as well. The re-creation and re-presentation of history interwoven with a fictional narrative was now seamlessly joined to a dénouement that fell into the realm of fiction but followed in the sequence of actual events.

Once introduced, the practice of supplying a fictional ending for an actual beginning continued to be used for the life span remaining to military spectacle as a boulevard attraction. This is not to say that the critics became totally comfortable with the solution or device, although audiences do not seem to have noticed any dissonance in the combination. The critics' reservations are eloquently expressed with regard to *Les Massacres de Syrie* (1861), one of the last large-scale national dramas to be presented on the boulevard before the genre was relegated by official decree to the café-concerts. Its appearance on the stage and in the arena of the Théâtre Impérial du Cirque was announced for several weeks by a series of notices in *Le Constitutionnel* which promised "a great military epic, dazzling in its luxury, ostentation, and oriental richness, and which combines the appeal of drama with the attraction of actuality" (January 13, 1861).[26] The wording of the publicity notice confirms the now easy alliance of fiction and actuality. The review following the play's opening, however, expresses no such acceptance of dramatic forecasting:

Such is, to the extent it can be rendered in a necessarily abbreviated analysis, this drama—so moving, so current, that it is taking place in reality, so to speak, at the very moment that it is being performed.—The intentions are excellent, the success was immense. However, despite the perfect seemliness of the execution, it makes us a little uneasy to see drama precede history, and the poet open the as yet closed hand of destiny to snatch events from it. Must matters not have the sanction of completion? And to portray them while they are still in the making, is this not a premature ambition? (January 7, 1861)[27]

This critic's sense that the natural order of things was disturbed by having "drama precede history" would perhaps be less acute today when it has been successfully argued that history cannot precede discourse. The debate, in any case, was cut short by the banning of the *pièces nationales* from the new theaters of Haussman's reconstructed Boulevard du Temple, and this final point of contention regarding the proper balance between the imaginary and the real would remain unresolved. In the meantime, it would seem that altered thresholds of credibility resulting from the advancement of cinematic and electronic representations of reality have precluded the type of speculation into the future decried in 1861, and the experiments of this brief period in the mid-nineteenth century have yet to be repeated.

7
Oriental Campaigns in Print and on Stage

IN THE LATE TWENTIETH CENTURY scholars of Orientalism are not the only ones to have found theatrical metaphors useful in describing the relationship of the West to the Middle East. A headline in the commentary section of the July 31, 1994, issue of the *Washington Post* warned that "in the next act" the United States must become more than a "bit player in the Mideast drama." Edward Herman and Gerry O'Sullivan, in their book *The "Terrorism" Industry: The Experts and Institutions That Shape Our View of Terror*, note that the metaphor is applied by expert analysts not, as one might expect, to the geopolitical arena but to the media that serve as "theaters" for the drama of terrorism.[1] One of the most recent studies of the triangular relationship between events in the Middle East, journalism, and drama takes this relationship out of the realm of metaphor. In an essay on the 1985 hijacking of the *Achille Lauro* entitled "The Myth of My Widow: A Dramatistic Analysis of News Portrayals of a Terrorist Victim," Jack Lule traces the linking of news and drama as modes of representation back to the 1920s and 1930s. Around this time, George Herbert Mead noted that communications media "report situations through which one can enter into the attitude and experience of other persons. The drama has served this function in presenting what have been felt to be important situations" (Lule 88).

But the practice of recounting "newsworthy" events in a manner designed to invite the emotional engagement of readers is not an exclusively twentieth-century phenomenon. It predates even the nineteenth-century emergence of the popular press. Elements of dramatization, namely a personalized perspective and sensationalized presentation, accompanied the first news bulletins made possible by the hand-operated printing press in the late fifteenth century. At this time, the first *feuilles d'information* (news bulletins) appeared in the form of occasional publications designed to keep at least a small segment of the public (primarily the nobility and the haute bourgeoisie) informed as to the progress of Charles VIII's campaign in Italy.[2] These bulletins, the first of which appeared in 1494, for the most part reproduced the text of letters written by the king or members of his entourage to various correspondents back home. Apparently, although the letters took the form of a private correspondence, their authors were not unaware of the public uses that might be made of them (Seguin, *Nouvelles* 10–11). Very early on, the range of coverage of the *occasionnel* was extended to the *fait-divers*, which offered detailed accounts of portentous or otherwise remarkable events such as the sighting of a dragon in the skies over Paris or the birth of a monster to a heretical woman. This kind of mélange would continue to characterize the *canard*, the nineteenth-century version of the tabloid. In these publications, "preference was always given to individual exploits, to sensational details at the expense of facts which were more important but held less appeal for the imagination" (Seguin, *Nouvelles* 19).

With the appearance of periodicals such as *Les Nouvelles ordinaires* and *La Gazette* (1631), the task of reporting "dry" facts was increasingly taken over by periodicals that evolved into the *presse d'information* of the nineteenth century. These publications—exemplified by *Le Moniteur*, *Le Journal de Paris*, and *La Gazette de France*—reversed the proportions of rhetorical style employed in the *occasionnel* and *canard*: while elements of the sensational and appeals to the imagination remained to enliven accounts, the emphasis was on the timely, accurate, and supposedly disinterested reporting of actuality. The rhetorical strategies (both verbal and visual) and narrative structures designed to achieve this end can be illustrated by comparing journalistic accounts and staged representations of the three major nineteenth-century French expeditions into the Middle East and North Africa. The first of these incursions, which would eventually lead to full French colonization of large regions in the Middle East and North Africa, was the Napoleonic invasion of Egypt in 1798. This opening would be followed by several other major expeditions, notably the invasion of Algeria in 1830 and interventions in Syria in 1860. All three of these campaigns would receive extensive coverage in the daily papers of Paris and, to varying degrees, provide the subject matter for stage representations.

Egypt, 1798–1799

The special relationship enjoyed by newspapers, war, and government was renewed in 1796, just three hundred years after the appearance of the first published bulletins from the front. In order to track the progress of *la Grande Armée*, *Le Journal des défenseurs* commenced publication on the 28 Germinal in the Year 4 (April 17, 1796). The editors of this "semiofficial" publication described their mission in the following manner:

The government thought that at this time when a campaign is about to get under-way, it would be of interest to have a newspaper whose purpose would be . . . to make known the marches of the armies, their position, their battles, their victo-ries, the heroic actions of the defenders of the country, [and] the prodigious acts of courage engendered every day by the love of liberty.[3]

The daily paper had become such an integral and useful part of French everyday life by the close of the century that printing presses were brought to Egypt by the army. The presses were used to produce two publica-tions: *Le Courrier de l'Egypte*, intended for the troops, reported news of Egypt and France and had the express purpose of maintaining the morale of the army; and *La Décade égyptienne*, addressed to officers and scholars, contained articles on political, economic, literary, and scientific problems relating to Egypt.

For the majority of French citizens, news of the expedition to Egypt led by General Bonaparte came through the official dispatches published in the *quotidiens* (daily newspapers) or from the condensed reprints of this material that appeared in the *occasionnels*. Although the social reading prac-tices outlined in Chapter 2 would have allowed for circulation of this in-formation through all class levels even without the material support of the cheaper *occasionnels*, which did not require subscription, the reproduction of these dispatches in the popular press created an additional form of dis-course around these events. This news was avidly sought, for as the author of an article entitled "De l'Égypte" noted:

There are very few of our fellow citizens who do not have a son, a brother, or a friend in this army; there are none who do not follow its operations with the inter-est inspired by national pride, the curiosity aroused by great enterprises, especially when, like this one, they have as their goal the future improvement of mankind's destiny. (*Gazette nationale/Moniteur universel*, October 14, 1798)[4]

A nineteenth-century painting by Louis-Léopold Boilly captures the avidity with which the *Bulletin de la Grande Armée* was read and the mo-mentous effect it could have on a family (Figure 8).

The dispatches, however, generally arrived in France some two months after the events themselves had transpired. This delay reflected

Figure 8. Louis-Léopold Boilly. *La Lecture du Bulletin de la Grande Armée* (1807). The Saint Louis Art Museum, gift of Mr. & Mrs. R. Crosby Kemper through the Crosby Kemper Foundations.

the state of land and sea transportation at the time and also the fact that the Egyptian expedition was part of a larger war against the English, in which the British navy's control of the Mediterranean Sea impeded French communication. Accordingly, the first reports of the expedition's progress came in tantalizing bits and pieces, as sightings of the French fleet were reported by travelers arriving from various points around the Mediterranean. The steady flow of information began only on September 29, 1798, when two pages of "Nouvelles intéressantes de l'Égypte et proclamations de Bonaparte à son entrée dans ce pays" appeared in the official government paper *La Gazette nationale/Le Moniteur universel*. Bulletins reporting the fleet's arrival at Alexandria followed by the army's advance on Cairo provided the main fare (along with related filler material on the history and geography of the region) until October 20, when Napoleon's own account of events to the Directoire exécutif was first shared with the public.

Over the next several days, additional dispatches from Napoleon as well as others written by General Alexandre Berthier, chief of staff of the army, to the minister of war, were published in installments. General Bonaparte's self-proclamation as governor-general of Egypt and his reorganization of the government were reported along with the army's victories. The earliest dispatches appeared first in *La Gazette nationale/Le Moniteur universel* and then were reprinted in other major publications, such as the *Journal de Paris*, a few days afterward. Later, bulletins seem to have been released simultaneously to all the major papers. Letters from independent sources began reaching France in early November, confirming the happy situation of the French army.[5] The celebratory tenor of these reports was subdued only when they reported the destruction of the French fleet—highlighted by the explosion of the French flagship, the *Orient*—by the English navy under Lord Nelson in the port of Aboukir. About this time, letters also began to offer indications of some of the hardships being endured by the French troops, largely due to the heat of the desert and the attacks made by Bedouin Arabs on stragglers. One letter reported that the French army had suffered little damage from the organized defense of the Mameluks, but that many Frenchmen who had become separated from the main body of troops had been "mercilessly massacred" by bands of Bedouins (*Gazette nationale/Moniteur universel*, November 20, 1798). Another letter published in *Le Journal de Paris* said that some of the young men who encountered the Bedouins escaped with their lives, but only after being "beaten, robbed, raped and sent back naked after having served the pleasure of the horde" (October 19, 1798).

In light of subsequent developments in the reporting of conflicts in the Middle East, it is important to note the clear distinctions that were made between different groups of Arabs and Muslims. In his account of the aftermath of the French defeat at Aboukir, M. Julien, "commissaire des guerres de l'armée d'Orient," noted that the Mameluks did not do the French much harm, but the Bedouin attacks were a renewal of "les horreurs de la guerre de la Vendée"—bloody counter-revolutionary insurrections that occurred in Brittany, Poitou, and Anjou in 1793. This comparison between Arabs and French recalls the identifications made across European/non-European lines in the censors' reports (see Chapter 2). It was also well known that similar attacks were carried out on Egyptian refugees fleeing Cairo after the French entry into the city. 'Abd-al-Rahman al-Jabarti, an Egyptian official living in Cairo at the time, wrote in his journal that "[w]hen these people, after having passed the city gates, reached the open desert, the Bedouins and fellahs robbed them of their possessions; they took their clothing and baggage, leaving them with nothing even to cover their nakedness or calm their hunger" (35).

While the events were momentous in themselves and the gradual unfolding of reports created additional suspense, dialogued scenes added drama to the coverage in a very literal sense. One such scene published in the November 27, 1798, edition of *Le Journal de Paris* was entitled "Entrevue de Bonaparte membre de l'Institut national, général en chef de l'armée d'Orient, et de plusieurs muphtis et imans, dans l'intérieure de la grande pyramide, dite pyramide de Chéops." What followed purported to be the transcript of an actual conversation, a debate in fact, between Napoleon and Suleiman over the relative merits of Christian and Islamic civilization as exemplified by the histories of France and Egypt. Needless to say, Napoleon's arguments proved to be the more convincing.

What the newspapers reported the stage soon represented—with considerable embellishment. As the decade following Napoleon's victories in the Middle East witnessed countless re-creations of these events, one work that typifies the process of transformation from print to stage was MM. Cuvelier and Augustin's *La Bataille d'Aboukir, ou les Arabes du désert*, first performed at the Cirque Olympique in 1808 and then expanded for a revival in 1809. Generically, the work was designated an "action pantomime militaire." In the earlier version, the action begins in the desert, not far from the Egyptian port city of Aboukir. A small party of wounded French foot soldiers, who have been unable to keep up with the main body of troops, stagger on stage. Physically exhausted and dangerously dehydrated, they are easily overpowered and taken prisoner when attacked by a band of Bedouin Arabs. Following their departure from the scene, a French officer named Derville arrives with his wife, Célestine, and their young son, Adolphe. Derville confides his family, also exhausted from crossing the desert, to the care of an old Turk (who is offered a a handsome sum of money as an incentive to protect them) and leaves to rejoin his regiment. Following his departure, English troops disembark from their ship and enter; their commander, Sir Tiger-Bold, catches sight of Célestine and falls in love with her. Skirmishes over the lady ensue between the Englishmen, assisted by Turkish soldiers, and Derville, supported by his men, with some attacks by Arabs thrown in for variety.

This personally motivated local engagement merges into the outbreak of the second Battle of Aboukir, which culminates in the taking of the fort itself, the complete rout of the Turkish troops, and the retreat of the English forces to their ships. All except Sir Tiger-Bold, that is, who, in a last vengeful gesture worthy of a boulevard villain, tries to blow up the tower of the fort where he had succeeded in imprisoning Célestine before the beginning of the battle. Gratifyingly, not only does his effort fail, but he himself is killed by the detonation. The joyful family reunion of Derville, his wife, and his son takes place amid the greater celebration of the French victory. (Needless to say, the French never bothered to re-create the earlier naval battle of Aboukir in which the French fleet was destroyed.) The seamless blending of melodramatic structure and military action was highly praised by critics and well received by audiences.

Algeria, 1830

In contrast to the secrecy and delays in reporting that surrounded the 1798 Egyptian campaigns, the launching of the Algerian invasion of 1830 was carried out in what would today be called the full glare of publicity. From the beginning, this expedition was heavily advertised as part of an effort to restore the ultraroyalist Restoration monarchy to favorable public opinion and to counter both bourgeois and working-class dissatisfaction. The May 7, 1830, edition of *Le Moniteur universel* contained an impressive enumeration by class of the vessels that would make up the French fleet. The next day, the paper reported that "[a]ll letters from Toulon assure us that both French and foreigners of both sexes are flocking there in an unheard-of manner. The neighboring communes are equally congested with military personnel and travelers."[6] The arrival and activities of the Dauphin formed the centerpiece of what was openly described as a spectacle, one that attracted crowds estimated to include over ten thousand people.

The continued status of the expedition as a public spectacle was assured by outfitting the invasion force with telegraphic equipment that would not only facilitate ship-to-shore communication but also assure that public interest could be sustained through the rapid dissemination of news. The average time it took for news from the north coast of Africa to reach Paris was ten days, as opposed to the two months required during Napoleon's time. In addition to being very open about the size and disposition of the French forces, official sources seemed remarkably well informed as to the counterpreparations being made by the dey of Algiers. The measures described in the May 25 issue of *Le Moniteur* were minimal and apparently not of an order to pose any threat to the French forces. The piece concluded that "[t]he French army has nothing to fear but the contrariness of the winds and the difficulties of disembarkation."[7] To judge by official accounts, the French forces encountered no such difficulties and swept to an inevitable if noisy victory over the defenders of the fort of Algiers.

But in contrast to the univocal coverage of the Napoleonic expeditions—the result of both widespread support for the war and effective censorship—contradictory views about the Algerian enterprise were being expressed in the news organs of the liberal opposition. *Le Journal des Débats* presented a "responsible" challenge to the official accounts and managed to cast doubts on the motives and honesty of the government of Charles X and his council president, the prince de Polignac, without criticizing the expedition in a way that could be construed as antipatriotic or demoralizing to the troops. On July 14, a front-page story strongly hinted that the government was not being entirely forthcoming in the information it released regarding the progress of the invasion. In particular, the story pointed out that only excerpts from Admiral Duperé's dispatches appeared in *Le Moniteur* and suggested that the suppressed passages described severe reverses the fleet had suffered due to storms along the Algerian coast. In support of this claim, *Le Journal des Débats* published a letter from a naval lieutenant that described the ordeals of shipwrecked crew members who fell into the hands of Bedouins. This report included a vivid, indeed dramatic, account of the heroic escape of two sailors who apparently made their way through the mountain wilderness, surviving on a diet of roots, to surrender to the dey's officers in Algiers. In a similar vein, on June 26, *Le Journal des Débats* stated:

It would seem that the African expedition has taken on a more serious complexion than was generally anticipated. Instead of fleeing before our disciplined batallions, the barbaric hordes that line the coast of Africa attacked our positions, and it took all the valor and sang-froid of our young army to triumph over the obstacles that separated them from the walls of Algiers.

The affair of the 19th must have been spirited to judge by the results. We are astonished not to find in the official bulletin the slightest allusion to the losses that that day must have cost us.[8]

The editors of *Le Journal des Débats* had the opportunity to strike one last blow at the "*réticences singuliers*" of the official reports before the announcement of victory put a temporary halt to their criticisms of the enterprise. In the June 29 issue a pointed comparison was drawn between France and England where, it was said, the government kept its citizens fully informed of "the least event of the most distant expeditions." This openness was attributed to the fact that whatever their political differences, Whigs and Tories alike understood that "truth and publicity are the element and very life of constitutional government."[9]

These calculated subversions of the official position took a more lively form in *Le Corsaire: Journal des spectacles, de la littérature, des arts, moeurs, modes*, a publication with no party affiliation to restrain the irreverent creativity of its writers. *Le Corsaire*'s satirical treatment of the Algerian campaign included a variety of parodic forms. M. de Bourmont, the commander-in-chief of the expeditionary forces, was a favorite target for its acerbic commentaries. While the political analysts writing for more serious papers discussed the constitutional violations involved in Bourmont's double appointment as minister of war and commander in chief, *Le Corsaire* took a more humorous approach to the potential conflict of interest and loss of accountability: "M. Bourmont, minister of war, will no doubt approve all the operations of M. Bourmont, commander in chief, and whatever blunders the latter may commit, he can be sure that he will never be deprived of his command by the minister" (May 11, 1830).[10] The prospect of Bourmont the minister naming Bourmont the general a *maréchal de France* allowed for even more "*bizarres effets*" in the form of the logistical problems posed by the need to bear and exchange various ritual objects during the ceremony of investiture. A parody of a letter from le *Généralissime*, as Bourmont was dubbed, to the prince de Polignac included a postscript that acknowledged receipt of a cargoload of blue and yellow spectacles to protect the eyes of the soldiers against the sun. The *Généralissme* reported that "I had two regiments try them on yesterday; the infantry wore the yellow glasses and the cavalry the blue; this produced an admirable effect in formation" (May 4, 1830).[11]

By the time of the conquest of Algiers, the *canard* had become a well-established source of news, popular with the middle as well as the lower classes. Its distinctive format consisted of an elaborate and detailed "headline," sometimes extending over the entire first page, that summarized the principal incidents of the lead story in phrases that could easily be shouted out by the street vendors. The woodblock illustrations that usually decorated the front page were occasionally created for the issue, but usually they were mere generic renderings of more or less related subjects. For example, the illustration that accompanied one *canard*'s coverage of the early phases of the Algerian expedition was a seventeenth-century woodblock that depicted a fleet of ships before a city of many steeples and spires labeled "COLONIA" (Seguin, *Nouvelles* 113).

As the French occupation continued and Algiers was employed as a base for attempted expansions into the Maghrib, events provided the *canards* with a rich flow of material. One story appearing in an 1843 issue featured the tale of the "TRAIT DE COURAGE D'UN OFFICIER FRANÇAIS EN AFRIQUE." [12] Apparently, a young French officer had left his post to rescue a father and his "jeune et jolie demoiselle" who were being attacked by Bedouins. Convicted of deserting his post in the face of the enemy, the young officer was condemned to execution by a firing squad. His brother, also stationed in Algeria, announced that his sibling would not die alone, for no human power would tear him from his arms. In a speech worthy of the boulevard stage, the condemned soldier replies: "My brother . . . what are you thinking of? You know that our poor mother has need of you. Will she not be unhappy enough when she learns of my death? Is she then destined to be entirely bereft of support? Think of her, I beg you, of this good mother to whom we owe so much and renounce your fatal design, for she will die of grief." [13] His brother was undeterred, but—in what can only be described as a theatrical tableau—the firing squad remained immobile, moved to tears, as were, it was to be hoped, the readers. This touching story, illustrated by four woodblock prints, appeared along with a report of the military engagement with the Arabs in which "large numbers of the enemy were left on the field of battle" (Seguin, *Canards* 48–49).

The original victory in Algeria produced a spate of celebratory spectacles, notably a festive "Prise d'Alger" at the Tivoli Gardens in which an opening exchange of gunfire between French and Arab riflemen (seemingly orchestrated as a prelude) was joined by stirring martial music that announced the arrival of full regiments who charged through the smoke to scatter the enemy: "[E]xplosions cross-cutting through the sky in all directions; the noise and din make a frightful tumult, and in the midst of all this, the French banner floats in the air." As the *Corsaire* writer put it succinctly, "Nous voilà sous Alger" (July 22, 1830). Given the magnitude of the event—considerable even if one did not know how French-Algerian relations would progress over the next 160 years—it might seem surprising that the conquest of Algiers would never qualify for the elaborate dramatizations that followed the Syrian expeditions of 1860, which were of far less strategic and economic significance. The explanation would seem to lie in the rapid sequence of events that, within a few weeks of the victory in North Africa, would result in the overthrow of the absolute monarchy of Charles X and the transference of succession to the Orleanist line represented by Louis-Philippe. With the principles of constitutional government reestablished along with the Monarchie de Juillet, it was unlikely that an enterprise so strongly associated with the deposed ultraroyalist government would be resurrected for public acclaim.

If the invasion of Algeria never qualified as a favorite subject for dramatization, the subsequent occupation and colonization of Algeria did find its way onto the boulevard stages. By 1837, the French presence in Algeria was well enough established to be easily integrated into a melodramatic structure. *Zara, ou la Soeur de l'Arabe*, by MM. Valory and Montigny, was first performed at the Folies-Dramatiques in May 1837 and then revived for the Gaité more than four years later in September 1841. The play used the tensions between the Algerians and the French to intensify the traditional dramatic conflict created by a love triangle. The terms of the conflict are made eminently clear in a single speech:

HASSAN: I know how to take revenge . . . revenge on all whom I hate. On you, Léon Dervigny, who are French and my rival! on you, woman, who rejected, scorned my love!

(4.7)[14]

The woman in question is of course the Zara of the title. And, as the title suggests, Zara's brother is also a significant figure in the play. Named Mohamed, he spoils Hassan's ambush of the couple by leading French troops to the rescue. Finally, he shoots and kills Hassan as the villain rushes at Léon and Zara with his dagger drawn in a last attempt to exact revenge. This moment, captured in the title illustration reproduced here (Figure 9), would seem to have had larger allegorical implications as well, for Mohamed's parting words to Léon are, "And your union [with my sister] will be the pledge of the unending devotion of my tribe to the cause of the French nation" (4.8).[15] The sentiments expressed in the final scenes of *Zara* were not merely the product of theatrical imagination. In January 1834 a French officer stationed at Bone had written: "We are on very good terms with the Arabs. We have had the good fortune, after a show of strength, to inspire them with great confidence; they like French domination and are constantly proving it. . . . [Several tribes] have joined their fate to ours without reservation" (qtd. in Guiral 48).[16] The authors of *Zara* were able

Figure 9. Title illustration for *Zara, ou la Sœur de l'Arabe,* by MM. Valory and Montigny (1842). *Magasin Théâtral*, vol. 31. The New York Public Library, Astor, Lenox and Tilden Foundations.

to preserve the illusion of pacification by bringing down the curtain. In actuality, the drama of Algerian resistance had only just begun.

Syria, 1860

The theatrical potential of the Syrian expedition of 1860 would not be diminished by the divisions associated with the Algerian invasion. From the first rumors of widespread massacres of Christians to the actual embarkation of eight thousand troops sent to support the Mideast Christians, French indignation and support for intervention cut across party lines. On July 21, 1860, a long and detailed account of the events leading to the attacks of Druze Muslims against the Maronite Christian population appeared in *Le Moniteur universel*. The actual massacres took place over a period of three days, beginning the morning of June 20:

[T]he Druzes, after having disarmed the Christians, began the pillaging that lasted the entire night of the 19th to 20th of June. In the morning, the Druzes from the mixed districts began arriving to take part along with their wives and children, without the slightest effort being made on the part of the soldiers to stop them. The massacre followed the pillages; no one was spared; children had their throats cut on their mother's knees, women and girls were raped and disemboweled before the eyes of their husbands and fathers.

Men were dismembered by hatchet blows in the streets; women were burned after being drenched in the blood of their children; not even nuns were spared. The city was strewn with corpses, and the streets ran with blood.[17]

The report continues to tell how, "excités par le carnage," the Druze mob demanded that five hundred Christians and their families who had found shelter in the governor's palace be handed over. The very soldiers assigned to protect them drove the Christians out of their refuge in the seraglio with blows from the bayonets of their rifles.

Disturbingly evocative as these accounts are, they seem measured and almost dispassionate compared to the version of events presented in *L'Opinion nationale: Journal politique quotidien*. Here we can see a radical departure from previous journalistic presentations of conflicts in the Middle East and North Africa. A new inflammatory rhetoric uses bestial metaphors to link the commission of atrocities with anti-Christian fanaticism, a connection that has yet to be dislodged:

We know that the savages of this part of Asia have disemboweled women after having dishonored them, that they have quartered priests and old men, killed small children with atrocious refinements of cruelty before the eyes of their mothers, whom they then forced to bathe in the blood collected from this new massacre of the innocents.

The steamship from Beirut will inform us as to whether or not these atrocities continue in Syria. . . .

We would like to hear that this terrible explosion of hateful passions has finally subsided, and that the ferocious beasts, sated with carnage, have retreated to their lairs to sleep off their intoxication. But we dare not hope for this; we fear that, on the contrary, fanaticism has only enlarged the field of its monstrous operations. (August 1, 1860) [18]

Compared to the assault on the sensibilities effected by this passage, *L'Opinion nationale*'s analysis of the outbreaks of violence in Lebanon and Syria as being symptomatic of a deeply seated "religious hatred, rekindled by political struggles and racial antagonism" (July 20, 1860) seems almost judicious in its passing acknowledgment of particular historical circumstances. But in a move that makes sense only in the context of Second Empire imperialist ambitions, the local attacks on Christians were discursively escalated into "[un] vaste complot ourdi par les musulmans contre les chrétiens" (a great plot hatched by the Muslims against the Christians [July 30, 1860]). The cry of conspiracy had in fact been sounded as soon as the first dispatches appeared in *Le Moniteur*. As early as July 18 an article in *La Patrie* stated: "There can no longer be any doubt: there is a great conspiracy against the lives of all the Christians of Asia, and this conspiracy, which has already claimed its separate victims . . . today has taken on fearsome proportions, and now proceeds only through mass murder."[19] In the face of this threat to Christianity, France was clearly being summoned to assume a position of military and moral leadership: "As a military power, as the home of science and ideas, France marches at the head of all the nations of the world. She occupies the first rank among civilized peoples, and the unhappy fate of the Christians of Syria must inspire noble outbursts and a manly resolve" (*L'Opinion nationale*, July 25, 1860).[20] These ringing words were not only an invitation to active intervention, they were also a call for epic dramatization, a call that would be answered by Victor Séjour with his *Massacres de Syrie*.

Occident versus Orient

Les Massacres de Syrie and the
Recasting of History

Acts of Atrocity

Fewer than six months would separate the first newspaper reports of the disturbances in Lebanon and Syria from a fully elaborated dramatic representation of those events. The writer responsible for bringing those events to the stage was Victor Séjour (1817–1874), a Creole from Louisiana, who had come to study in France at the age of nineteen and had remained to establish a highly successful career as a writer and dramatist.[1] He was at the height of his career when *Les Massacres de Syrie*, "drame en huit tableaux," had its premiere performance on December 28, 1860, at the Théâtre Impérial du Cirque. The success of the play was immediate and overwhelming. A week after the first performance a notice in *Le Constitutionnel* remarked, "[T]he success of *Les Massacres de Syrie* has surpassed all expectations" (January 7, 1861).[2] A month later the same newspaper informs us that "the immense success of *Les Massacres de Syrie* seems to grow still greater with every performance" (February 9, 1861).[3]

The regular notices keeping the public informed as to the activity of the theaters confirm the solid alliance of dramatic interest and current events with a third element, exceptional visual and sensory effects, as the great drawing attractions of Séjour's drama. The series of notices appearing in the theater section of *Le Constitutionnel* following the opening present variations on this theme. *Les Massacres de Syrie* is variously described as:

A great spectacular play, to which contemporary events add a powerful draw of curiosity and interest. (January 10, 1861)

A great military epic, with dazzling displays of extravagance and oriental sumptuousness, and which joins to the interest of the drama the attraction of actuality. (January 15, 1861)

A great spectacular play, to which contemporary events add a powerful draw of actuality and timeliness. (January 19, 1861) [4]

One of the last notices in this series offers the appreciation that there could be "[n]othing more engaging than this work which joins to the dramatic interest, to the prestige of actuality, the richness of a dazzling staging" (February 9, 1861). [5] The interest created by dramatic narrative was now fully integrated with that generated by contemporary military action and political or diplomatic maneuvering.

The full acceptance of the national drama as a genre with broad public appeal, rather than as a special-interest theatrical form, is reflected in its designation as both a *grande pièce à spectacle* and an *épopée militaire*. The interchangeability of the terms indicates that the overlapping of these forms and of their audiences had become commonplace by this time. Both appellations reflect the vast scale of production that had become commonplace for such enterprises. Vestiges of the original format of the military theater piece can be recognized in the main organizing unit of the play: the tableau. In *Les Massacres de Syrie*, the eight tableaux are subdivided into anywhere from five to twenty scenes. This proliferation of scenes was accompanied by a multiplication of the cast, with almost forty actors assigned speaking parts in *Les Massacres*.

True to form, this proliferation of sets and characters corresponds to a more complete representation of the sites of social, political, and economic activity and the full hierarchy and range of interested social subjects. The reproduction—always selective as we shall see—of familiar and recognizable social structures and relations was essential to establishing a mode of reception designed to draw on actuality in producing its effects, and then to stimulate responses that could have an impact on that actuality. In other words, the reproduction of key features of social organization would both require and open the way to free circulation between internal and external circuits of theatrical communication.

It is interesting to note that of the three prime drawing factors mentioned in these bulletins, the only feature that is mentioned in one form or another in every one is the "attrait d'actualité et d'à-propos," "the appeal of actuality and timeliness." Such verbal insistence can be safely assumed to reflect the actual presence of such an interest or awareness among the majority of spectators or potential spectators and confirms for us that this level of context was in fact active in shaping the reception of the work. At no time was this dialogue more visibly and deliberately engaged than at the premiere of the play, when Napoleon III himself was in the audience:[6]

That the popular fiber should vibrate at the memory, at the recounting, what am I saying? at the faithful and vivid representation of these cruelties, of these per-fidies, and of these bloody slaughters that the sword of France was neither able to prevent nor to avenge completely, what could be more natural? That the audience profited from the august presence of the Sovereign to acclaim him and thank him for having understood so well the sentiments of the nation, what could be more legitimate? (January 7, 1861)[7]

This engagement with actuality is marked internally from the moment the curtain is first raised. In sharp contrast to the constant remove from reality signaled by the sets and opening tableaux and scenes of *Les Ruines de Babylone*, the opening of *Les Massacres de Syrie* immediately places the action in a socioeconomic context. The former's rendering of fantastic, festive palace gardens, offering glimpses of a cheerful and picturesque countryside through ornamental openwork, has given way to the latter's depiction of a fertile farm caught at harvest time—the moment of greatest productivity. The spectator's entry into the fictional world is here guided by signposts of reality rather than those of fantasy. The opening stage directions read:

THE MORÉAC FARM

THE INTERIOR COURTYARD OF A RICH ORIENTAL FARM

A well in the corner. In the background, a vista showing the sky of Syria. At the rise of the curtain, the farm is full of activity; the wheat and hay is being stored by the farmhands, who bring it in from the back gate and carry it to the inside granaries by exiting left. The farmhands are dressed either in the French fashion or in the style of Brittany; others according to the taste of the country.[8]

As the means of production that provide the material support of the community are displayed in the background, its spiritual foundations are illustrated in the foreground. In the first scene of the first tableau we find that

(Marthe [the owner's daughter] is preparing a light meal on a tray. Father Simon is seated across from her; he is reading his breviary. The workers are finishing bringing in the wheat.)

MARTHE: (*To the Sisters of Charity.*) Come in, Sisters, come in . . . we will have the honor of serving you ourselves.

(*The Sisters enter right.*)

FATHER SIMON: Noble heart! . . .

MARTHE: These pious and holy Sisters! (*To Father Simon.*) Two of them are from Brittany like us, father. We talked about home. But they have such lofty souls, so detached from our passions, that they find their home-land everywhere that suffering calls them. You did well to choose us as their hosts.[9]

In this scene both church and "management" are initially presented to the audience in their most innocuous or unthreatening forms, through the most disempowered representatives of these institutions. The church is represented by a local parish priest and the Sisters of Charity, while the pro-prietors of the farm are represented by the young daughter of the family.

The first fully developed scene evolves into the second one, in which only the workers occupy the stage. Given the context created by the open-ing scene, they are presented if not in circumstances of authority, at least in a situation of autonomy. The more authoritative members of the Moréac family appear gradually, one scene at a time, and in order of ascending power: Madame de Moréac enters in the third scene to direct the prepara-tion of the meal; her son Georges returns from hunting in the fourth scene and has on his mind only Gulnare, a young Arab woman adopted as a child by the Moréacs; while the appearance of the "patron" himself, Pierre de Moréac, is postponed until the sixteenth scene. He makes this entrance in the company of a band of his workers. The audience therefore first par-ticipates in the life of this "Oriental farm" through the perspective of the working-class characters as they go about their business without apparent supervision.

It is in their midst that Papillon, an itinerant barber, first brings up the topic of tensions between the Druze Muslims and the Maronite Christians:

PAPILLON: . . . Have you heard that the Druze of the Bekkaa have met in arms on the Djebel-Sunnin? . . . We have to watch out, you know. Not only do they detest the Maronites, they hold a grudge against all the Chris-tians of Lebanon.

(1.2)[10]

His call for vigilance is met with enthusiasm by his co-workers, most of whom have served in the army or the national guard. This implicit incorporation of working-class interests under the heading of larger—most properly national but here Christian—interests, and the linking of both with armed defense and military service, respects the genre's traditional interpellation of the lower ranks of the army veteran. It also more hopefully—but with less certain success—represents the interpellation of the potential recruit under the circumstances particular to France's international situation in the late 1850s and early 1860s and the ambitions of Napoleon III's regime. Finally, it recognizes the growing consolidation of working-class identity and the increasing awareness of the disparity of their interests and those of even the liberal bourgeoisie with whom they had frequently been allied since the the the French Revolution.

The initial address of working-class spectators in terms of parity sets the condition for subsequent, more pointed exchanges. In scene 18 of the first tableau, Ben-Reschid enters in the wake of the first attacks of the Druze on Maronite villages to warn them that "[t]he vultures with human faces who devastated the neighboring villages are already hovering around our town" and to obtain assistance. The elder Moréac then issues a rousing call for volunteers:

MOREAC: Friends, they are killing, slaughtering Christians . . . they are killing our brothers! . . . Hasbeiya needs defenders! . . . Are there those among you who will consent to leave their work for the only thing that is even more sacred . . . fighting for a sacred cause? [11]

The response to this call for volunteers is, of course, enthusiastic. While it was essential to establish the full participation of all segments of society in the community being represented, the interpellation of separate groups was not the principal resource of the military or national drama. In keeping with the designation of the genre, it was naturally a common identity as Frenchmen, and for the most part only *men*, that was stressed. Pierre de Moréac, in a statement clearly transmitted along both internal and external lines of communication to characters and audience alike, maintains that "là où il y a un Français, l'honneur de la France est engagé: la France ne doit pas répudier sa mission: protection aux faibles, dévouement aux droits" (wherever there is a Frenchman, the honor of France is at stake. France must not repudiate her mission: the protection of the weak, devotion to rights" [1.18]).

In cases involving the Middle East and other non-European regions, the appeal to nationalism that was synonymous with the military play was allied to an appeal to the identity of the spectators as Europeans and

even more importantly as generic Christians. The terms of the local conflict made this last allegiance by far the overriding consideration in *Les
Massacres de Syrie*. By 1860, the terms of Orientalist or more broadly speaking colonialist discourse had been as firmly established in the theater as in
other areas of cultural activity. Abdul JanMohamed describes the dominant
structural feature of all forms of colonialist representation, institutional as
well as discursive:

> The dominant model of power- and interest-relations in all colonial societies is the
> manichean opposition between the putative superiority of the European and the
> supposed inferiority of the native. This axis in turn provides the central feature
> of the colonialist cognitive framework and colonialist literary representation: the
> manichean allegory—a field of diverse yet interchangeable oppositions between
> white and black, good and evil, superiority and inferiority, civilization and sav-
> agery, intelligence and emotion, rationality and sensuality, self and Other, subject
> and object. ("Colonialist Literature" 63)

The inevitable consequence of this determined dualistic structuring of
thought and representation in imaginary texts is that "Instead of being
an exploration of the racial Other, such literature merely affirms its own
ethnocentric assumptions; instead of actually depicting the outer limits of
'civilization,' it simple codifies and preserves the structures of its own mentality" (65).

In large part because of its antecedents in melodrama on the one hand
and the military tableau or pantomime on the other—both structured
along lines of an inherent dualism—the national dramas constituted one of
the most hospitable host forms for presenting variations on the Manichean
allegory. This twofold representational framework placed France, Christianity, the Occident—and sometimes Europe—as wholly congruent and
interchangeable terms on one side of the conceptual divide and the Arabic,
Islamic, or the Oriental on the other. When sufficiently clear-cut and simple
oppositions—geographical, political, or religious—did not exist, the move
to posit such equivalencies in organization or institutions led to negative formulations and to the inevitable conclusion that the non-European
model was defective or degenerate. All these moves are indicative of the
linguistic and intellectual failure to perceive Middle Eastern societies and
cultures on their own terms. In *Les Massacres de Syrie* the very sequence and
conception of the early tableaux incorporates this mode of comparison.

The opening tableau, as we have seen, displays the productivity, order,
and communal cooperation of the farm owned and operated by the de-

scendants of French Crusaders. The message intended to be conveyed by these initial glimpses into the Moréacs' lives is summed up by Théophile Gautier in his review of the play: "[T]he Moréacs have not forgotten their old homeland, and are still faithful to the religion of their ancestors. The traditions of the Occident are being maintained by this small group lost in the heart of the mountain among the multiple sects that divide these populations" (*Le Moniteur universel*, January 7, 1861).[12]

The set of the second tableau presents a striking contrast to the impression made by the first set:

THE GREAT RAVINE

An immense ravine the rich vegetation of which contrasts with the arid slopes that lead down to it. Scattered Bedouin Arabs are lying in front of their tents. —Ben-Yacoub is standing, in the background, leaning on his horse, mechanically caressing the horse's mane. Ali-Bey watches him. — At the highest summit, a spahi on guard with his reed spear in hand. — An enormous tiger skin, at right, is stretched before Ben-Yacoub's tent: it is his bed. At left, a large tree on a precipice. —Beyond, the desert.[13]

In contrast to the cultivated fertility of "la ferme de Moréac" and its rich harvest produced by laborers of European stock in the opening scene, here the only sign of fertility is that of nature, the land itself. The implication of this contrast, that only Europeans could realize the potential of the natural resources of the Middle East, was a repeated notion in scientific discourse, in newspaper articles arguing for European colonization of the region, and even in travel literature. The arid slopes that surmount the green ravine and the desert that surrounds it suggest that it is the lot of the native Arab inhabitants, who are represented not by permanent residents but by transients, to accept and adapt themselves to the arbitrariness of nature.

The speeches Victor Séjour assigned to Ben-Yacoub, the man elected to organize and lead the Druze Muslims in their massacres of Maronite Christians, constantly invoke the more dangerous and unattractive animal inhabitants of the most inhospitable habitats. Overlooking the dispersion of the bloodthirsty sheiks who had assembled to plan the murder of Christians and the looting and destruction of their property, he observes with satisfaction, "There they go! . . . Like a band of vultures in search of a great prey!" (2.4).[14] As he gives orders for the ambush of Georges Moréac, who is on his way to Damascus to summon aid from the European powers, Ben-Yacoub says: "Choisis cinq de mes meilleurs tireurs; qu'ils se glissent à plat ventre et sans bruit, comme des serpents, dans les crevasses et les plis de la montagne" (Choose five of my best marksmen; let them glide silently on their bellies, like snakes, in the crevices and fissures of the mountain [2.6]). In the context established by previous settings, connotations very different from those produced in *Les Ruines de Babylone* adhere to the representation of a band of Bedouins. In the melodrama, the depiction of a Bedouin encampment, following as it does upon two settings designed to recall the most fantastic and ornamental aspects of Oriental architecture, continues the exercise in decorative exoticism, the main purpose of which was to procure for the spectator the sensory novelty of a removal in time and space. But in *Les Massacres de Syrie* a comparison is posed between two modes of living, European and Arab, and the conduct of every aspect of social, economic, and political activity, themselves considered reflective of fundamental differences between two civilizations and even two races— the one clearly superior and the other irremediably inferior. The tableaux present visual confirmation of words pronounced by "le père Simon" in the third scene of the first tableau with regard to the tensions that exist between the Druze and the Maronites:

FATHER SIMON: . . . a deadly hatred exists between the Druze and the Maronites: hatred of party, because the Druze execrate France and the Maronites love us; hatred of custom, because they pillage and the Maronites work; hatred of religion, because they are idolaters and the Maronites are Christians.[15]

The gathering of Muslim Arabs in the wilderness, following as it does upon the scenes of French farm life in Lebanon, invites unfavorable contrasts in the realm of economic productivity and resource management. A similarly disparaging contrast in styles of diplomatic negotiation emerges in the light of the succeeding tableau situated in Damascus and entitled

THE FRENCH CONSULATE

A small salon at the home of the French consul, opening onto an illuminated gallery. —A ball. —Music can be heard. —Servants come and go, offering refreshments.[16]

Featured amid these refinements of European civilization are the counterparts of the dozen Arab sheiks who just met to plan their military strategy: the consuls of France, England, Russia, Prussia, and Austria. The meeting of sheiks is characterized by its utter lack of deliberation or discussion of the situation at hand. The following exchanges are typical of their decision-making process:

(The twelve horsemen descend at a gallop and arrange themselves in a semicircle around Ben-Yacoub.)

BEN-YACOUB: (*Solemnly.*) By the eternal Hackim, our Lord and God, I answer for the sultan of the Osmanlis, and the last hour of Christians has sounded!

THE D'JEMMALA-D'JEZZAR: The holy war! the holy war! . . .

SECOND SHEIK: Yes, the holy war! . . . The mountains and the valleys will see us! . . . I will attend to Hasbeiya: there is an emir there of the family of Shebah whom I hate; the emir included, I will not leave one Christian house standing, nor a head of those who make the sign of the cross. I have two thousand men known as the Pack of Wolves. . . . I will attend to Hasbeiya! . . .

THIRD SHEIK: (*Indicating the two horsemen who are at his side.*) We will attend to Zahleh: we will be known by the cries of the vanquished; we will not leave one stone atop another. . . .

THREE SHEIKS: We will attend to Deïr-el-Kamar!

SIXTH SHEIK: We, to Beirut!

SEVENTH SHEIK: We, to Damascus!

EIGHTH SHEIKH: We, to Tripoli!

BEN-YACOUB: Good! and I, I shall be everywhere! . . . yes, Damascus, Beirut, Tripoli! the triple key that we must have! . . . We are the soldiers, the elected of the god Hackim. . . . Those whom he has condemned will perish! . . . They will perish by the sword, by water, by fire! . . . Death to the Christians! death to the giaours! . . .

ALL: Death to the Christians! death to the giaours!

(2.3)[17]

The uniformly exclamatory style and the unrelenting rhetoric of fanaticism that dominate almost every exchange among the Arab or Muslim characters find their antithesis in the soberness, restraint, and careful reasoning of the conversation of European diplomats. Anxious to avoid any premature hints of a European alliance until the full implications and extent of the Arab unrest can be ascertained, they have arranged an informal meeting at a ball. It is of course the French consul who shows the proper initiative, whereas the English consul misjudges the situation:

THE ENGLISH CONSUL: . . . I will confess to you, monsieur, that your fears seem exaggerated to me; and on the other hand. . . .

THE FRENCH CONSUL: What does it matter, if they enable us to prevent a great calamity.

$$(3.1)^{18}$$

As to their objectives, it is understood that the French consul is acting as the spokesman for all the European powers when he demands protection for those of his religion.

The contrast of motivations is indicative of what is perhaps the most pernicious and persistent feature of the misrepresentation of the Middle East and Islam in Western theater, film, and now television. Europeans are portrayed as motivated by concrete concerns or demands for protection of lives and property that are threatened by specific and immediate cirumstances. The acts, scenes, and tableaux have been constructed to present those institutions and practices of public and private life that are in danger of being disrupted or destroyed. Military action or intervention is a clear response to the need to defend, but never promote, these interests at a specific historical juncture. Europeans and Christians never appear to act with any thought of the political, commercial, or strategic advantages to be gained. The Muslims, on the other hand, are pictured as motivated by one factor only: an ahistorical, seemingly primordial, hatred of Christians which translates into a vague yet obsessive desire to exterminate them. The spontaneous generation of this hatred and hostility is moreover an entirely internal affair, independent of anything the Christians might or might not have done in the past and anything they might or might not do in the future.

Nowhere is this opposition more succinctly expressed than in the fourth tableau, entitled "Le Drapeau Français" (The French flag). The climax of this scene is a confrontation between the enigmatic character known as "La D'Jemmala D'Jezzar" and Abd-el-Kader, an Algerian emir. The former incites the crowd to desecrate the French Tricolor while the latter attempts to prevent her:

THE D'JEMMALA: (*Shaking the Tricolor.*) Here is the symbol of honor and courage of these Franks who have come to defy us at our own doorstep. . . .

ALL: Down with the flag! Down with it!

THE D'JEMMALA: Yes, for behind this rag there is an infamous and cowardly people. . . .

ALL: Underfoot! underfoot!

THE D'JEMMALA: A people that mocks Mohammed, the true prophet!

ALL: In the gutter! in the gutter!

THE D'JEMMALA: An accursed people that I would like to pull down like this tattered old cloth, and trample beneath my feet like this rag.[19]

She is about to cast the flag to the ground when she is stopped by the timely arrival of Abd-el-Kader.

Abd-el-Kader was a historical figure who would have been well known to French audiences by 1860. A longtime adversary of the French in North Africa, he was finally defeated by the French army. His engagements with the French had received considerable coverage in the popular *canards* as well as the official newspapers. For example, an 1845 Parisian *canard* presented the typically narrativized and illustrated adventures of a French trumpeter and his comrades captured by the forces of Abd-el-Kader (Figure 10). A reversal of fortune the next year resulted in the "Fuite d'Abd-el-Kader" (The flight of Abd-el-Kader) being reported on April 15, 1846. The issue reported that the emir's force of two thousand Arabs had been defeated by a unit of three hundred French troops. His defeat was illustrated by a characteristically crude woodcut depicting the capture of the emir's baggage train, which included booty that earlier had been taken from France's allies.[20] But the French press was never totally unsympathetic in its coverage of Abd-el-Kader. Indeed, as Seguin notes, the emir was in fact regarded with respect and admiration, and the press helped make him a truly popular figure. In 1852, when Louis-Napoleon finally released Abd-el-Kader from imprisonment in France so that he might retire to Syria with his family, the occasion was reported in a *canard* along with the following description of his physical appearance:

The emir is of average height; although there is nothing remarkable about his face, it does possess a certain majesty; his complexion is white or rather pale, although somewhat tanned by the sun; his face is oval and his features regular, his beard is light and of a dark chestnut color; his gray-blue eyes are handsome and very expressive; he has a pensive and almost shy aspect, but when he speaks, his eyes become animated and flash. (Seguin, *Nouvelles* 116)[21]

Following the events of June 1860, Abd-el-Kader occupied an even more prominent position in the press and politics of France. Hailed as the savior of Christians, he was decorated by several European rulers, Christian and non-Christian alike. Napoleon III made him a member of the

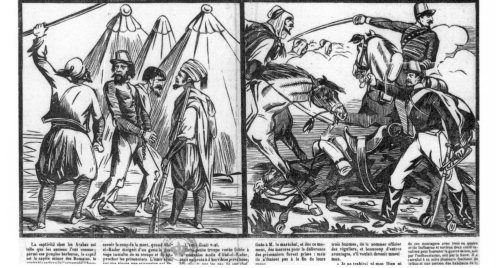

Figure 10. "Captivité du trompette Escoffier et de ses camarades chez Abd-el-Kader." Illustration from *canard* published by Dupont (Paris, 1845). Bibliothèque Nationale de France, Fol. Ln²⁷.2139.

Legion of Honor. This was promising material indeed for the stage, and in *Les Massacres de Syrie* Séjour would build on this foundation and provide a scene worthy of such a noble figure:

ABD-EL-KADER: Defilers of sacred objects, back!

ALL: Abd-el-Kader!

ABD-EL-KADER: Yes, it is I!. . . and the Franks are a noble people because they can find defenders even among their former enemies!

ALL: (*Furious.*) The flag! the flag!

ABD-EL-KADER: I have seen the French fight. . . . I know how they will triumph or die. . . . I replace the most resolute among them at this moment. . . . I will fight and die for this flag! (*Cries.*) Here is my breast, here my heart, strike, or make way for me!

(*The ranks open. Abd-el-Kader passes.*) ²²

The confrontation between La D'Jemmala and Abd-el-Kader represented more than a conflict between two individuals. Théophile Gautier, or
perhaps his son,[23] described La D'Jemmala as "[a] kind of black prophetess,
her reason troubled by the sun of Africa and the reflections of the sands, a
bloody and fanatical madwoman who travels among the tribes mounted on
a horse as black as she is" (*Le Moniteur universel*, January 7, 1861).[24] In the
play she reports with pride that her most notable accomplishments were
the stabbing of a monk who was officiating at a service in a convent and
the strangling of two Christian newlyweds, whose bodies she had dumped
in the Damor River that flows past Damascus. She had killed her own husband, a camel driver from Cairo, when he converted to Christianity. Following these isolated murders, she gained an even more fearsome reputation among the Christians of Lebanon. Georges de Moréac recounts how,
during an attack on a Christian village, La D'Jemmala became the very
"genius of the massacre" as "she ran through the streets screaming, killing,
pillaging, ransacking. . ." and then, "the night being dark, she had the four
corners of the city set afire the better to see" (1.13).[25] Gautier's summation
accurately captures her intended and perceived function in this epic play:
"Djemmala is the monstrous personification of superstition; she is the
night that protests against the light; the dark race attempting a last effort
against the white race."[26] The terms if not the words of Gautier's comparison reflect her role as the personification of the new stage Oriental of the
imperial era as primitive essence in human form rather than as social being.

The crucial confrontation in the above scenes is not between La
D'Jemmala and Abd-el-Kader, but between La D'Jemmala and the French
Tricolor. On the one side is a people shaped by their environment and governed by passions and "superstitions" personified by a possessed being;
on the other is a people organized into a nation, a state symbolized by a
flag. So central was this scene to the meaning of the play as a whole that
it was chosen for the first page illustration when *Les Massacres de la Syrie*
was published in the *Magasin Théâtral* (Figure 11). The illustration shows,
surrounded by a restive but intimidated mob of Arabs, a stalwart and composed Abd-el-Kader in white robes who holds the unfurled French flag
aloft as a shadowy figure clad in black cowers before it. It is an image for
which Gautier had composed the ideal caption.

When placed in this sequence of events, the obligatory Oriental palace
setting (tableau 5) performs an entirely different function and carries a
meaning entirely different from that of comparable sets in melodrama. We
are now

Figure 11. Abd-el-Kader upholding the honor of France. Title illustration for *Les Massacres de la Syrie*, by Victor Séjour (1861). *Magasin Théâtral*. The New York Public Library; Astor, Lenox and Tilden Foundations.

AT THE PALACE OF BEN-YACOUB, AT SAIDA

A magnificent room in the oriental taste; arcades, in the background, closed off with rich hangings; these hangings can be raised at will to reveal a gallery or terrace that runs around the palace. Some women, in the background, reclining on cushions.[27]

The set depicting the residence of Ben-Yacoub, rather than serving as a reminder of magnificent Arab achievements in architecture and design or as a decorative signal to release the imagination from the constraints of realism, takes its place in the gallery of images of Oriental sensuality. This association is strengthened by the opening scenes that focus on Ben-Yacoub's obsessive love for Gulnare, the adoptive daughter of the Moréacs, who has made it clear that she prefers the more tempered sentiments and appropriately inhibited advances of Georges de Moréac. Despite the fact (one would suppose) that he spends the greater part of his time in residence at a palace that is the product of the most refined sensibilities of Arab craftsmen and engineers, Ben-Yacoub's behavior and emotional responses are more in keeping with the wild and barren portions of the Lebanese landscape:

BEN-YACOUB: . . . my love is fierce, I admit; but it is God who must be accused. . . . It is he who is to be blamed, along with these rugged mountains of Lebanon who have given me their harshness and their loftiness! . . . I feel their savage grandeur and their depths in me!. . . I don't know how to pray . . . my passions are storms . . . the air that I breathe sets me ablaze . . . the sun that burns me has molded me with bronze and iron as a threat or a danger! . . . I am thus!

(5.4)[28]

The advantages to be gained from the operations discussed above have been analyzed by JanMohamed in relation to African colonialist literature. He argues that European colonialist writers transform "social and historical dissimilarities into universal, metaphysical difference." He goes on:

[If] African natives can be collapsed into African animals and mystified still further as some magical essence of the continent, then clearly there can be no meeting ground, no identity, between the social historical creatures of Europe and the metaphysical alterity of the Calibans and Ariels of Africa. If the differences between the Europeans and the natives are so vast, then clearly the process of civilizing the natives can continue indefinitely. The ideological function of this mechanism, in addition to prolonging colonialism, is to dehistoricize and desocialize the conquered world, to present it as a metaphysical "fact of life," before which those who have fashioned the colonial world are themselves reduced to the role of passive spectators in a mystery not of their making. (68)

While this "denial of history and normal social interaction" could be applied very successfully to the tribally and feudally based societies of the Middle East, supplemental strategies had to be developed to account for those segments of Arabic and Islamic civilization whose exceptional achievements in all areas of human activity could not be overlooked. It should be stressed that European writers were compelled to take these achievements into account not merely because they existed, but because they were already known and familiar to European society at large; indeed, they had been incorporated into European culture over a period of hundreds of years, under circumstances in which Europe did not occupy a position of unquestionable dominance.

Consequently, in *Les Massacres de Syrie*, the pervasive dualistic structuring of representation at almost every level, with Muslims and Arabs on one side and Christians and Europeans on the other, appears to be relieved with the introduction of characters such as Abd-el-Kader and his family and Gulnare. These apparent concessions to a broader perspective on the Arab population, however, soon prove to be false. Those Arab figures who are shown to possess, within the limits of the conventions of nineteenth-century boulevard theater, the full range of human intellectual and emotional capacities, organized according to some system of moral values, are sooner or later shown to be essentially French or Christian. If the hypothesis of irremediable difference cannot be supported, the only alternative is identity. For example, from her first appearance, Gulnare has been contemplating the idea of converting to Christianity. By the time of her final confrontation with Ben-Yacoub, he is able to note with great accuracy, "ces chrétiens t'ont déjà donné leur âme!" (these Christians have already given you their soul!" [5.4]). Her conversion will become official before the end of the play.

The religious dilemma of another character will have far broader implications. Abd-el-Kader's daughter Aïssa rescues Georges de Moréac from Ben-Yacoub's ambush and will in turn be protected by him as mobs run wild in the streets of Damascus when the massacre of Christians gets under way. Greatly moved by reports of the massacres of Maronite Christians in Lebanon, she had responded with a religious gesture, but not the one her family would have anticipated. Instead of going to pray in the mosque, she had found herself drawn by "an irresistible force" to a church. She tries to explain this impulse to her father

AïSSA: The horrible cruelties carried out against the Christians of the mountain had just been retraced before my eyes. My heart was filled with tears. I told myself that one could pray better in the house of the martyrs; a church presented itself, and I entered.
ABD-EL-KADER: (*Sadly.*) Your soul is moving in that direction, my child. . . I don't blame you. But remember that you are of the blood of Mohammed.

(7.1)[29]

After Aïssa leaves for the mosque, Abd-el-Kader laments: "[I]n the face of empires that are collapsing and dead civilizations! . . . Oh! Mohammed, the race of Islam is fading, and your name is being erased even from my daughter's heart! . . . Sad! sad! sad!"[30]

The conclusion is clear: given the choice, the younger generation of Muslims who are morally sensitive and open to sentiments such as compassion and justice will inevitably be drawn to Christianity as the more appropriate faith. But the immediate context of the dialogue and the sense of the play as a whole make it clear that it is not merely Christianity itself that is at stake here, since the Eastern Christian sects had been very present options for centuries. There has been a conflation of Christianity with European civilization of which France is the finest example. What is being proclaimed is actually the superiority of Europe and Europeans in their capacity to revive the "dead civilizations" of the Middle East, a capacity that the younger generations of Arabs, who can best benefit from their formative influence, can and will appreciate.

An even more telling "conversion" (since even by 1860 the women of Asia, Africa, the Middle East, and the Americas had already proven themselves in print and on stage to be notoriously easy to seduce away from their original religious, social, and cultural allegiances) is that of Abd-el-Kader himself. As the above fragment of dialogue has already indicated, his is not a religious conversion, but an acceptance of the authority and superiority of France. Having acted as the flag-bearer for the French in the fourth tableau, he carries Napoleon III's sword into battle in the seventh, with the following declarations:

ABD-EL-KADER: (*Taking his sword . . .*) Napoleon III gave me this sword . . . I felt great enough to accept it; I feel worthy enough to use it! . . . I will prove to the sultan of France that this hand which he has touched is his, that this heart he has moved belongs to him, and that he has a devoted servant and a soldier in me.

(7.6)[31]

A generous construction of these characterizations could see them as being inspired by reforms in the economic and political systems of the Middle East and North Africa which were instituted to counter the spread of European power and influence during the first half of the nineteenth century. These attempts at reform involved the accommodation of

European trade practices and in some cases the adaptation of European models of political and military organization. In certain locations, notably Egypt, new schools and missions to Europe were introduced to educate a socioprofessional elite of doctors, engineers, and officials. However, in the process of change—which it should be noted was confined to coastal centers—at no time was it suggested that Islamic societies would benefit from a wholesale conversion to Christianity. The European litany—here voiced by the fictionalized Abd-el-Kader in an apparent echo of a letter written by the historical figure—regarding the hopelessly moribund and degenerate state of Islamic civilization notwithstanding, the leaders of the Ottoman Empire recognized the need to reconsider the traditional foundations of their administrative systems. This reconsideration, moreover, was not seen as incompatible with the fundamental tenets of Islam. A royal proclamation issued following the death of Sultan Mahmud II in 1839 stated:

All the world knows that since the first days of the Ottoman state, the lofty principles of the Qur'an and the rules of the *shari'a* were always perfectly preserved. Our mighty sultanate reached the highest degree of strength and power, and all its subjects of ease and prosperity. But in the last one hundred and fifty years, because of a succession of difficult and diverse causes, the sacred *shari'a* cannot survive. . . . Full of confidence in the help of the Most High, and certain of the support of our Prophet, we deem it necessary and important from now on to introduce new legislation in order to achieve effective administration of the Ottoman government and provinces. (Qtd. in Hourani 272)

As with any attempt to effect major reforms in an established religion, there would be dissension and resistance to change. Far from being symptomatic of the death of a civilization, however, such controversy, it would seem, should be seen as a sign of its viability.

On the rare occasions when Muslim characters in *Les Massacres de Syrie* do show signs of sharing the values actively promoted by the various French sociocultural institutions, including the theater, it is only to highlight either the perversity or the gullibility of the characters concerned. The most prominent example concerns the incident designed to incite Arab mobs to attack the Christians of Damascus. This incident is engineered by a local pacha, Daoub-Kaïbar, a thoroughly despicable character of whom the critic of *Le Constitutionnel* had this to say: "This Machiavellian and rapacious Musulman, who does not even have fanaticism as an excuse, obeys the most perverse and lowest instincts, the most shameful and cruel passions" (January 7, 1861).[32] Daoub-Kaïbar accedes obsequiously to the

French consul's demand that some Druze children who desecrated the symbols of Christianity be punished by being forced to sweep the streets of the Christian quarter. His intentions, however, prove not to be not so pure. As La D'Jemmala reports back to Daoub-Kaïbar, "The sentencing of the Druze children to sweep the streets has produced its effect. I believe that we can profit from it to rouse Beirut" (4.1).[33] The Arab citizens of Beirut are indeed aroused. The character Ali-Bey expresses the crowd's indignation and outrage when he cries, "Ils ne balayeront plus, ils ne balayeront plus! Assez d'humiliation et de honte ainsi!" (They will sweep no more, they will sweep no more! Enough humiliation and shame!). Needless to say, it was not only Daoub-Kaïbar and La D'Jemmala who were engaged in manipulating emotions attached to children and childhood. In the gap between the way children are used for dramatic interest in *Les Ruines de Babylone* or *Les Maures d'Espagne* and the way they are used to arouse audience hostilities in *Les Massacres de Syrie* can be seen the implication of theater in the greater imperialist project of justifying the domination of one people by another.

One of theater's unique contributions to this project resided in its capacity to reenact the acts of violence and disorder that could only be described in newspaper accounts. These accounts are echoed in tableau 3, scene 3 in *Les Massacres* when Georges de Moréac brings word of the attacks to the French consul:

GEORGES: Finally, odious excesses broke out around Hasbeiya . . . men massacred everywhere . . . women kidnapped, dishonored, their throats cut! . . . They don't simply kill, they torture! . . . They take their time as though the better to perform the horrible task.[34]

Mirroring the structure of newspaper accounts, his general account passes to a specific case as he tells of a family who ran into a band of marauders just outside a house of worship—whether church or mosque he could not remember. The father offered his life if those of his wife and children could be spared. In answer, his outstretched hand was cut off, as were his lips and chin, before a cross was carved into his forehead. Within the play, this outrage is perceived not so much as one against individual human rights and dignity but as a violation of the sanctity of the family. In demanding justice, Moréac cries out, "It is about widows mourning their husbands . . . desperate children calling for their fathers . . . heads that have been cut off that I am speaking . . . it is spilled blood that is my concern, and I demand an accounting!"[35] The specific is then personalized to further manipulate the family sentiments that first bourgeois tragedy and then melodrama had constructed over the preceding one hundred years.

The cult of motherhood is desecrated in the person of Mme de Moréac, who is kidnapped and sold into slavery. Beaten, and then thrown out into the street when she becomes too ill to perform the hard labor demanded of her, she struggles back to the once peaceful farmhouse. The formerly prosperous woman is now starving and in rags. The bloody tragedies are no longer relegated to the wings by *la bienséance* as in the past. The final tableau shows Christian families who had been offered false refuge in the palace of one of the Arab leaders being routed out of their hiding place and slaughtered. The stage directions echo the account given in *Le Moniteur universel* five months earlier: "The victims pour out of the seraglio tumultuously uttering fearful cries; they are still defending themselves; some their wives and daughters; others their newborn babies whom they press to their heart" (8.4).[36]

This staged atrocity drew on the combined effect of a maximum assault on the physical senses and a maximum assault on the moral sensibilities of the audience. These assaults were carried out along both the theatrical and diegetic circuits of communication. The audience's moral outrage was solicited by the dramatic structure in the manner already outlined. It was coordinated with a theatrical attack on the senses of the spectators involving noise (shouts, screams, commotion, music), visual chaos, and kinesthetic responses to violent struggles and physical mutilation. In national and military dramas, the spectacular excesses and intensified emotions of nineteenth-century popular drama reinforced a narrative designed to have an inflammatory effect. In *Les Massacres de Syrie*, in a move new to fictional representations of the Orient, these deliberate acts of cruelty are no longer classed among the brutalities of war or attributed to particular groups, but are tied instead to the fundamental tenets of Islamic doctrine. When one of the Arab leaders states (admittedly in bad faith) that the culprits will be punished, the following exchange takes place:

DAOUB-KAÏBAR: The law condemns them, the law strikes them down . . . we will let the law speak and act.
GEORGES: Which law? . . . Yes, which law? The law of Mohammed, that justifies and glorifies the murder of Christians? . . . Is it the law of your god Hackem, who orders the extermination of infidels?

(3.3)[37]

When Daoub-Kaïbar offers to give his solemn oath that justice will be done, Georges cuts him short, saying, "Don't swear . . . these are Christians you have before you: the Koran has already given the lie to any vows you may make."[38] The Koran, once the enabler of comic effect through its prohibition of the drinking of alcoholic beverages, assumes a new role in Western drama. Henceforth, it is the origin of what was conceptualized in the press as a "vast Muslim plot against Christians" and more poetically designated in the theater as "la lutte de l'Orient contre l'Occident" (the struggle of the Orient against the Occident).

Rewriting History

The implication of theater in this great struggle was not always recognized or admitted. In an opinion consistent with the reporting of the events in the capital's newspapers, his own among them, the theater critic of *Le Constitutionnel* wrote:

Some have tried to see in *Les Massacres de Syrie* a play that is at the same time political and literary, a manifesto, a proclamation, I was almost going to add a declaration of war. As for me, I saw only an energetic and powerful drama, a bitter struggle between two rivals of different race and religion who love the same woman; the whole having for a frame a splendid land, and *recalling without any exaggeration, in their naked truth and with an eloquent simplicity, contemporary events that have moved all Europe.* (January 7, 1861; my emphasis)[39]

In fact, the absolute dualism of *Les Massacres de Syrie* could not, of course, have been realized without a significant and pointed rewriting of history. The eloquent simplicity praised in *Le Constitutionnel* was a gross reduction of a complex situation. The "naked truth" was fully clothed in representational strategies designed to serve both domestic and foreign policies. These complications are signaled from the outset in the very title of the play. While both title and settings are in fact as problematic as those of *Les Ruines de Babylone*, it is interesting that the successors of those who were so ready to "quibble" over Babylone, Baghdad, and Séleucie (see Chapter 3) made no mention of the geographical, ethnographic, or historical inconsistencies that run through *Les Massacres de Syrie*.

As with *Les Ruines de Babylone*, the first question arises with the title and setting. Apparently in keeping with his profession's concern for evoca-

tive titles, Séjour opted for the more impressive sonorities of *Les Massacres de Syrie*—or *Les Massacres de la Syrie* in the later published text—
over the comparatively flat *Les Massacres du Liban*. The opening notation
in the published text confirms "La scène se passe en Syrie en 1860"—despite the fact that internal references make it clear that the Moréac farm is
in Lebanon (and correctly located there by both Gautier and the *Constitutionnel* critic in their reviews) and that the play deals as much, if not more,
with the massacres of Christians in Lebanon than in Syria.

Legitimate arguments can be advanced, however, to prove that it was
not entirely inaccurate to present all these events as taking place in Syria.
Séjour could claim to be using "Syria" to refer to a geographical region
of the Middle East, which stretched from the Taurus Mountains in the
north to the Sinai Peninsula in the south, and from the Mediterranean
Sea on the west to the Syrian Desert on the east, rather than to the more
narrowly delimited province of the Ottoman Empire. This practice was
apparently shared by many Oriental scholars of the time and continued
until after the First World War, when the area was divided into French and
British mandates. Even then, "Syria" might be used at times to refer to
the entire French mandate, which included Lebanon. It is true that by the
mid-nineteenth century the indigenous populations of the region and the
administrators of the Ottoman Empire recognized very distinct political,
religious, ethnographic, and historical differences between the provinces
of Lebanon and Syria. But these differences would not have provided sufficient grounds to call for a revocation of Séjour's artistic license had the
historical conflations in *Les Massacres* remained as innocuous as the geographical ones.

While the decision to prefer "la Syrie" over "le Liban" can be geo-
graphically justified and artistically preferred for its rhythm and euphony,
the blending of the massacres of Maronites by the Druze and the massacre of Damascene Christians by the Muslims of the city is not so benign.
The two events are presented as being intimately connected, planned, or
instigated by the same personages and executed by the same groups out
of the same timeless hatred of Christians. It would seem, however, that
this intimacy, even identity, was one generated by French perceptions and
representations—including this play—rather than one reflective of circumstances themselves. In fact, as will be discussed below, it was possible for a
lifelong resident of the area who lived through the Damascus massacres to
perceive the two events as being completely dissociated. With the benefits
of hindsight and overview, modern scholars acknowledge at best an in-

direct or peripheral relationship of causality between the two outbreaks of anti-Christian violence. The events are seen instead as equally symptomatic of tensions arising from broad transformations that in turn resulted from a confluence of circumstances. As Albert Hourani makes clear, direct hostility against Christians was only one manifestation of this unrest: "The dislocation of the economy, the loss of power and influence, the sense of the political world of Islam being threatened from outside: all these expressed themselves in the middle of the century in a number of violent movements directed against the new policies, against the growing influence of Europe, and in some places against the local Christians who profited from it" (277). Antoine J. Abraham, while reiterating the complexity of the situation, represents the massacres of Maronites by the Druze as the culmination of an internal struggle for power that was tied to the Maronite initiative to win greater independence from Ottoman rule. He also emphasizes the instigatory role of European interference, which other sources specify as having been mainly French and British:

It would not be accurate to place the blame for the Maronite-Druze civil wars of 1841, 1845, and 1860 upon any single group or cause. The conflict was motivated by many factors and all the inhabitants of the region contributed to the tensions which impinged upon the formerly cordial atmosphere in Lebanon. Also, the European powers interfered in Lebanese affairs during that period and in so doing they contributed to the polarization of the religious factions which only served to create further unrest rather than stability. However, the nucleus around which the conflict revolved was the national aspirations of the Maronite establishment. (81)

Abraham's statement presents a picture of the political situation in Lebanon that is strongly at odds with the narrative put together by Séjour, his journalistic sources, and other public discourses. Most importantly, the Christian community of the region did not consist of struggling churches, isolated convents, and missionary outposts as *Les Massacres de Syrie* would suggest. Instead, it was an extremely well organized and politically potent institution:

In the period lasting from 1841 until 1860, the Maronite clergy exhibited an unparalleled zeal directed towards the acquisition of Lebanese independence from the Ottoman Empire. The Maronites had emerged from the conflict of 1840 with their candidate in the office *hakim*, military support, organizational strength, an ideology and the charismatic leadership of their patriarchs which made them capable of leading a revolt. No other sect or faction in Lebanon could have matched the Maronite establishment in its progressive drive towards independence. . . . Nevertheless, in part, Lebanon was "bi-national," a home for both the Maronite and the

Druze sects. Therefore the first step taken by the Maronite clergy was an attempt to gain a political foothold in the Druze districts partially inhabited by their co-religionists. (81–82)

Popular representations like Séjour's not only disregard the fact that the Maronites could be seen as provoking the conflicts leading up to the 1860 massacres, but also conveniently fail to mention that the British supported the Druze in their resistance to Maronite incursions on their political and geographical positions in Lebanon.

To bring up this point would spoil the dualism so critical to the structure of the *épopée militaire* and to the preservation of the myth of the French mission in the Middle East. It would have posed the playwright an almost impossible task to depict what Ben-Yacoub heralded as "la lutte de l'Occident et de l'Orient" (1.7), when different nations of the Occident were offering financial and military support to different factions of the Orient. By integrating the Lebanese and Damascene disturbances, Séjour is able to extend the specific circumstances leading to the Damascus massacre to other major incidences of anti-Christian violence that occurred in 1860.[40]

The extent and direction of the revisions made in *Les Massacres de Syrie* are clear when the play's narrative is compared to an extremely vivid personal account and analysis of the Damascus massacres that has survived in the memoirs of Mikhayil Mishāqā.[41] Born in Mount Lebanon in 1800, Mishāqā was a Greek Orthodox Christian who converted to Protestantism. He served as financial comptroller to the emirs of the House of Shihab in Hasbayya until the line ended in 1841. In 1859 he was appointed vice-consul for the United States in Damascus and was serving in this capacity when the massacres and street riots of 1861 broke out. As Christians, he and his family were forced to flee from their home; while attempting to reach the sanctuary of the residence of Emir 'Abd al-Qadir—the Abd-el-Kader of *Les Massacres de Syrie*—they were attacked by mobs in the street. Mishāqā was injured, but survived. His memoirs recount his personal experiences of the disorders and also give his assessment of their causes:

The Damascus incident had no connection with the incidents in the Lebanon but had special causes that grew out of the conduct of ignorant Christians when the intelligent among them no longer had the power to curb them. As the Empire began to implement reforms and equality among its subjects regardless of their religious affiliation, the ignorant Christians went too far in their interpretation of equality and thought that the small did not have to submit to the great, and the low did not have to respect the high. Indeed they thought that humble Christians were on a par with exalted Muslims. They did not want to understand that, just as equality was based on regulations and legal rights, the people of stature had to maintain their proper dignity before whatever community, especially when it came to Christians vis-à-vis Muslims. They should have known that the leaders and important people of the area were Muslims, as the power structure, with its viziers, soldiers and might, was all Muslim. The Christians in Syria were the smaller and weaker portion in everything, and in all regards the Christians should have not only paid great respect to the Muslims but given total obedience to the authorities. (244)

While the analyses of twentieth-century scholars omit Mishāqā's vigorous indictment of short-sighted Christians, they stand in general agreement that it was the new liberties accorded Christians that placed untenable pressures on the social structure. Abraham gives this more judicious but corroborative summary of the causes of the Damascus massacres:

In Syria, the conflict was intrinsically religious and it had only a superficial relationship to the conflict in Lebanon. Ever since Ibrahim Pasha had attempted to obtain greater freedom for the Syrian Christians and Sultan Abd Al-Mjid had issued the *Khatt-i-Sharif* (Noble Rescript, 1839) and *Khatt-i-Humayun* (Imperial Rescript, 1856) to placate the European Powers by eliminating injustice to the Christians, the Muslim and the Christian communities in Syria began to draw apart and suspect the intentions of each other. For centuries, the Christians had been relegated to an inferior status in the Muslim lands and, therefore, these decrees were impractical since no effective preparation had been made for a drastic change in the social system. (105)

The massacres of Christians in Lebanon by the Druze in May 1860 added to the strain by trapping many Christian migrant farm workers in Damascus. These Christian families, who had come down from the mountains to work in the villages and farms around Damascus during the harvest, were afraid to return on roads that were watched by the Druze. Aggravating these conditions still further were deliberate attempts on the part of certain Muslim leaders to incite an outbreak of violence. In an original combination of statistical evidence and colorful conjecture, Mishāqā describes the pattern of this incitement during an already advanced state of tensions. Ahmad Pasha, the governor of Damascus, for instance, had cannon mounted at the gate of the Umayyad Mosque for Friday prayers, ostensibly to protect the Muslims from any Christian treachery. According to Mishāqā, however, the Christians were not likely to pose any true threat since the Muslims greatly outnumbered the Christians both in the city and in the surrounding villages. Furthermore, whereas the Muslims were well armed, the Christians, apparently, were not only hard put to come up with even a hunting rifle, but also lacked the temperament to commit the slightest act of aggression:

Most of [the Christians] took their chickens to the butcher for slaughter because it was impossible for a Christian to screw up the courage to cut a chicken's head off himself. Could any rational person imagine that the Christians might murder Muslims? However, when they saw how the pasha was and that his desire was in line with theirs, the ignorant among them—not the intelligent—were incited to annihilate the Christians, most of whom kept to their houses. So also did the Muslims and Druze of the villages of Damascus change toward the Christians. (248)

The alleged reluctance of Christians to slaughter their own poultry aside, this passage suggests why the circumstances of the Syrian massacres provided a far more congenial model for the dramatic imperatives faced by Séjour and for the political and dynastic interests of Napoleon III's regime. But in order to cross the threshold of credibility that the national drama required for its effect—at a time, moreover, when a wide range of newspapers were disseminating information on these events to all segments of society—Séjour had to observe a certain degree of faithfulness to the facts as they were being commonly circulated. This negotiation between accuracy or at least consistency on the one hand and generic and political reshaping on the other is demonstrated in two clear-cut cases, both already mentioned. The first pertains to the alleged incitement of mobs, and the other concerns the figure of 'Abd al-Qadir.

Contemporary and modern accounts agree that there was undoubtedly some official sanction for and probably active incitement of the Damascus violence. Mishāqā's recital, however, makes it clear that it was "adult Muslims who had been jailed for crimes against Christians" who were "paraded through the markets in chains" and not children forced to sweep the streets along which they had desecrated Christian symbols. The motives for and implications of this rewriting of history have already been suggested. The purpose of the gesture was certainly to incite; the targets of this provocative action, however, were not just the Muslims in the fictional world of the play. It was the arousal of the spectators in the Théâtre Impérial du Cirque that was equally desired.

As for 'Abd al-Qadir, it has been historically recorded by a great variety of witnesses that he did in fact take extraordinary measures to protect the Christians of Damascus, sheltering thousands of them within the compound of his own home and moving about the city with his armed followers to rescue countless others. As already mentioned, his name was well known to the Parisian public from his prior encounters with French troops in Algeria in the 1830s and forties. His role in the Syrian massacres was honored by one *canardier* with the publication of a *Notice historique et biographique de l'emir Abd-el-Kader Sauveur de 13,000 Chrétiens en Syrie* (Seguin, *Nouvelles* 116). Hourani sums up his significance in the region as follows:

> Deriving prestige from belonging to a family with a religious position, connected with the Qadiri order, he became the point around which local forces could gather. For a time he ruled a virtually independent state, with its centre lying in the interior, and extending from the west into the eastern part of the country. This inevitably brought him into conflict with French power expanding from the coast. The symbols of his resistance to the French were traditional ones—his war was a *jihad*, he justified his authority by the choice of the *'ulama* and respect for the *shari'a*— but there were modern aspects of his organization of government. (270)

'Abd al-Qadir's cordial relations with the representatives of France and other European powers, as well as the high esteem he enjoyed among Muslims, have been generally recognized. (It can be assumed, however, that his good relations with the French fell well short of the subservience suggested by Séjour's portrayal.) What Séjour's play does not indicate is that the Algerian emir was not alone in his commitment to the protection of the Christian population; indeed, that many prominent Muslims offered them refuge. As one would suspect, neither they nor 'Abd al-Qadir acted out of unbridled admiration for the French and their emperor. Mishāqā gives a detailed account of a meeting that took place among Muslim leaders as it became evident that the unrest would turn to violence:

> That evening Emir 'Abdul-Qadir went to the governor and met with the Muslim council members. They deliberated about what was happening, and Emir 'Abdul-Qadir testified that according to Islamic law it was not permissible. If the insurgents did not cease their actions, the authorities would be religiously obliged to fight them. The *mufti*, Tahir Efendi, was present and could not deny it. They agreed, and Emir 'Abdul-Qadir returned to arm his men and accompany the vizier to fight the insurgents. While he was preparing his band, word from the governor came ordering him to desist, so all he could do was to try to save as many as possible. [The emir] ordered his band to patrol the Christian quarter and bring him everyone they could find, man, woman and child. This was also done by His Excellency Sharif As'ad Efendi Hamza . . . ; he armed himself and his coterie to rescue every Christian he could find, take him to his house and provide him with necessities. So also were there many religious and virtuous Muslims . . . who followed the example of Emir 'Abdul-Qadir and took Christian men and their families into their homes. (251)

Such a view of Muslims was incompatible with the purposes of mid-nineteenth-century Orientalism and unprovided for by its discourse. Incompatible with French academic and administrative discourses, and inimical to French military ends, the notion of justice and compassion as inherent to Islamic law could not be promoted.

In 1855, just five years before he would be portrayed on the Parisian stage as a staunch defender of French national honor and cultural values, 'Abd al-Qadir sent a work written in Arabic to the president of *La Société Asiatique* in Paris. The modern translator of this work, René R. Khawam, has provided the most faithful translation of the title: *Lettre aux Français: Notes brèves destinées à ceux qui comprennent, pour attirer l'attention sur des problèmes essentiels* (Letter to the French People: Brief notes intended for those who understand, to draw their attention to vital problems). This work set out 'Abd al-Qadir's understanding of contemporary Franco-Arab relations and provided a historical context for this vision. The style was poetic and philosophical rather than polemical. The argument was advanced indirectly through the structure of the piece, which consisted of a preface, three body chapters, and a general conclusion. The first chapter expounded upon the merits of scientific knowledge. The second chapter discussed divine legislation or the juridical sciences and defended the authenticity of the (Islamic) Prophecies. The third chapter spoke of the importance of writing and literary composition. In essence, the author conceded that in the nineteenth century "[t]he inhabitants of France had become a model for all mankind in the domain of the sciences and knowledge" (227). In the other two areas, however, he maintained that it was the Arabs who excelled and surpassed all other civilizations in their accomplishments.

Khawam explains that those familiar with classical Arabic forms of composition would understand that 'Abd al-Qadir was suggesting that the Arab world should adopt modern Occidental scientific techniques and methods, but without sacrificing any of the practices or values of their original heritage. According to 'Abd al-Qadir, this was by no means an unnatural evolution since the French and Arabic nations were to be counted among the elite civilizations of the world:

Understand that mankind is divided into two groups: one group includes those who are concerned with the sciences, which have given rise to different forms of knowledge, so that they constitute the elite among God's creatures; the other group includes all those who have not succeeded in applying themselves to science so as to have their work recognized.

The first group comprises several nations, including those of the Indians, the

Persians, the ancient Greeks, the Byzantine Greeks and the Romans, the Franks, the Arabs, the Hebrews, [and] the Egyptians. The second group is made up of all other nations. (207)

When asked to make a recommendation to the minister of public instruction regarding the disposition of this document, the president of *La Société Asiatique* at first proposed that it be deposited in the Bibliothèque Impériale but not translated. In other words, it was to remain inaccessible to all but a few scholars. As it turned out, the document was translated into French (although far from accurately, it would appear) shortly after it was received and quietly published in 1858, but it was never widely distributed. 'Abd al-Qadir's open letter to the French people would not become available to the general public until 1977, when Khawam's translation was published.[42] What was behind this apparent lack of interest in, even efforts to suppress, the emir's writings during the height of his celebrity in France? In retrospect the answer seems only too evident. At a time when the full-scale French colonization of Algeria was just getting underway and Napoleon III was forming his plans for a new French empire, it was not convenient to publicize a highly respected and still influential Arab leader's vision for a new Arab world that would meet Europe on its own terms. Furthermore, the man revealed in the *Lettre aux Français* far exceeded the selective and reductive images that were being propagated in print and on the stage. Neither the forms of representation nor French interests of the time could accommodate the ambitions and complexities of the living 'Abd al-Qadir.

Conclusion: From Stage to Screen

WHEN READ AS AN ENSEMBLE OF TEXTS, the dialogue and stage directions of the plays themselves, the *procès-verbaux* of nineteenth-century censors, the critical reviews of the period, and contemporary newspaper accounts reveal distinct developments in the representations and modes of reception attached to the Orient. In the melodramas of the first decades of the nineteenth century exemplified by Guilbert de Pixerécourt's *Les Ruines de Babylone* (1810), purely imaginary representations of Middle Eastern subjects were governed primarily by generic considerations. These plays displayed a full distribution of melodramatic roles over an Oriental cast and relied for their effect on the audience registering an appropriate emotional response to these characters. These early nineteenth-century dramatic representations followed in a tradition established over the seventeenth and eighteenth centuries when Oriental figures and motifs participated in intellectual, social, or political discussions, notably those surrounding absolutism. Any restrictions on such representations in the nineteenth century were designed to respect domestic concerns to preserve the social and moral order and to avoid politically sensitive issues, and bore little relation to overseas developments. Such restrictions were, however, significantly rare. The censors' reports reveal and the plays themselves confirm that Oriental settings and subjects effectively served as a barrier to any transfer of meaning from the realm of fiction to that of reality. This blocking effect seems to have derived from the absence of homologous social structures in nonindustrialized societies that corresponded to those of industrialized societies.

As at first France's and then the rest of Europe's material involvement

with the Middle East intensified, beginning with the Napoleonic expeditions, Western Europe eventually came to dominate the region through its
military and industrial superiority. Thereafter, the relatively benign theatrical consignment of the Orient to an imaginary realm disconnected from
actuality could not continue. Paralleling the developments in academic,
scientific, and administrative discourses on the Orient, the possibility of
any form of "sympathetic identification" via the drama was progressively
precluded. The tragic, melodramatic, and romantic presentations of the
Orient and the Oriental, so frequent until the 1830s, could not survive
the confrontation with the actuality of French colonial and military activity in these regions. Not only had this activity increased in scale, but
reports offering considerable detail were being disseminated with ever
greater efficiency to an ever broadening public. The realism characteristic of nineteenth-century dramatic forms could only accommodate either
the dramatization of military events or the fictionalized accounts of adventures of exploration, colonization, and conquest. In staging these conflicts, national or military dramas such as Victor Séjour's *Les Massacres de
Syrie* deployed a Manichean aesthetic within a genre already predisposed
to dualistic representations by its antecedents in melodrama and the early
military tableaux and pantomimes.

The inception of the military play in fact coincided with the emergence of modern Orientalism as it has been defined by Edward Said.
Henceforth, representations of the Orient, rather than guaranteeing the
closure of the diegetic or fictional circuit of theatrical communication,
would instead be engaged in an active dialogue with other Orientalist discourses and real events often simultaneously unfolding in the Middle East.
Furthermore, these transformations in staged representations bore witness
to the emergence of a new perception of reality, as for the first time recent,
even current, historical events were re-created in a realistic mode and a narrativized context before a general audience. The particular apprehension
of reality fostered by these plays could not survive the maturation of the
silent film. The tableaux, plays, and finally full-fledged dramas depicting or
inspired by overseas conflicts would, however, have a marked influence on
their twentieth-century incarnations: newsreels, documentaries, and spectacular cinema.

Nicholas Vardac concludes his argument regarding the splitting of the
sensational and the realistic modes of theatrical representation—and with
it theater audiences—during the latter part of the nineteenth century by
crediting film with reinstituting the alliance between the sensational and

the realistic. This new cinematic alliance, like the old theatrical one, was able to attract a truly popular mass audience. As Christine Gledhill puts it, cinema "offered to twentieth-century society a new site of cultural cohesion" (27). The categories of Orientalist representation employed by this new agent for cultural cohesion corresponded in significant respects to nineteenth-century models. Vardac has demonstrated that this correspondence was not accidental; rather, it involved a direct transfer of structures of representation. On a practical level, the interchange of practitioners—writers, directors, actors, composers, designers, and so on—between the two industries assured continuity in the sociocultural functions of theater and film, if not in the actual techniques used to perform those functions. The Orient of the *féeries* and historical melodramas that facilitated the *dépaysement* of the spectator found a new home in fantasy films such as *The Thief of Baghdad* and desert romances such as *The Sheik*. The drama of colonial relations continued to be enacted in films of empire, while major battles and campaigns were fictionalized for war films.

In the second half of the twentieth century, the creation of the state of Israel and the uncovering of vast oil reserves in the region have brought new complications to the relations between Western and Middle Eastern nations. These developments and internal contests for power following the break up of the European empires have added new inflections to the popular representations of the Arab worlds in Europe and America. The global circulation of American popular culture, particularly in the form of Hollywood studio films, has further altered the situation. Whereas for preindustrial and early capitalist Europe the conflicting tenets of the doctrines of Islam and Christianity were seen as the fundamental source of difference, in the late twentieth century it is the East's concerted resistance to the secularization and commercialization of society that seems to have become the ultimate sign of disparity between it and the West. Just as they did in the previous century, popular forms of culture both construct and reinforce these Western perceptions of difference and draw on them to collect commercial and professional rewards.

Despite the radically altered historical situation and the evolution of new cultural institutions and genres (due largely to technological advances), the current popular representations of Middle Eastern societies in the West are by no means completely divorced from their nineteenth-century predecessors. The interviews and essays collected by Edmund Ghareeb in *Split Vision: The Portrayal of Arabs in the American Media* attest to the resilience of stereotyped images in print and television journalism, cartoons, comic books, novels, films, and educational materials. In all cases, these imaginary constructions, whatever the nature of their institutionally or generically defined relationship to reality or actuality, have continued to be shaped by the repertory of prior representations, which through repeated use and continued dissemination have attained a certain status as truth or knowledge. Oriental luxury, Oriental despotism, Oriental barbarism, and Oriental irrationality have found their late twentieth-century incarnations in oil-rich sheiks, fundamentalist religious leaders, military dictators, and terrorists.

The only nineteenth-century figures who have shown no sign of returning are the morally superior heroes and heroines of classical melodrama who just happened to be Oriental. The historical circumstances leading to their disappearance have already been detailed. It should be recalled that the permanent exit of such sympathetic figures from the field of cultural representation came about with the demise of classical melodrama following the collapse of the sociocultural conditions that had made it a viable form. It is therefore ironic that in the 1990s the fundamental dynamics of melodrama that continue to operate in popular film and television should now retard a more favorable reconception of the Middle East, Arabs, and Islam. The end of the cold war era deprived two of the dominant genres, the action-adventure movie and the political thriller, of the sinister Other needed to complete the central Manichean opposition. Political, economic, and military tensions, combined with a long-standing tradition of unfavorable representation have made the Muslim Arab one of the prime candidates to fill this vacancy.

As the history of nineteenth-century theater has already shown, significant modifications of institutional representations cannot take place without a fundamental change in the societies that produce those representations. As we move toward the twenty-first century, it has become evident that significant alterations in social structures are being effected by the global movement of populations. With increased immigration from the Middle East and North Africa to European countries and the United States, the cultural boundaries required to sustain stereotypical popular representations are being breached. As more cultural groups gain access to the means of self-representation in a full range of sociocultural institutions—whether that access is freely accorded or acquired only through contention—the silence that fosters unidimensional representations has been broken.

Meanwhile, relieved of the responsibility for providing popular dramatic entertainment, European and American theater in the late twentieth century has been able to establish new relationships with the cultures of the Middle East, Africa, and Asia. Intercultural theater projects, such as those of Eugenio Barba, Peter Brook, Ariane Mnouchkine, and Robert Wilson, have aimed at using performance to create sites and events where bodies, objects, and practices from disparate cultural traditions can be brought together in a way that fosters international dialogue. The intention of practitioners engaged in intercultural performance has been to effect exchanges founded on mutual respect and regard between artists and audiences from different parts of the world. These exchanges, however, have proven to be subject to their own cultural politics—politics that are inseparable from the economic disparities that persist between former colonizers and the formerly colonized.[1]

If, in cross-cultural contexts, it has become difficult if not impossible to sever theatrical activity from the history of imperialism, there is at least one product of this association that has proved to be of value for the societies that were once exoticized or vilified on the stages of Europe. A rich array of postcolonial theaters and forms of drama have taken their place among the sociocultural institutions that both reflect and define the ever complex and changing organization of the many societies of Africa, Asia, and the Middle East.[2] At these sites, new metaphors and narratives are being formulated through words, gestures, and sound to give voice and visibility to cultures performing their histories of the twentieth century.

Notes

Introduction

1. The only dramatic works Said does bring up in *Orientalism*, Aeschylus's *The Persians* and Euripides' *The Bacchae*, date from the fifth century B.C. Mozart's operas *The Magic Flute* and *The Abduction from the Seraglio* are also briefly mentioned.

2. Jacky S. Bratton et al., eds., *Acts of Supremacy: The British Empire and the Stage, 1790–1930*, and J. Ellen Gainor, ed., *Imperialism and Theatre: Essays on World Theatre, Drama and Performance, 1795–1995.*

3. See, for instance, the essays collected in Craig Calhoun, Edward LiPuma, and Moishe Postone, eds., *Bourdieu: Critical Perspectives.*

4. For instance, speaking of twentieth-century boulevard and bourgeois theater, Patrice Pavis has asked: "[W]hy bother to theorize about a kind of theatre that gets by with tried and tested recipes, that only takes any interest in sociological reflection so as to find out how the market and audience tastes are developing?" (*Theatre at the Crossroads* 93). Pavis readily admits the elitist nature of his remarks and makes no apology for them.

5. Michele Root-Bernstein reviews the historiographical debate opposing *culture savant* to *culture populaire* in her book, *Boulevard Theater and Revolution in Eighteenth-Century Paris* (see 3–6).

Introduction to Part I

1. Emile Deschamps, "Lettre à M. de Pixerécourt," Paris, May 4, 1841, in Guilbert de Pixerécourt, *Théâtre choisi* (Geneva: Slatkine Reprints, 1971), 4–5.

C'était à Sceaux, dans une charmante maison, toute blanche, au milieu de la verdure de son parc; noble asile d'amitié, temple élégant des arts. Le maître du lieu aimait à s'y reposer du soin des affaires publiques, dans un cercle intime . . . ; la châtelaine y venait tenir sa cour d'amis en quittant celle de l'Impératrice; . . .

Ce jour-là, Madame la comtesse Duchâtel ne fit point de musique. . . . Mais elle nous emmena au second salon, et vous demanda les *Ruines de Babylone*, en souriant au manuscrit qui s'entr'ouvrait de lui-même. Les conviés ont pris place sur de larges ottomanes; le maître et la maîtresse de la maison avaient à leurs pieds, sur des carreaux de soie, leur jeunes enfants. . . . De scène en scène, d'acte en acte, l'intérêt se répandait et grandissait dans l'auditoire, comme dans votre oeuvre. . . . Je doute que les trois cents représentations des *Ruines de Babylone*, à Paris, et le bruit de leurs succès dans les provinces et sur tous les théâtres étrangers, aient valu pour vous cette première victoire, cette matinée d'élite. . . .

2. Those with articles most relevant to nineteenth-century French melo-drama include *La Revue des sciences humaines*, *New York Literary Forum* (edited by Daniel Gerould), and *Europe*.

3. See, e.g., Joseph Roach's "Mardi Gras Indians and Others: Genealogies of American Performance" and Jeffrey D. Mason's "The Politics of *Metamora*."

4. Richard Demarcy has discussed the function of the exotic in twentieth-century boulevard theater in *Eléments d'une sociologie du spectacle*.

Chapter 1

1. "Que le domaine du mélodrame est vaste! Sans parler des ressources que lui offrent les théâtres étrangers, ni de la mine cent fois plus fertile que trouvent dans leur imagination les auteurs qui lui ont consacré leur plume, le mélodrame exploite tour-à-tour l'histoire de tous les temps et de tous les pays, et les fables con-sacrées par les diverses mythologies."

2. This transformation has been thoroughly chronicled by Catherine Nau-grette-Christophe in "La Fin des promenades: Les Bouleversements de la carte des théâtres dans le Paris du Second Empire." The article includes the plan for the demolition of the Boulevard du Temple and the new map of Parisian theatres. In *Places of Performance: The Semiotics of Theatre Architecture*, Marvin Carlson places Haussman's plans and the evolution of boulevard theatres in the larger context of the history of theater architecture and its relationship to the urban environment.

3. Maurice Descotes traces this phenomenon of *embourgeoisement* in *Le Pub-lic de théâtre et son histoire*. As Hemmings, in *The Theatre Industry in Nineteenth-Century France*, and McCormick point out, this process applied more to some theatres than to others. The Funambules and the Acrobates, for instance, remained resolutely working-class theaters, while the Gaîté and Ambigu-Comique courted a more middle-class public as the century progressed.

4. Susanna Barrows discusses the growing fear of crowds that would result from violent proletarian uprisings in *Distorting Mirrors: Visions of the Crowd in Late Nineteenth-Century France*.

5. The complete quotation reads: "La pièce, l'une des meilleures qu'on ait composées depuis longtemps dans ce genre, et la seule, peut-être, où la liaison des idées réponde à l'enchainement des faits, offre à l'examen d'un jugement calme tout le degré d'intérêt qu'elle avait excité lors de son succès d'enthousiasme."

6. Douglas A. Reid advances a similar argument in his article on "Popular Theatre in Victorian Birmingham." Using a variety of contemporary sources, Reid counters both hostile and patronizing stereotypes of working-class audiences, dem-

onstrating that regular theatergoers were both knowledgeable and sophisticated in their appreciation and tastes.

7. Roger Chartier has demonstrated the complex relationship between published texts, performance contexts, and the production of meaning in his exemplary study on Molière's *George Dandin* in *Form and Meaning: Texts, Performances, and Audiences from Codex to Computer*.

8. John McCormick has been one of the few to correct this bias. At the close of his chapter on audiences he notes the steady growth in literacy rates among men, with a 52 percent increase between 1828 and 1846. He also points out that, following the establishment of the popular press, audiences were "coming to see in flesh and blood on the stage the characters with whom they were already familiar in popular novels which had often appeared in serial form in the 'feuilletons' of the newspapers" (87).

9. As one would suspect and as recent studies have confirmed, there was generally a discernible distance between the family as it was portrayed on stage and familial relations as they were actually constituted in society or as they were envisioned by many contemporary social thinkers. See Catherine Hall, "The Sweet Delights of Home," and Michelle Perrot, "The Family Triumphant," in *The History of Private Life*, vol. 4, *From the Fires of the Revolution to the Great War*.

10. In the *Melodramatic Imagination*, Brooks devotes an entire chapter to the special significance of muteness in classical melodrama.

11. ". . . une âme de feu qui sente et exprime les passions; un sentiment doux et persuasif qui intéresse tous ceux qui vous écoutent; une physionomie qui soit tour-à-tour leur fidèle interprète."

12. Extensive discussions of music in melodrama are to be found in Thomasseau's studies on melodrama and in an article by David Mayer on "The Music of Melodrama." As Thomasseau notes, very few scores have survived.

13. ". . . nous croyons que la pantomime doit se borner à traiter des sujets connus, de même que la musique dans le drame lyrique doit accompagner la parole: elles peuvent et doivent renforcer le sentiment; mais si ces deux arts s'arrogent le droit de vouloir exprimer par les moyens qui leur sont propres des sujets absolument inconnus, l'un devient une gesticulation vague et insipide, l'autre une succession de tons, qui, bien ordonnées charmeront l'oreille, et n'en auront pas moins une signification équivoque que chacun peut varier et interpréter à sa fantaisie."

14. See Roland Barthes, "Rhétorique de l'Image" and Christian Metz, "On the Impression of Reality in the Cinema," in *Film Language*.

15. It would seem that even the realm of visual and sensorial experience could not remain untouched by the hierarchizing tendencies of the professional critics. In a review of L'Ambigu-Comique's *Les Mexicains* designed by Daguerre (who had begun his career as a scene painter for the Opéra), it is suggested that the hierarchization of taste and appreciation assumed for literary material applied to the appreciation of visual effects as well. A notice in the May 20, 1819 issue of *Le Camp Volant* by M. H*** declared, "Sa décoration de second acte, représentant le lever de la lune, est le plus étonnant morceau que l'on puisse produire en ce genre. La nature y corrigerait quelques'unes de ses imperfections" (His design for the second act, representing the moon rise, is the most astonishing that this genre is capable of

producing. Nature has some of its imperfections corrected here). A couple of weeks later on June 6, 1819, H***'s colleague L*** suggested that Daguerre's talent and refinements of the scenic arts were wasted on the public of the Ambigu-Comique, which in his view was largely incapable of appreciating subtle visual effects:

> [Le décor] du second acte est d'une beauté surprenante, et si j'osais dire ce que j'en pense, j'affirmerais qu'il a trop de mérite pour plaire à la multitude. La magie qui respire dans le tableau de cette nuit si calme, si imposante, si vraie, n'est pas faite pour l'admiration de tous. Le plus grand nombre veut des effets chauds, heurtés, voyans; mais qu'il est facile de les produire, et que M. Daguerre est sage de ne pas leur prostituer ses pinceaux enchanteurs!

> [The décor] of the second act is of surprising beauty, and if I dared to say what I think of it, I would assert that it has too much merit to please the multitude. The magic that breathes in the tableau of this night, so calm, so imposing, so true, is not made for the admiration of all. Most people want showy effects, animated and striking; but these are easily produced and M. Daguerre is wise not to prostitute his enchanting brushes for them!

16. Although for the reasons stated in the Introduction, I will not be focusing on the third major nineteenth-century genre to generate the Orient—the *féerie*—it should be noted that fantasy also relies on the impression of reality generated by its medium. In Metz's words, "Fantastic art is fantastic only as it convinces (otherwise it is merely ridiculous), and the power of unreality in film derives from the fact that the unreal seems to have been realized, unfolding before our eyes as if it were the flow of common occurrence—not the plausible illustration of some extraordinary process only conceived in the mind" (5). Fantastic representations, however, made no claims of authenticity.

17. "Au surplus, la pompe de la scène, la beauté des décorations, la richesse des costumes, et tout l'éclat qui convient particulièrement au mélodrame, tout annonce combien les directeurs sont animés de l'amour des arts et du zèle de plaire au public; et à cet égard le mélodrame de *Pisarre* l'emporte peut-être sur tout ce qu'on a vu de mieux dans ce genre."

18. "Nous ne pouvons donc qu'engager l'administration à redoubler d'efforts pour varier les plaisirs d'un public qui aime qu'on ne lui présente toujours la même chose. Il lui faut surtout de grands effets."

Chapter 2

1. If there was any difference, it was that the boulevard theaters were often known to exceed the state-subsidized theaters in the quality of their sets and costumes. The capacity of the boulevard theaters to produce spectacular "grands effets" was often held up as an example for the Grands Théâtres to emulate. The opening

of Pixerécourt's *Koulouf, ou les Chinois* at the Opéra-Comique in 1806 brought the following observations in the *Courrier des Spectacles* (no. 3602, December 22):

On reprochoit depuis longtems aux sociétaires de l'Opéra-Comique d'apporter un peu trop d'économie dans l'appareil du spectacle, et de n'offrir le plus souvent au public que des costumes et des décorations dont les couleurs jaunies de fumée attestent leur antique existence dans les magasins, mais pour cette fois ils ont déployé un luxe dont on doit leur savoir gré. Il est impossible de rien voir de plus pittoresque, de plus vrai, de plus riche. C'est de l'argent place à intérêt. Ce n'est pas assez de parler à l'esprit, il faut aussi faire quelque chose pour le plaisir des yeux. Nos Premiers Théâtres sont, sous ce rapport souvent fort au-dessous des théâtres du second-ordre; et c'est peut-être à la magie des décorations que nos Boulevards doivent une partie de la fortune dont ils jouissent.

For some time now, the sociétaires of the Opéra-Comique have been criticized for applying a little too much economy in the apparatus of the spectacle, and most of the time offering the public only costumes and sets, the colors of which are yellowed with smoke and attest to their ancient existence in storage, but this time they have deployed a luxury for which we must be grateful. It is impossible to see anything more picturesque, truer, richer. It is money invested with interest. It is not enough to speak to the mind, one must also do something to please the eyes. Our principal theaters are, in this regard, often far inferior to the secondary theaters; and it is perhaps to the magic of the sets that our Boulevard [playhouses] owe a measure of the fortune they enjoy.

2. An audience member observed: "Le parterre, où les ennemis contrebalançaient les amis, était tumultueux et ne laissait pas tomber quelques négligences provenant de la hâte et de l'effervescence avec lesquelles l'ouvrage avait été écrit" (The parterre, where friends were offset by enemies, was tumultuous and did not allow certain oversights, resulting from the haste and excitement with which the work had been written, to escape). M. G. Desnoiresterres, qtd. in "Avertissement" to *Zaïre* 533.

3. "Une gloire qui n'appartient qu'à Voltaire, c'est celle de varier de la manière la plus vraie son style selon les personnages qu'il met en scène; c'est celle de mettre avec un art surprenant les moeurs étrangères en opposition entre elles et avec les notres; les pinceaux qu'il emploie pour peindre Zaïre, Tancrède et Mahomet ne sont pas les mêmes; il est impossible de marquer plus naturellement qu'il ne le fait encore dans *Zaïre*, comme dans l'*Orphelin de la Chine* et dans *Alzire*, les traits distinctifs des moeurs ottomanes et françaises, chinoises et tartares, espagnoles et mexicaines."

4. Voltaire himself was known to have criticized Racine for his shortcomings in this regard. Bajazet's language, he wrote, was that of "un Français qui s'exprime avec élégance et avec douceur" (A Frenchman who expresses himself elegantly and gently). To his mind, "A la bonne heure qu'un courtisan poli, qu'une jeune prin-

cesse ne mettent dans leurs discours que de la simplicité et de la grâce. Mais il me semble que certains héros étrangers, des Asiatiques, des Américains, des Turcs, peuvent parler sur un ton plus fier, plus sublime" (It's all very well for a refined courtier or a young princess to express themselves with nothing but simplicity and grace. But it seems to me that certain foreigners—Asians, [Native] Americans, and Turks—could speak with a prouder, loftier tone [qtd. in Badir]).

5. "Peut-être Orosmane n'offre-t-il pas avec assez de vérité le caractère oriental; mais aussi peut-être intéressoit-il moins s'il étoit franchement Turc; d'ailleurs il est si beau dans son amour, dans ses transports jaloux, que l'on perdroit trop si Voltaire en le peignant n'eût pas adouci la rudesse musulmane."

6. "OROSMANE: . . . The sultans whom the universe contemplates on its knees, / Their customs, their rights, do not set an example for me; / I know that our laws, favorable toward pleasures, / Open an unlimited field for our vast desires; / That I can at will lavish my affections, / And receive at my feet the incense of my mistresses; / And in the tranquillity of the seraglio, dictating my commands, / Govern my country amid sensual delights."

7. "OROSMANE: . . . Do not believe that my honor will entrust / The virtue of a spouse to those monsters of Asia, / The abusive guardians of the sultan's harem, / Who serve the pleasures of their odious overseers. / I will respect you as much as I love you, / And trust you to protect your own virtue."

8. "OROSMANE: . . . / I have not sprung from Asian blood: / Born amid the rocks in the heart of Tauric Scythia, / I retain the pride of my Scythian ancestors, / As well as their manners, their passions, and their generous hearts."

9. "OROSMANE: . . . Let my seraglio be closed forever; / Let terror dwell within the gates of the place; / Let all within feel the bonds of slavery. / Let us follow the ancient ways of Oriental kings. / One may put aside one's rank and on a slave / Let a favorable glance fall; / But it is too shameful to fear a mistress; / Let us leave such submission to the ways of the Occident. / While this dangerous sex, which aims at conquering all, / May reign in Europe, here it must obey."

10. In the eighteenth century the essentialist debate was addressed primarily through discussions regarding cultural relativity. In *Zaïre*, the issue is broached when Zaïre expresses the enlightened view that a person's religion is essentially a matter of historical accident: "ZAIRE: . . . / La coutume, la loi plia mes premiers ans / A la religion des heureux musulmans. / . . . les soins qu'on prend de notre enfance / Forment nos sentiments, nos moeurs, notre croyance. / J'eusse été près du Gange esclave des faux dieux, / Chrétienne dans Paris, musulmane en ces lieux. L'instruction fait tout. . . ." (1.1) (ZAIRE: . . . Customs, laws guided my early years / Towards the religion of happy Muslims. / . . . the care we receive in childhood / Forms our feelings, our customs, our beliefs. / Living near the Ganges, I would have been the slave of false gods, / In Paris, a Christian, and here, a Muslim. / Instruction is everything . . .).

But despite the fact that this realization was a prerequisite for the universal tolerance Voltaire so strongly advocated, in this case the demands for a dramatic climax were greater than the need for philosophical argumentation. Consequently, the call of her Christian "blood" proves too compelling and when called upon by her father to declare, "Je suis chrétienne," she replies, "Oui . . . seigneur . . . je le suis" (2.3).

11. "... forme de gouvernement dans lequel le souverain est maître absolu, a une autorité sans bornes, un pouvoir arbitraire, qui n'a pour règle que sa volonté. Tel est le gouvernement de Turquie, du Mogol, du Japon, de Perse et presque de toute l'Asie. Le principe, le caractère et les maux qu'entraîne le despotisme sont suffisamment développés dans nos meilleurs écrivains."

12. "OROSMANE: ... But indolence is sweet and its aftermath cruel; / I see the cowardly successors of Muhammed, / These caliphs trembling amid their sorry grandeur, / Lying on the debris of their altars and thrones, / ... / I see these proud Christians, ready to ravage; / Drawn to our borders from the lands of the Occident."

13. "... le deuxième acte de *Zaïre*, la première fois qu'il fut joué, produisit peu d'effet, et même excita des murmures dans le parterre pendant qu'on pleurait dans les loges; ... mais ce moment d'injustice fut très-court, et, dès la seconde représentation, la pièce fut aux nues."

Given the disparaging assessments of the emotional susceptibilities of the lower classes in the following century, it is worth pointing out that on this occasion it was the wealthier and aristocratic members of the audience seated in the loges who were moved to tears. Anne Vincent-Buffault's analysis, which is discussed in Chapter 1 of this book, sheds light on this reaction. In the early to mid-eighteenth century, it was not only accepted but expected that members of the upper classes would display their refined sensibilities in public. It would be another century before the ability to contain emotions would be used as a sign for distinguishing the aristocrat and the grand bourgeois from the common masses.

14. The work was apparently begun in 1738 and completed in 1740. It was first performed in Lille in 1741 so Voltaire could have the opportunity to gauge its effect far from the cabals of Paris. The Paris premiere took place on August 9, 1742 ("Avis" to *Le Fanatisme, ou Mahomet le Prophète, Oeuvres completes* 4:97).

In *Voltaire et l'Islam*, Djavâd Hadidi devotes a chapter to *Mahomet* and situates the play in the evolution of Voltaire's views on Islam.

15. "Je prends donc la liberté de lui envoyer ce premier acte d'une tragédie qui me paraît, sinon dans un bon goût, au moins dans un goût nouveau. On n'avait jamais mis sur le théâtre la superstition et le fanatisme."

16. Hadidi points out (57–58) that "the play was full of anti-jansenist *tirades*," including verses such as the following:

MAHOMET: (addressing his lieutenants) ...
Promettez, menacez; que la vérité règne;
Qu'on adore mon dieu, mais surtout qu'on le craigne.

(2.3)

(Promise, threaten; let the truth triumph; / Let my god be worshipped, but above all let him be feared.)
The god to be feared was recognized by eighteenth-century audiences as the Jansenist god, who dispensed his grace at will to followers who were required to submit with unquestioning obedience. Jansenists were not pleased to hear lines such as the following placed in the mouth of an unscrupulous and fanatical religious leader:

MAHOMET: . . .
Quiconque ose penser n'est pas né pour me croire.
Obéir en silence est votre seule gloire.

(3.6)

(Whoever dares to think was not born to believe in me. / To obey in silence is your only glory.)

17. "Soit que, dans la rapidité de la représentation, ils n'eussent pas suivi assez le fil de l'ouvrage, soit qu'ils fussent peu accoutumés au théâtre, ils furent blessés que Mahomet ordonnât un meurtre, et se servît de sa religion pour encourager à l'assassinat un jeune homme qu'il fait l'instrument de son crime. Ces personnes, frappées de cette atrocité, ne firent pas assez réflexion qu'elle est donnée dans la pièce comme le plus horrible de tous les crimes, et que même il est moralement impossible qu'elle puisse être donnée autrement."

18. For instance, his "Traité sur la tolérance" appeared in 1763, following his highly publicized posthumous defense and rehabilitation of Jacques Calas, a sixty-eight-year-old Protestant who had been tortured to death for allegedly having hanged his son to prevent him from renouncing the Protestant faith.

19. "ZOPIRE: I blush for you alone, for you whose deception / Has brought your country to the edge of a precipice; / For you whose hand has committed heinous crimes, / And caused war to break out in the midst of peace. / Your name alone divides our families, / Spouses, parents, mothers and daughters; / And a truce for you is nothing but a new way / Of plunging a dagger into our hearts. / Civil discord lies everywhere in your wake."

20. "J'auray encor le temps d'attendre que L'ambassadeur turc soit party, car en vérité il ne seroit pas honnête de dénigrer Le profète pendant qu'on nourit L'ambassadeur et de se moquer de sa chapelle sur notre théâtre."

21. "Un préjugé [reçu] suffit pour un peintre et pour un poëte. Où en seraient Virgile et Homère si on les avait chicanés sur les faits? Une fausseté qui produit au théâtre une belle situation, est préférable en ce cas à toutes les archives de l'Univers."

Chapter 3

1. The primary sources on which this chapter is based include the censored manuscripts themselves and the reports or *procès-verbaux* that were prepared for every play that was to be presented in Paris, whether at one of the state-subsidized Grands Théâtres, the secondary boulevard theaters, or the small cafés-concerts. These documents are collected in the Archives Nationales in Paris.

For the specific project of attempting to define the forms, strategic concerns, and modes of reception attached to the representation of non-Europeans in various types of boulevard drama, I reviewed dossiers F 21–974 (L'Ambigu-Comique), F 21–975 (La Porte-Saint-Martin), F 21–976 (La Gaîté), F 21–991 (Le Cirque Olympique), and F 21–993 (Le Panorama Dramatique). Reports of all works (dramas, comedies, vaudevilles, *féeries*, melodramas, and national or military tableaux, plays, or pantomimes) that treated a historical subject, a military campaign or engagement, and/or were set outside the industrialized regions of Western Europe were considered.

Odile Krakovitch has written a comprehensive study of censorship and nineteenth-century French theater, *Hugo Censuré: La Liberté au théâtre au XIXe siècle*, based on the material in the Archives Nationales. Jean-Marie Thomasseau includes a chapter on melodrama and censorship in *Le Mélodrame sur les scènes parisiennes*.

2. "La commission d'examen avait principalement à combattre les tendances continues des auteurs à chercher des situations et des effets scéniques:

"1) dans l'antagonisme des classes inférieures et des hautes classes *où ces dernières sont invariablement sacrifiées*;

"2) dans les attaques contre le principe d'autorité, contre la religion, la famille, la magistrature, l'armée, en un mot contre les institutions sur lesquelles repose la société;

"3) enfin, dans la peinture plus ou moins hardie des moeurs dépravées des femmes galantes et de la vie de désordre que l'on présente souvent à la jeunesse sous des couleurs d'autant plus dangereuses qu'elles sont plus attrayantes."

3. "Le théâtre est une façon d'histoire intime d'un peuple; il reproduit la physionomie d'une époque, il en révèle l'esprit moral, il se fait l'écho des bruits qui courent, il transmet les caprices de la mode, enfin il commente, souvent même il explique les mouvements politiques. Certes, il serait d'une exagération puérile de placer le *Mariage de Figaro* parmi les causes de la Révolution . . . ; mais qui pourrait se refuser à voir dans ces oeuvres, et plus encore dans le succès fiévreux qui les a accueillies, un reflet exact de la marche des idées, de l'état des esprits, des aspirations et des hardiesses des diverses classes de la société?

"En contact incessant avec les hommes, avec les passions, avec les incidents de l'heure présente, le théâtre se laisse fatalement entraîner à lâcher la bride à sa verve prime sautière, libre agressive. Le jour où des pièces ont, soit blessé la conscience publique par des tableaux de moeurs trop libres, soit froissé les gouvernements par des satires et des personnalités trop acerbes, l'autorité est intervenue et a mis terme à ces excès. Alors s'est établie entre le pouvoir et l'écrivain une lutte, lutte féconde en enseignements. Que l'on connaisse les sacrifices imposés, ainsi que les libertés accordées à l'écrivain, et la pièce interdite et la scène approuvée ne révèleront-elles pas tout ensemble l'esprit public et l'esprit du gouvernement au jour de l'interdiction, à l'heure de l'autorisation? C'est à ce point de vue particulier que nous voulons envisager l'histoire du théâtre."

4. "Il n'en est pas, en effet, du drame comme du livre. Celui-ci se lit dans le silence du foyer; les idées qu'il propage, les paradoxes qu'il émet, les tableaux qu'il présente n'influent sur l'esprit du lecteur que dans la mesure de son imagination et de ses opinions individuelles. Les lois et les tribunaux ordinaires auront toujours le temps de faire utilement leur devoir.

"L'oeuvre dramatique éclôt avec une soudaineté qui exige une autre action. Voyez ces masses attentives au spectacle qui se déroule devant leurs yeux, étudiez ces physionomies haletatnes qui reflètent toutes les passions du drame, écoutez les appréciations brèves et brutales, les conclusions d'une logique parfois imprévue, les jugements sans appel qui partent de mille bouches pour courir du salon à l'atelier, du café au cabaret, et vous comprendrez avec quelle énergique puissance le théâtre s'empare des imaginations populaires, quel germe, mauvais ou bon, il dépose dans les esprits."

These observations were apparently accepted as general truths, at least by those occupying the office of censor. Hemmings cites remarkably similar sentiments expressed by a censor of the previous century, Jean-Baptiste-Antoine Suard, in the *Journal de Paris* on August 27, 1789: "Freedom of the press is not attended by the same inconveniences as freedom of the stage. One reads a book on one's own, quietly, and communicates the impression it has made only in conversation with a few individuals. Theatrical performances, on the other hand, address themselves to the imagination and the senses; they can excite every passion, and the resulting impressions acquire an extraordinary energy by the simultaneous interaction of all the impressions received by a great multitude in concourse" (52).

5. See also Reid.

6. "Le courage ou plutôt la lâcheté anonyme est une force si puissante! . . . Une allusion maligne, souvent même sanglante, n'effarouchera pas des esprits timorés, alors que, perdus dans la foule, ils ont le plaisir, et non le danger, de la manifestation. Les théories sociales les plus osées et les plus fausses exalteront un peuple qui, dans l'emotion du drame, ne saura pas discerner la perfidie des déclamations et des peintures qu'on lui présente."

7. As censors were reduced to being mere executors of directives from above, their preoccupation with allusions or obvious challenges to authority obscured the subversive potential of the new social melodramas of the 1830s and 1840s. In her article "Robert Macaire ou la grande peur des censeurs," Odile Krakovitch points out the risks of mechanically and uncritically applying any single approach to reading. She concludes by noting that "[c]ensorship has always been one battle behind. . . . [The censors] censored what was most familiar and what they could recognize as being dangerous" (58).

8. Throughout *Hugo Censuré*, Krakovitch cites statistics for various epochs. In general 2 to 4 percent of the manuscripts submitted were denied approval. The years from 1835 to 1841 seem to have been typical: 123 out of 3,825 plays or about 3 percent were rejected (74).

9. "L'action se passe dans l'armée française en Egypte lorsque Kléber en est devenu général en chef. Le nom de Kléber ne rappelle rien de favorable pour Bonaparte. La gloire de cette fameuse expédition appartient à la France. Sa Majesté l'a adoptée en continuant d'en faire publier l'histoire à ses frais. Je n'aperçois donc aucune nécessité à priver le théâtre de ces images pittoresques, surtout quand elles se rapportent à l'époque choisie par l'auteur, le commandement de Kléber."

10. "L'action se passe en Egypte à l'époque de Kléber, et je crois qu'on a assez parlé des guerres de Bonaparte, pour pouvoir laisser reposer un pareil sujet. Si l'auteur peut faire passer la scène dans un autre pays, et dans un autre temps, on pourra représenter son ouvrage. Jusque-là, j'ai l'honneur de proposer à votre excellence d'en ajourner la représentation."

11. "Lorsque je conçus le plan du mimodrame intitulé *La Vivandière*, je ne pensai nullement au lieu de la scène non plus qu'à l'époque. Il est aisé de voir à la lecture de cet ouvrage, que je n'avais cherché qu'une action dramatique capable de

produire de l'effet au théâtre. Cette action appartient à tous les temps et à tous les âges. Si l'on a porté la scène en Egypte, sous les ordres du Général Kléber, ce n'a été que pour varier les costumes et les plaisirs des spectateurs. Plusieurs mimodrames dont l'action se passe en Espagne viennent d'être joués. Je ne pouvais donc la placer dans ce pays.

"S'il est impossible de conserver l'Egypte, je consens de tout mon coeur, que la scène se passe en Bohème sous Chevert, lors de la Bataille de Fontenoy, ou durant la guerre de 7 ans. Je m'en rapporte entièrement à la décision qu'on voudra prendre, sur une de ces trois époques."

12. "Mais l'inquisition ne figure là que comme machine dramatique, sans allusion, sans réflexion, sans vérité locale. Tout se passe dans la plus grande innocence."

13. "Cette circonstance est toujours utile dans les pièces de ce genre, où les gens du peuple, qui en sont les spectateurs, n'y voient qu'un *spectacle curieux appartenant à un monde qui n'est pas le leur* [my emphasis]. Je tiens en ce sens à l'apparition de l'ayeule, qui dépaise encore plus le public français et répand sur tout l'ouvrage une couleur purement fantastique."

14. Authors of tragedy for the Comédie-Française or Théâtre de l'Empereur were not above resorting to the same subterfuge, not always with success. Marvin Carlson recounts an effort by Charles Brifaut to get a play entitled *Philippe II* (1813) passed by the censors by changing Spaniards to Assyrians and changing the title to *Ninus II*. Apparently the censors were satisfied, but the Emperor himself was not so easily appeased and the play was closed. (*The French Stage* 22)

15. "Mais l'auteur vient de faire cesser les motifs de cette décision en transportant l'action et les personnages de la pièce dans le pais des mille et une nuits. Il ne s'agit plus que d'un Sultan, de janissaires, d'Arabes du désert. . . ."

16. "Il n'est pas besoin de remarquer que ces voleurs des contrés barbares de l'Asie n'ont rien de commun avec les malfaiteurs des pais civilisés, et que leur apparition au théâtre ne produit point le même effet."

17. "La scène est dans un pays dont les habitans naturels sont des sauvages à qui nos moeurs et notre religion sont étrangères, qui n'ont pas la même horreur que nous du meurtre et de la suicide. L'exemple de ce qui se peut passer aux bords du Mississippi n'est pas contagieux pour les habitans des rives de la Seine."

18. "Une considération qui nous a paru ne pas être indifférente, c'est que les auteurs ont eu la précaution de faire d'Harris, ce maître odieux qui maltraite les nègres, un mulâtre, autrefois esclave lui-même.

"Nous pensons que ce drame peut-être autorisé, moyennant les modifications introduites et qui ont eu surtout pour object de faire disparaître toute assimilation entre les nègres esclaves et les travailleurs européens."

19. "Ce mélodrame, tiré d'un roman d'Eugène Sue ainsi que reporte la brochure, a été représenté en 1832, alors qu'il n'y avait pas de censure, alors aussi que les idées socialistes qui se sont produites au grand jour en 1848, n'existaient encore qu'en germe dans quelques mauvais esprits et dans les ouvrages de certains auteurs.

"Depuis 1850, le drame d'*Atar-Gull* a été porté sur la liste des pièces interdites et nous sommes consultés aujourd'hui sur la question de savoir s'il y a lieu de l'y maintenir ou au contraire d'en autoriser la représentation. Après un examen consciencieux, sans préventions aucune, il nous a semblé que les cruautés des colons, suivies des vengeances atroces et presque légitimes des nègres ne déguisent mal l'antagonisme entre les patrons et les ouvriers, entre les riches et les pauvres.

"La mesure d'interdiction prise par l'administration a été évidemment le résultat de craintes de même nature et nous pensons qu'il y a lieu de la maintenir."

20. "Un nègre est le héros de cette pièce, les intentions du poète sont un peu surannées. On pouvoit, il y a vingt ans, louer beaucoup les vertus des nègres, pour décrier davantage les blancs; car alors il étoit question de soumettre les blancs au noirs, en faisant jouir ceux-ci des grands bienfaits de la liberté, de l'égalité et de la fraternité. On pouvait aussi s'extasier devant des moeurs patriarchales et presque celestes des paysans, car il falloit chassait leurs seigneurs et dépouiller les propriétaires. Aujourd'hui, les noirs, les paysans, et la populace des villes nous ont donné une idée juste de leur perfection, et St. Domingue suffit pour attester ce qu'il faut attendre d'une multitude déchaînée qui ne peut avoir d'autre intérît que d'égorger ses anciens maîtres pour se mettre à leur place."

Chapter 4

1. On the title page of volume 4 of this edition of Pixerécourt's selected works, the various contributors are described as "ses amis, membres de l'Institut, de l'Académie française, et autres hommes de lettres" (his friends, members of the Institute, of the Académie française, and other men of letters).

2. While many late-twentieth-century sources continue to credit Pixerécourt with being the founder of classical melodrama, there have always been scholars and critics who placed other names alongside his. For example, John McCormick cites an 1809 treatise by Armand Charlemagne, *Le Mélodrame aux boulevards*, that designates J. G. A. Cuvelier de Trie's *C'est le diable, ou la Bohémienne* (1798) as the first melodrama (160–61). In Maurice Albert's opinion, "la gloire, selon les uns, la honte, selon d'autres, d'avoir créé le mélodrame" (the glory according to some, the shame, according to others, of having created melodrama) was to be shared by Pixerécourt, L. C. Caignez, Cuvelier, and Corse (244).

3. "Le mélodrame . . . quand la saine morale est sa boussole, surtout quand rien ne s'y passe qui ne soit à la portée de l'intelligence de la classe ouvrière et manufacturière, ne peut qu'être utile, politique même, et contribuer de plus à maintenir cette même classe dans le bon chemin des qualités morales, si nécessaires au repos de chaque famille et de la société entière."

4. This body of Pixerécourt's writings offers an interesting illustration of the role dominant discursive forms and generic conventions play in structuring accounts—and perhaps even perceptions—of experience. In his *Histoire de la littérature dramatique* (1855), Jules Janin paraphrased an excerpt from one of Pixerécourt's autobiographical essays, remarking that "en certains esprits, chaque événement, chaque incident prend une teinte singulière qui rappelle tout à fait les habitudes de ces sortes d'esprits" (in certain minds, every event, every incident takes on a certain cast that closely reflects the habits of that sort of mind). The "habitudes" in this case were those of a melodramatic author. Willie Hartog, citing this passage

in his own study, agrees that when reading Pixerécourt's "Souvenirs du jeune âge," one gets the impression that "Pixerécourt s'est conduit pendant toute sa vie d'une façon mélodramatique. Sa vie est une suite de 'Précipices inattendus, d'événements incroyables, d'accidents qui n'arrivent qu'à lui seul'" (Pixerécourt lived his entire life in a melodramatic fashion. His life is a series of 'Unexpected peripeties, unbelievable events, accidents that happen only to him'"; [21]).

5. "Il était bien naturel que je fusse irrité contre ces paysans avec lesquels j'avais constamment vécu familièrement; d'ailleurs, ma mère était si charitable, si attentive pour eux tous, qu'il était juste de croire qu'ils nous étaient dévoués. Cet affreux mécompte me bouleversa; dès ce moment je les pris en haine, et la révolution me fit horreur."

6. According to Hartog (19), Pixerécourt's father sold the *seigneurie* de Pixe-récourt in 1789 to buy the lands of Saint-Vallier in the hopes of obtaining the marquisate. With the abolition of all seigneurial rights on August 5 of that year, he lost the newly acquired lands along with the remainder of his fortune.

7. ". . . avec des idées religieuses et providentielles, . . . avec des sentiments moraux qu'[il s'est] lancé dans la carrière épineuse du théâtre."

8. "Tout le monde connaît la loi génante que le calife Haroun-al-Raschid avait imposée au vaillant Giafar, le Barmecide, son visir, et le soutien de son trône, en lui faisant épouser sa soeur Abassa. Giafar n'avait obtenu l'honneur insigne de s'allier à la famille des Abassides, qu'en jurant sur l'Alcoran de traiter la princesse comme sa soeur, et de ne jamais réclamer auprés d'elle les droits d'un époux. L'engagement était téméraire et difficile à tenir, près d'une femme jeune, belle et spirituelle; aussi fut-il promptement violé. Le Calife en fut instruit: Giafar et plus de quarante Barmecides furent immolés à sa vengeance, et la malheureuse Abassa ne conserva la vie que pour la traîner dans l'humiliation et la misère."

9. "L'un s'est assez scrupuleusement conformé à la vérité de l'histoire, tandis que l'autre, usant dans toute son étendue du privilège de son art, ne s'est embarrassé que de composer un roman plein d'intérêt."

10. ". . . riche en situations pathétiques, en incidents merveilleux, sans être cependant hors du domaine de la vraisemblance poétique théâtrale."

11. "Tout autre que l'orgueilleux Haroun eût été attendri de ce spectacle; jamais faute ne fut plus pardonnable, si un despote savait pardonner."

All quotations from Geoffroy's synopsis are taken from his "Notice sur *Les Ruines de Babylone*," 8–11.

12. ". . . par ce trait de générosité, [Giafar] désarme la vengeance de ce monarque."

13. This notice appears under the cast listing in the published version of the play.

14. "Quelques écrivains, obligés à une plus grande exactitude qu'un auteur de mélodrame, sont cependant tombés dans cette erreur, et leur opinion, quoique fausse, suffirait pour excuser M. de Pixerécourt. . . ."

15. ". . . c'est même une sorte d'avantage pour l'auteur qui les a mis en scène; ses acteurs sont déjà connus des petits et des grands; il n'y a point d'enfant qui ne tremble au nom du commandeur des croyants et de son premier visir."

16. "L'administration a prodigué dans cette pièce tout ce que le luxe asiatique

offre de plus brillant et de plus recherché, tant pour les costumes que pour les décors."

17. "Les décorations, les costumes, tout est d'une fraicheur, d'un éclat qui ne laisse rien à désirer, et *qui fait oublier aux spectateurs le pays où ils sont*" (my emphasis).

18. "Le théâtre représente l'intérieur des jardins du sérail. A gauche, l'appartement de Zaïda, dont une croisée donne sur le jardin. A droite, un kiosque fort simple en apparence. Dans le fond une grille très-riche. En ouvrant les persiennes dont elle est garnie, on voit le Tygre qui baigne les murs du palais et le pont couvert jeté sur ce fleuve. L'autre rive présente une campagne riante ornée de jolies habitations."

19. "Le théâtre représente un joli pavillon circulaire ou octogone, dans une forêt agréable. On voit les arbres de chaque côté du pavillon, ainsi qu'à travers les portes et les croisées. Ces dernières sont garnies de stores en treillis peints. Cette construction doit être élégante et surtout très-légère. Elle occupe toute la largeur du théâtre."

20. "Le théâtre représente la partie des ruines de Babylone, qui s'étendait vers le Tygre. A droite, au second et au troisième plans, les murs d'un château fort, dont une petite porte dérobée donne sur le théâtre. Tout près de l'avant-scène, du même côté, une masure couverte avec des feuilles de palmes."

21. ". . . une halte de Bédouins; des ballots, des chameaux, des esclaves, des draperies jetées sur des branches de palmier, etc."

22. "Jamais 'Iphigénie en Aulide immolée'; jamais le *Misanthrope* ou le *Tartuffe* n'ont peut-être vu une foule aussi considérable se porter à leurs premières représentations, que le mélodrame d'hier. Toutes les loges louées sans exception, le Boulevard encombré d'un nombre immense de spectateurs ou d'aspirants à l'être; enfin, les barrières qu'une sage prévoyance opposait à leur impatience, renversées par eux, voilà ce que nous avons vu hier à nos risques et périls."

23. "Jamais, peut-être, on n'a vu au théâtre des Boulevards des décorations aussi fraîches, des costumes aussi riches, des ballets aussi gracieux. Le tailleur, le chorégraphe, le décorateur ont fait assaut d'imagination et de talent, et chacun d'eux mérite une couronne. . . ."

24. ". . . L'auteur a donné pour ange tutélaire aux proscrits, un Français nommé Raymond, dont toutes les saillies réjouissent le calife: ce jeune homme, plein d'esprit, de gaîté et de courage, se dévoue aux intérêts de Giafar, le suit partout, le délivre des plus grands dangers. . . ."

25. ". . . l'auteur a tiré de son cerveau un comique français plein d'adresse, de présence d'esprit et de courage."

26. "Sans doute la faute en est au genre de la pièce, qui est tout à fait sévère, tandis que mes autres drames sont tous mêlés de gaîté."

27.

RAYMOND: Où est votre fils?
GIAFAR: Dans sa retraite.
RAYMOND: Est-elle impénétrable?
GIAFAR: A tous les yeux.
RAYMOND: Puissiez-vous dire vrai!

GIAFAR: D'où nait ce trouble? Viens-tu m'annoncer quelque malheur?
RAYMOND: Non. Mais je crains tout des ruses de votre ennemie. Je ne sais quel secret pressentiment me dit que le départ d'Haroun n'est qu'une feinte pour mieux connaître vos démarches. Redoublez de prudence, Seigneur, où vous êtes perdu.

28. "Raymond dirige tout. Ses recommandations et son activité impriment un grand mouvement à ce tableau."

29. "RAYMOND: . . . j'ai de grandes obligations à Giafar: pendant le séjour que ce ministre fit à la cour de Charlemagne, j'eus occasion d'éprouver la bonté de son coeur. Ma famille était opprimée; il lui rendit tous les biens à la fois, l'honneur et la fortune. Je m'attachai à lui, et je quittai la France pour le suivre à Bagdad. Il me regardai comme un autre lui-même et me communiquait ses plus secrètes pensées. . . ."

30. It is possible that Raymond's costume(s) might have given some hint of the character's presumed social status, although it seems likely that the theatrical aspects rather than the social origin of the character would have been conveyed by his costume.

31. "Ce rôle est joué par Tautin, avec une vivacité, une finesse et un enjouement dignes de la nation française."

32. "RAYMOND: . . . Tenons-nous sur nos gardes; redoublons de ruse et d'activité; n'oublions pas que les méchants ne sont point découragés par les revers: ils trouvent sans cesse, dans l'envie de nuire, le courage et la fermeté nécessaires pour former de nouveaux projets. Il est donc juste que ceux qui sont forcés d'obéir soient plus ingénieux que celui qui commande."

33. "Haroun-al-Raschid fut le cinquième calife de la race des Abassides. On l'a comparé à Charlemagne; mais combien était grande la supériorité que le monarque français avait sur le despote oriental! Dans toutes les grandes choses que fit Haroun, on vit toujours près de lui son visir Giafar le Barmecide, né d'une famille de tout temps célèbre en Orient par sa générosité; ce ministre partageait la gloire de son maître, prévenait les fautes qu'il pouvait faire, et lui donnait d'excellentes leçons. Or, il serait difficile de nommer le ministre de Charlemagne. . . ."

34. "Haroun-al-Raschid était contemporain, mais non pas rival de Charlemagne. L'illustre empereur d'Occident fut toujours un monarque aussi sage que courageux; le calife de l'Orient fut trop souvent un despote insensé: à quelques traits de justice et de générosité, il a mêlé un trop grand nombre d'actions bizarres, extravagantes et cruelles, triste destin des princes orientaux, qui peuvent tout ce qu'ils veulent: il leur arrive rarement de vouloir ce qui est raisonnable."

35. "Qui mieux que moi connaît ce despote orgueilleux, si étonnant par le mélange inconcevable des meilleures et des plus mauvaises qualités. Je sais que ce prince, justement renommé dans l'Orient par sa bravoure, sa liberalité, les bienfaits qu'il répand sur ses peuples, s'est montré souvent capricieux, ingrat, cruel même; qu'il sacrifie, sans scrupule et sans regret, les droits les plus sacrés de la reconnaissance et de l'humanité, à ses injustes soupçons et à la bizarrerie de ses goûts."

36. ". . . il sert la haine de la sultane Almaïde contre le visir, qui a dédaigné ses faveurs."

37. "GIAFAR: . . . Tu le vois, Haroun, ta situation ne présente aucun espoir de

salut; tes gardes me sont dévoués; les Bédouins sont tes ennemis; te voilà seul au milieu des plus affreux dangers, et tu n'as plus même pour te défendre, le soutien de ta couronne, ton ami le plus zélé, Giafar."

38. "GIAFAR: (*avec énergie.*) Hé bien, imitez-moi. (*Il lève son cimeterre. Les soldats et les Bédouins en font autant.*) Tombez tous aux pieds de votre légitime Souverain. (*Tous posent les armes et se prosternent devant le Calife. Des Esclaves, des Bédouins sont accourus et garnissent les ruines.*)

"HAROUN: Ah! Giafar! . . . combien je fus injuste, et que ta vengeance est noble! (*Il le relève et lui tend les bras. Giafar s'y précipite.*) Zaïda, Naïr, Hassan, Raymond, venez tous dans mes bras.

"GIAFAR: O mon maître! (*La toile tombe.*)"

39. "O vous, êtres privilégiés que le hasard, la naissance ou les talents ont placé à la tête des nations; montrez-vous toujours justes et bons envers les peuples qui vous sont soumis: sachez par des bienfaits sagement répartis, gagner les coeurs de ceux qui vous entourent; au milieu de votre gloire peut-être un revers vous attend, vous trouverez un ami dans chacun des heureux que vous aurez faits."

40. "La renommée grossit les objets et fait souvent à un général une très grande réputation, aux dépens de tel ou tel de ses officiers ou même de ses soldats, qui a contribué, plus que lui, à ses succès."

41. "GIAFAR: . . . Tu l'as forcé d'abandonner ta cause, et par ton injustice et par tes cruautés. Reconnais enfin combien il est dangereux de se livrer à l'impétuosité des passions. Celui qui gouverne un grand peuple lui doit des grands exemples. Si, réprimant un aveugle transport, tu n'avais écouté que la voix de la justice, en conservant une épouse et un fils à celui qui venait de sauver tes Etats, tu n'aurais point, en un seul jour, terni ta gloire, outragé l'amitié, méconnu la nature et compromis le rang suprême."

42. "De jolies ballets, des décorations fraîches, voilà pour les yeux; mais le coeur et l'esprit ont aussi besoin d'être intéressés, et l'affluence prodigieuse qui se porte aux représentations multipliées de cet ouvrage, prouvent suffisamment que l'auteur n'a négligé aucun moyen de plaire et de toucher."

43. I laugh to myself at your Mahomet;
May the Prophet himself forgive me!
But to the pleasures promised by his law,
I prefer a kiss someone gives me.

To true believers, in his holy book,
After death, he promises ambrosia.
Ah! rather than wait for uncertain bliss,
Let's move along to the next life now.

Ah! if I were master of this place,
Finding the sure way to true bliss,
I would banish Mahomet from my court,
And let Epicurus dwell there forever.

Chapter 5

1. "Représenter des batailles sur nos théâtres, c'est une tentative un peu difficile. Leur étroite dimension ne permet pas d'y faire manoeuvrer beaucoup de troupes. Des armées de 20 à 30 hommes au plus couvrent ce petit espace, engagent des combats, prennent des villes d'assaut et remportent des victoires; mais ces moyens, tout foibles qu'ils sont, produisent souvent beaucoup d'effet, lorsqu'ils sont ménagés et combinés avec adresse. Alors l'art supplé au nombre, et le spectateur, déjà porté à se faire illusion, transforme ses yeux en multiplians, et se représente, au lieu de quelques hommes qui défilent, des armées entières qui manoeuvrent."

2. Especially informative among the more recent treatments of the subject are Marvin Carlson's *The Theatre of the French Revolution* (1966), Daniel Hamiche's *Le Théâtre et la Révolution: La Lutte des classes au théâtre en 1789 et en 1793* (1973), Michèle Root-Bernstein's *Boulevard Theater and Revolution in Eighteenth-Century Paris* (1984), and Graham E. Rodmell's *French Drama of the Revolutionary Years* (1990).

3. "La Révolution triomphe sur tous les théâtres. Tout est prétexte à des pièces populaires, la mort de Mirabeau aussi bien que la fuite du roi. Cette malheureuse tentative de Louis XVI fut une bonne fortune pour les auteurs patriotes."

4. "Malgré la liberté des théâtres décrétée . . . elle doit cependant avoir des bornes, et il pourrait y avoir le plus grand inconvénient de remettre sur la scène ce qui a déjà excité tant de mécontentement."

5. See Bruce Jenkins's *Nationalism in France: Class and Nation since 1789* (1990).

6. "Le théâtre a gardé la trace du mouvement de l'esprit public à Paris, en ces heures penibles. Sur toutes les scènes retentit le cri d'alarme. On cherche, dans l'histoire, les crises analogues que le pays a dû traverser; Philippe Auguste, St. Louis, Charles Martel, Bayard, Jeanne Hachette, sortent de leur tombe pour redire par quel élan national on chasse l'étranger du sol de la patrie. . . ."

7. "Malgré la revanche éclatante que la France a prise, malgré la place glorieuse que l'Empereur Napoléon III lui a réconquise parmi les nations, nous pensons que sous la dynastie Napolénienne, le spectacle profondément affligeant et humiliant des calamités que l'esprit de parti a reprochées au premier Empire et présentées comme la cause de sa chute, ne peut être mis devant les yeux du public."

8. "Pour exposer sur la scène, sans compromettre la dignité royale, la mascarade et la démence de Charles VI, il faudrait un art et un talent qu'on ne peut se flatter de trouver au Cirque Olympique."

9. "Notre théâtre occupe, depuis le milieu du 18e siècle, un tel rang en Europe, il a conquis une influence si grande, que les nations étrangères ont toujours l'oeil ouvert sur les spectacles de Paris, et que les ambassadeurs se préoccupent vivement de tout ce qui peut intéresser leur patrie. Avant 1789, l'interdiction de plus d'une pièce, avons-nous vu, fut imposée par ces susceptibilités diplomatiques. Il en sera de même sous l'Empire, sous la Restauration, sous le gouvernement de Juillet."

10. ."Ici s'arrête la compétence de la Censure dramatique, et c'est aux lumières

seules de l'autorité supérieure qu'il appartient de décider si un pareil sujet, purgé de tous les passages dont je propose la suppression, peut être sans inconvénient politique, transporté sur le théâtre."

11. "Pendant tout le course de ce drame, malgré une différence d'humeur constante et des taquineries mutuelles, l'anglais et le français ne cessent d'agir avec l'accord le plus complet.

"Les Russes sont peints dans cet ouvrage sous les couleurs les plus odieuses. Ils foulent impitoyablement la province envahie et y accomplissent les plus grandes cruautés. . . .

"Persuadés qu'il est mauvais de livrer en pâture aux passions populaires la majesté souveraine, même dans la personne d'un ennemi, nous avons fait supprimer de l'ouvrage tout ce qui pouvait avoir trait d'une manière fâcheuse à l'Empéreur Nicolas."

12. The most recent and concise overview of Napoleon's stage career is W. D. Howarth's "Bonaparte on Stage: The Napoleonic Legend in Nineteenth-century French Drama" (1986). More extensive treatments of the relations of Napoleon I and the theater were published early in this century. Two books were written by L.-Henry Lecomte. The first, *Napoléon et l'Empire racontés par le théâtre, 1797–1899* (1900), considers representations of Napoleon and the Napoleonic legend; the second, *Napoléon et le monde dramatique* (1912), is primarily concerned with the administration and regulation of the theaters under Napoleon I. Maurice Albert's *Les Théâtres des Boulevards* (1902) includes detailed chapters on the theater under the Directory, the Consulate, and the First Empire.

13. The history of these and other theaters featuring equestrian spectacle has been very thoroughly researched by Arthur H. Saxon in *Enter Foot and Horse: A History of Hippodrama in England and France* (1968).

14. "*Les tableaux historiques*, dans le genre Servandoni. Dans ces tableaux, les décorations devront être la partie principale. Chaque tableau pourra présenter un fait, un grand événement.

"*Les évolutions militaires*. Ce spectacle consistera en marches, assauts, combats de fantassins ou de cavalerie."

15. ". . . on y a retracé en effet deux ou trois époques glorieuses pour le nom français, et nous avons été les premiers à faire l'éloge de ce zèle civique dont la présence des personnes du rang le plus élevé et les applaudissemens de tous les bons citoyens ont été la récompense."

16. See in particular Nichols's chapter 5, "Sticking to Reality: Rhetoric and What Exceeds It," in *Representing Reality*.

17. Martin Meisel illuminates the symbiotic relationship between pictorial and dramatic representations of the Napoleonic legend in his "Napoleon, or History as Spectacle," a chapter in *Realizations: Narrative, Pictorial, and Theatrical Arts in Nineteenth-Century England* (1983).

18. Meisel defines the crucial distinction in function between the dramatic tableau of effect and situation and the *tableaux vivant*: "Both present a readable, picturesque, frozen arrangement of living figures; but the dramatic tableau arrested movement, while the *tableau vivant* brought stillness to life" (47).

19. "Ce n'est qu'une légère esquisse mais dans laquelle il règne beaucoup de

mouvement. On aime d'ailleurs à avoir sous les yeux, même en petit, l'image des combats, et lorsqu'ils rappellent la constance et la gloire des héros qui on immortalise, par leurs exploits, les plaines de la Saxe et de la Pologne, ils acquièrent un nouveau degré d'intérêt."

20. ". . . embelli de tout ce que la fiction peut offrir de dramatique et d'imposant à l'imagination."

21. "M. Labrousse, lui, n'a pas d'ambition littéraire: à cheval sur le Cirque, il fait tranquillement sa petite bataille. Sans se soucier de style ou d'inventions: aussi n'avons-nous rien à dire à ses oeuvres, qui demanderaient un général grand tacticien pour critique. Nous devons nous borner à constater le plus bruyant, le plus étourdissant succès que l'on ait entendu depuis qu'il se brûle de la poudre au théâtre. De magnifiques décorations, encadrant magnifiquement de magnifiques évolutions, et l'on sort de la assourdi par le canon et les applaudissements, aveuglé par le feu et la fumée, et parfumé de poudre comme un vieux de la vieille. Une représentation compte pour une campagne."

22. "Nous avons vu ou revu un *Bonaparte en Egypte*;—les mêmes chevaux, les mêmes guerriers, les mêmes coups de fusil qui attirent pendant cent représentations les amateurs de gloire et de fumée. . . . Le mimodrame de M. Labrousse remplit toutes les conditions du genre. Comment en serait-il autrement? L'auteur a pour sa part fait deux fois au moins chaque campagne de Napoléon; il ne doit pas être embarrassée de les recommencer."

23. David Spurr's *The Rhetoric of Empire: Colonial Discourse in Journalism, Travel Writing, and Imperial Administration* (1993) identifies the basic rhetorical features of colonialist discourses as they appear in British, French, and American popular journalism of the nineteenth and twentieth centuries.

Chapter 6

1. The following three chapters are based on material drawn from the major Paris *quotidiens* and from newspapers that specialized in reporting on the theaters of the French capital. The latter type of publication served as the primary source of material for the first two decades of the nineteenth century; during this time the major daily papers included reviews of new productions or reports on theatrical activity only rarely. The most complete source by far was *Le Courrier des Spectacles*, published daily from 1796 (or 1797) to 1807, when it changed its format to include coverage of political events and took the title of *Le Courrier de l'Europe*. Over the next several years the *Courrier de l'Europe* became *Le Journal de Paris* (1811–1816), then *Le Journal des Débats politiques et littéraires* (1816–1817), and finally *Le Journal de Commerce, de Politique et de Littérature* (1817–1819). In 1819, a new publication, *Le Camp Volant*, appeared that once again focused on news about and reviews of the theaters of Paris. Its irreverent, flippant style contrasted with the more sober, judicious tones of the theater reviews that had preceded it. The next major publication to feature reportage on the theaters was ambitiously entitled *Le Courrier des Théâtres, Sciences, Histoire, Industrie, Littérature, Beaux-Arts, Moeurs, Librairie, Variétés, Nouvelles, Modes*. It remained active through the 1830s.

2. "La Campagne qui vient de s'ouvrir forme un si beau spectacle, et les nouvelles qui viennent d'être publiées présentent un si grand intérêt, que nous avons cru devoir aujourd'hui suspendre tout ce qui concerne les théâtres, pour ne présenter à nos Lecteurs que les scènes de bravoure et d'héroisme par lesquelles nos armées viennent d'ajouter de nouveaux lauriers à ceux dont elles sont couronnés depuis tant d'années."

3. "Nous avons donc pensé que si nous pouvions joindre au mérite littéraire celui d'une politique plus étendue et plus neuve, (objet d'un si grand intérêt en ce moment) nos abonnés n'auroient rien à désirer. . . ."

4. "J'ai un peu négligé les nouveautés dramatiques qui ont alimentés nos théâtres, depuis quelques jours; je l'ai fait à dessein. Il m'a semblé que dans un moment où une partie de la nation était appelée à exercer la plus précieuse comme la plus légitime de ses prérogatives, il ne fallait pas distraire de ces nobles soins les lecteurs d'un journal, particulièrement consacré à la défense des droits du peuple et des libertés constitutionnels. Quels attraits auraient pu avoir pour nos abonnés des discussions, des raisonnemens, des jugemens portés, sur des acteurs ou sur des pièces nouvelles, tandis que le plus imposant de tous les spectacles frappait tous les yeux, absorbait tous les esprits, commandait toutes les attentions?"

5. ". . . les théâtres se trouvaient abandonnés, ou n'étaient plus qu'un lieu de réunion, dans lequel on espérait apprendre le nom de quelques-uns des élus de la nation."

6. "Tout Paris retentit depuis plusieurs jours de chants d'allégresse; tout célèbre le retour de la paix, tout s'empresse de témoigner sa reconnaissance au héros qui nous l'a rendue. Sur nos théâtres, ce ne sont que des hymnes en l'honneur du vainqueur et du pacificateur de l'Europe. L'Ambigu a aussi voulu se distinguer en cette occasion mémorable par les témoignages de son zèle et de son dévouement. La façade du théâtre étoit avant-hier illuminée d'une mannière très ingénieuse. La foule qui se presse chaque jour sur les boulevards s'arrêtoit pour contempler l'image auguste de l'Empéreur dans un temple transparent et éclaire avec magnificence. L'intérieur étoit occupe par une multitude de curieux jaloux de mêler leurs applaudissemens à l'expression franche et naive des sentimens de reconnaissance et d'admiration dont les acteur devoient être les interprètes."

7. "Avec quel sentiment consolateur je détourne les yeux de cet affreux théâtre pour les tourner vers des spectacles de joie, de tendresse, de reconnaissance et de bonheur! Tous les soirs nos salles retentissent d'acclamations et d'applaudissemens si vifs si unanimes, qu'on croirait que les nombreux étrangers mêlés parmi nous se plaisent à oublier un instant leur patrie pour lutter d'enthousiasme avec les Français dans l'expression de leur amour pour ce prince auguste, pour ce *Bourbon* dont le nom rappelle de si doux souvenirs, dont les vertus et la bonté promettent tant de bonheur. Partout les allusions plus ou moins directes sont accueillis avec transport: Les pièces nouvelles se succèdent rapidement, les anciennes rajeunissent, et il n'est pas de jour ou Melpomène, Thalie, Euterpe, Polymnie et même le folâtre Momus ne paient un tribut au meilleur des rois. . . . "

8. "Etrangers à toutes les passions, nous avons exprimé notre opinion avec franchise, décence et liberté. Nous avons cru que le premier soin de l'homme de lettres, lorsqu'il rend compte d'un ouvrage, étoit d'en examiner le mérite independam-

ment des considérations de la personne. Nous avons imaginé que loin d'entretenir le feu des dissentions, par des censures amères et passionnées, loin de ranimer les parties, et de les mettre sans cesse aux prises l'un avec l'autre, le plus noble et le plus sacré de nos devoirs étoit d'entretenir entre tous les hommes les liens de la concorde et de la paix, sur lesquels repose le bonheur de la société et des Etats."

9. "Nous aurons toujours la même franchise, la même impartialité dans nos examens. Notre critique, tant des pièces que des acteurs, sera toujours dictée par notre amour pour l'art du théâtre, et le désir de le voir résister au mauvais goût, et le ramener, s'il est possible, à celui des grands hommes qui ont assuré à la France la priorité en ce genre sur toutes les nations du monde."

10. "Nous avons déjà attribué la décadence de l'art dramatique à plusieurs causes. Nous l'avons rejeté sur la naissance et le succès du genre appelé drame, qui, prêtant par sa facilité un appas séduisant aux auteurs, les détourne de l'étude longue et approfondie des anciens, qui, secondée par le génie, peut seule produire un auteur tragique, et de la méditation qu'exige la véritable comédie. Nous avons reconnu comme très-contraire à l'art dramatique cette indulgence, qui, née du mauvais goût, tend à le perpetuer. Nous nous sommes recriés sur cette habitude que l'on a prise au théâtre de s'opposer à ceux qu'un reste de goût engage à s'élever contre les mauvais ouvrages.

"Il est aisé de voir que c'est le mauvais goût seul qui produit toutes ces causes. Il est encore bien plus remarquable dans l'espèce de préférence que le public semble donner aux ouvrages médiocres, et même mauvais, sur les chefs-d'oeuvre de l'art."

11. "L'auteur a voulu tracer lui-même un fait historique, il s'est écarté de la fidelité des rapports et le fait est encore trop récent pour qu'on puisse à ce point altérer la vérité de l'histoire."

12. "On a discuté souvent sur les avantages et les inconvéniens des romans historiques, mais nos romanciers ont trouvé bien des imitateurs; vaudevilles, chansons, mélodrames, tout est historique maintenant, et il ne faudrait pas être surpris que l'on composât dorénavant des contes et des fables historiques. En attendant, voici un mélodrame dont le sujet, quoique tiré de l'Histoire de France est une conception presque fabuleuse, par les détails dont il est surchargé et par les incidens romanesques qui s'y succèdent continuellement."

13. "Faut-il en faire un reproche à l'auteur: il répondra qu'il a dû embellir un fait historique de tous les charmes de la fiction; qu'une pièce de théâtre n'est pas une leçon d'histoire, que si de graves auteurs se permettent de l'altérer dans des ouvrages représentés sur la première scène de la capitale, la même liberté peut bien s'excuser au théâtre de la Gaîté, où l'on apporte moins de prétentions; enfin il répondra par le succès brillant qu'il a obtenu.

"L'auteur auroit pu cependant, sans compromettre les grands effets du mélodrame, faire plus d'emprunts à l'histoire."

14. "Le but de l'histoire est . . . d'établir des faits, et de fixer les opinions, en s'appuyant de preuves et d'autorités. Quand un événement n'est point contesté, quand on n'a point réuni les témoignages qui en attestent l'existence, quand les écrivains varient entre eux, quand ils s'abstiennent d'émettre leur jugement, il n'y a plus d'histoire, il n'y a que du doute."

15. "Rechercher dans l'histoire l'origine des sujets que l'on a transportés sur

la scène, juger jusqu'à quel point le poète s'est rapproché ou écarté de la vérité des caractères et de l'exactitude des faits, blâmer ou justifier ses licences. . . . "

16. "Un des événemens qui ont le plus illustré les Français en Egypte et le héros qui les a toujours conduit à la victoire c'est la bataille des Pyramides. Pour peindre à nos yeux cette action célèbre, il falloit un pinceau exercé et digne de la retracer. Le Français ne désire rien tant que d'honorer par son suffrage le souvenir des victoires dont l'éclat rejaillit sur tous: mais lorsque le peintre est à une intervalle immense au dessous de son sujet, tout en applaudissant à son intention, on repousse impitoyablement son tableau, disons mieux, sa caricature. C'est ce qui arriva hier à cette première représentation. Rien de plus froid, de plus ridicule, de plus invraisemblable que l'intrigue amoureuse liée au plan de cet ouvrage. . . . "

17. ". . . depuis que [les Franconi] ont associé l'immortel Kléber à leurs travaux, tout Paris y a pris part; et loin que l'intérêt diminue, il va croissant d'une bataille à l'autre."

18. "L'héroïque Kléber, qu'une mort cruelle et prématurée enleva à l'armée française, dont il fut l'un des plus illustres chefs . . . a réparu en souvenir hier au soir au Cirque Olympique. Sa mort, dont on nous a présenté la douleureuse image, a offert au public un spectacle attendrissant et curieux. Les spectateurs ont mêlé des larmes à leurs applaudissemens."

19. ". . . lier une action attachante à l'intérêt qu'inspire le principal personnage et de donner à sa mort un aspect plus dramatique. . . . "

20. "Tous les éléments sont là: le vieux père aveugle qui n'a plus qu'un petit fils et qui le donne à la France, le jeune homme qui aime et qui redoute un moment le sort, parce qu'il aime; la jeune fille heureuse d'être aimée, qui craint pour son bonheur et pour celui d'un autre; mais à côté d'eux, le soldat devenu sergent, qui a déjà payé la croix de ses sueurs et qui demande à la payer encore; le commandant qui donne un fraternel rendez-vous à son sous-officier sur le champ de bataille; le mauvais ouvrier à qui le drapeau apprendra l'honneur; le gentilhomme oisif et ruiné qui veut se refaire gentilhomme avec son courage; partout le sentiment de la dignité des armes, de l'excellence de la discipline pour ennoblir, pour retremper, pour fortifier les âmes; l'expérience de la joie virile, et, comme conclusion, la fête du départ, les enseignes deployées, la marche solennelle des régiments, aux cris de Vive l'Empéreur et de Vive la France!"

21. "*La Guerre en Orient*, soit: c'est un titre heureux, mais ce n'est qu'un titre, et le début d'un drame dont les plus beaux spectacles sont encore entre les mains de Dieu."

22. "Ce n'est pas le poème du passé qu'il arrange en spectacle, c'est le bulletin militaire, c'est la gazette du dernier mois, c'est le récit de la guerre présente, de cette campagne du Danube, où la Russie semble provoquer le monde et où la Turquie forme l'avant-garde de la civilisation, aux applaudissements de l'Europe étonnée. La pièce suit les phases diverses de la lutte qui s'engage."

23. The representation of the Crimean War on the London stage and the impact of developments in telecommunications have been studied by J. S. Bratton (1980).

24. "Le Cirque est prêt à reproduire chaque soir la dépêche télégraphique, la note officielle."

25. ". . . prêt . . . à chanter le Te Deum avec nos soldats et publier les victoires qui sont encore entre les mains des armées. C'est une entreprise nouvelle et singulière, où l'à-propos peut tenir lieu de bien des choses et où la soudaineté de l'exécution doit être imputée à mérite."

26. ". . . une grande épopée militaire, éblouissante de luxe, de faste, de richesses orientales et qui joint à l'intérêt du drame, l'attrait de l'actualité."

27. "Tel est, autant que peut le rendre une analyse nécessairement écourtée, ce drame si émouvant, si actuel, qu'il se passe dans la réalité, pour ainsi dire, au moment même où il se joue.—L'intention en est excellente; le succès en a été immense. Cependant, malgré la convenance parfaite de l'exécution, cela nous inquiète un peu de voir le drame devancer l'histoire, et le poète ouvrir la main fermée encore du destin pour en arracher les événements. Ne faut-il pas aux choses la sanction de l'accompli? et les peindre pendant qu'elles se font, n'est-ce pas une ambition prématurée?"

Chapter 7

1. Edward Herman and Gerry O'Sullivan place the "media as 'theater' of terrorism" analogy in the context of a larger discourse that portrays the West as particularly vulnerable to terrorism because of the openness of its societies (42–44).

2. See Jean-Pierre Seguin's *Nouvelles à sensations: Canards du XIXe siècle* (1959).

3. "Le gouvernement a pensé qu'à l'instant où la campagne va se faire, il serait intéressant qu'un journal fût destiné à . . . faire connaître les marches des armées, leur position, leurs combats, leurs victoires, les actions héroïques des défenseurs de la patrie, les prodiges de courage que l'amour de la liberté enfante chaque jour."

4. "Il est peu de nos concitoyens qui n'aient dans cette armée un fils, un frère ou un ami; il n'en est aucun qui ne suive ses opérations avec cet intérêt qu'inspire l'orgueil national, avec cette curiosité qu'éveillent les grandes entreprises surtout lorsqu'elles ont pour but, comme celle-ci, l'amélioration future du sort de l'humanité."

5. Nineteen letters from François Bernoyer, an officer of the "Armée d'Orient," were discovered and published by Christian Tortel in 1981. This collection gives a clear idea of the great variety of information—personal impressions and feelings, accounts of daily life, unusual incidents, as well as the results of military engagements—contained in letters sent to family members in France. Also brought to light relatively recently are the *Mémoires sur l'Expédition d'Egypte* by Joseph-Marie Moiret, originally prepared for publication in 1818.

6. "Toutes les lettres de Toulon assurent que les Français et les étrangers des deux sexes y affluent d'une manière vraiment inouïe. Les communes voisines sont également encombrées de militaires et de voyageurs."

7. "L'Armée française n'a donc réellement à redouter que la contrariété des vents et la difficulté du débarquement."

8. "L'expédition d'Afrique paraît prendre un aspect plus sérieux qu'on ne s'y

attendait généralement. Au lieu de fuir devant nos bataillons disciplinés, ces hordes barbares qui couvrent le rivage africain attaquent nos positions, et il faut toute la valeur et tout le sang-froid de notre jeune armée pour triompher des obstacles qui la séparent encore des murailles d'Algiers.

"L'affaire du 19 doit avoir été vive, à en juger par ses résultats. Nous sommes étonnés de ne pas trouver dans le bulletin officiel la moindre allusion aux pertes que nous aura coûtées cette journée."

9. ". . . l'administration ne laisse pas le pays une minute dans l'ignorance du moindre événement des plus lointaines expéditions. C'est que là tous les partis, whigs et torys, comprennent que la verité et la publicité sont l'élément et la vie même du gouvernement constitutionnel."

10. "M. Bourmont, ministre de la guerre, approuvera sans doute toutes les opérations de M. Bourmont général en chef, et quelques bévues que fasse ce dernier, il est bien sûr de ne jamais se voir privé de son commandement par le ministre."

11. "J'ai reçu votre cargaison de lunettes et besicles à verre bleus et jaunes contre le soleil; j'en ai fait porter hier à deux régimens; l'infanterie avait les verres jaunes, la cavalerie avait les verres bleux; cela fait en ligne un effet admirable."

12. These pages are reproduced in Seguin's *Canards du siècle passé*.

13. "Mon frère, dit le lieutenant, à quoi penses-tu? Tu sais bien que notre pauvre mère a encore besoin de toi. Ne sera-t-elle pas assez malheureuse quand elle apprendra ma mort: est-elle donc destinée à n'avoir plus aucun soutien. Pense à elle, je t'en prie, à cette bonne mère à qui nous avions tant d'obligations, et renonce à ce funeste dessein, car elle en mourrait de douleur."

14. "HASSAN: Je sais me venger . . . me venger de tout ce que je hais. De toi, Léon Dervigny, qui es Français et mon rival! de toi, femme, qui as repoussé, méprisé mon amour!"

15. "Et votre union sera le gage de l'inaltérable dévoûment de ma tribu à la cause de la nation française."

16. "Nous sommes très bien avec les Arabes. Nous avons eu le bonheur, après nous être montrés fort, de leur inspirer une grande confiance; ils aiment la domination française et ils le prouvent tous les jours. . . . [Plusieurs tribus] ont associé leur sort au nôtre et sont sans arrière-pensée."

17. ". . . les Druses, après avoir désarmé les Chrétiens, commencèrent le pillage, qui dura toute la nuit du 19 au 20 juin. Dès le matin les Druses des districts mixtes arrivèrent pour y prendre part avec leurs femmes et leurs enfants, sans que les soldats fissent la moindre tentative pour les arrêter. Le massacre succéda alors au pillage, personne ne fut épargné; des enfants furent égorgé sur les genoux de leurs méres, des femmes et des filles violées et éventrées sous les yeux de leurs maris et de leurs pères.

"On dépeçait les hommes dans les rues à coup de hache: des femmes furent brulées, après avoir été baignées dans le sang de leurs enfants; les religieuses ellemêmes ne furent point épargnées. La ville était jonchée de cadavres, et les rues ruisselaient de sang."

18. "Nous savons que les sauvages de cette partie de l'Asie ont éventré les femmes après les avoir déshonorées, qu'ils ont écartelé les prêtres et les vieillards, tué avec d'atroces raffinements de cruauté, les petits enfants sous les yeux de leurs

mères, qu'ils forçaient ensuite de se baigner dans le sang recueilli après ce nouveau massacre des innocents.

"Le paquebot de Beyrouth nous fera savoir si ces atrocités continuent dans la Syrie. . . .

"Nous voudrions apprendre que cette explosion terrible de passions haineuses s'est enfin calmée, et que les bêtes féroces, rassasiés de carnage, se sont retirées dans leurs tanières pour cuver leur ivresse. Mais nous n'osons l'espérer; nous craignons au contraire, que le fanatisme n'ait étendu le champ de ses monstrueux exploits."

19. "On ne peut plus en douter: il y a une vaste conspiration contre la vie de tous les chrétiens d'Asie, et cette conspiration, qui déjà avait choisi séparément ses victimes . . ., prend aujourd'hui d'effrayantes proportions, et ne procède plus que par le meurtre en masse."

20. "Comme puissance militaire, comme foyer de la science et des idées, la France marche à la tête de toutes les nations du monde. Elle occupe le premier rang parmi les peuples civilisés, et le malheureux sort des chrétiens de la Syrie devait lui inspirer de nobles élans et de mâles résolutions."

Chapter 8

1. Victor Séjour's life and career are detailed by Michel Fabre in *From Harlem to Paris: Black American Writers in France, 1840–1980* and in an unpublished thesis by Era Mae Brisbane. Séjour's mother was a New Orleans quadroon and his father was "un homme de couleur libre" (a free man of color) from Santo Domingo. His first work for the Parisian stage, *Diegarias*, a five-act historical drama, was performed at the Théâtre-Français in 1844. From then until his death in 1874 he wrote a variety of plays, including histories, melodramas, adaptations of Shakespeare and Ben Jonson, and plays based on contemporary *faits-divers*. In 1862, Séjour wrote his one play that was set in the United States; *Les Volontaires de 1814* reflected his support for the Napoleonic dynasty, as had his much earlier ode, "Le Retour de Napoléon," composed when the emperor's remains were brought from Saint Helena to Paris.

2. ". . . le succès des *Massacres de Syrie* dépasse toutes les prévisions."

3. ". . . l'immense succès des *Massacres de Syrie* semble grandir encore à chaque représentation."

4. ". . . [une] grand pièce à spectacle, à laquelle les événements contemporains ajoutent un puissant attrait de curiosité et d'intérêt."

". . . [une] grande épopée militaire, éblouissante de luxe, de faste, de richesses orientales, et qui joint à l'intérêt du drame, l'attrait de l'actualité."

". . . [une] grande pièce à spectacle, à laquelle les événements contemporains ajoutent un puissant attrait d'actualité et d'à-propos."

5. "Rien de plus attrayant que cette oeuvre qui joint à l'intérêt dramatique, au prestige de l'actualité, les richesses d'une éblouissante mise en scène."

6. Apparently, Napoleon III was more than just an enthusiastic spectator.

According to Alphonse Lemonnier's reminiscences of boulevard theater, *Les Petits Mystères de la vie théâtrale*, the emperor himself had contributed suggestions for *Les Massacres de Syrie* (201–2).

7. "Que la fibre populaire ait vibré au souvenir, au récit, que dis-je? à la représentation fidèle et vivante de ces cruautés, de ces perfidies, de ces sanglantes hécatombes que l'épée de la France n'a pu ni empêcher, ni venger complètement, quoi de plus naturel? qu'on ait profité de la présence auguste du Souverain pour l'acclamer et le remercier d'avoir si bien compris les sentiments de la nation, quoi de plus légitime?"

8. "LA FERME DE MORÉAC. COUR INTÉRIEUR D'UNE RICHE FERME ORIENTALE. Un puits dans un coin. Au fond, une échappé laissant voir le ciel de la Syrie. Au lever du rideau, la ferme est en pleine activité; on rentre les blés et les foins que les garçons de ferme reçoivent de la porte du fond et transportent dans les greniers intérieurs en sortant par la gauche. Les garçons de ferme sont vêtus, les uns à la française, les autres à la mode bretonne; quelques-uns dans le goût du pays."

9. "*Marthe prépare une petite collation sur un plateau. Le père Simon est assis du côté opposé; il lit son bréviaire. Les ouvriers achèvent de rentrer les blés.*
"MARTHE: (A des soeurs de charité.) Entrez, mes soeurs, entrez . . . nous aurons l'honneur de vous servir nous-mêmes.
(*Les soeurs entrent à droite.*)
"LE PERE SIMON: Noble coeur! . . .
"MARTHE: Ces pieuses et saintes soeurs de charité! (*Au père Simon.*) Deux d'entre elles sont de Bretagne comme nous, mon père. Nous avons causé du pays. Mais elles ont l'âme si haute et si détachée de nos passions, qu'elles retrouvent leur patrie partout où la souffrance les réclame. Vous avez bien fait de nous avoir choisis pour leurs hôtes."

10. "PAPILLON: . . . Avez-vous entendu dire que les Druses de la Bekkaa s'étaient réunis en armes sur le Djebel-Sunnin? . . . Il faut y veiller, voyez-vous. Non-seulement ils détestent les Maronites, mais ils en veulent à tous les chrétiens du Liban."

11. "MOREAC: Amis, on tue, on égorge les chrétiens . . . on égorge nos frères! . . . Hasbeiya a besoin de défenseurs! . . . En est-il parmi vous qui consentent à quitter le travail pour la seule chose qui soit plus sacrée encore . . . le combat pour une sainte cause?"

12. ". . . les Moréac n'ont pas oublié leur ancienne patrie, et ils sont toujours fidèle à la foi de leurs ancêtres. Les traditions de l'Occident se maintiennent chez ce petit groupe perdu au sein de la montagne parmi les sectes multiples qui divisent ces populations."

13. "LE GRAND RAVIN: Un immense ravin dont la riche végétation contraste avec les pentes arides par lesquelles on y descend. Des Arabes-Bédouins sont couchés çà et là devant leurs tentes. —Ben-Yacoub est debout, au fond, appuyé sur son cheval, dont il caresse machinalement la crinière. Ali-Bey l'observe. —Au sommet le plus élevé un spahis en vedette avec sa lance de roseau à la main. —Une énorme peau de tigre, à droite, est étendue devant la tente de Ben-Yacoub: c'est un lit de repos. A gauche, un grand arbre sur un précipice. —Au-delà, le désert."

14. "Les voilà partis! . . . On dirait une bande de vautours à la recherche d'une immense proie!"

15. "LE PERE SIMON: . . . une haine mortelle existe entre les Druses et les Maronites: haine de parti, parce que les Druses exècrent la France et que les Maronites nous aiment; haine de moeurs, parce qu'ils pillent et que les Maronites travaillent; haine de religion, parce qu'ils sont idolâtres et que les Maronites sont chrétiens."

16. "LE CONSULAT FRANÇAIS: —Un petit salon chez le consul de France, ouvrant sur une galerie éclairée. —Un bal. —On entend la musique. —Des domestiques vont et viennent, offrant des rafraichissements."

17. "(*Les douze cavaliers descendent au galop et se rangent en demi-cercle autour de Ben-Yacoub.*)

"BEN-YACOUB: (*Solennellement.*) Par l'éternité de Hackem, notre Seigneur et Dieu, je réponds du sultan des Osmanlis, et la dernière heure des chrétiens a sonné!

"LA D'JEMMALA-D'JEZZAR: La guerre sainte! la guerre sainte! . . .

"DEUXIEME SCHEIKH: Oui, la guerre sainte! . . . Les montagnes et les vallées nous verrons! . . . je me charge d'Hasbeiya: il y a là un émir de la famille de Shebah que je hais; l'émir compris, je ne laisserai pas une maison chrétienne debout, ni une tête de ceux qui font le signe de la croix. J'ai deux mille hommes qu'on nomme la Horde des Loups . . . Je me charge d'Hasbeiya! . . .

"TROISIEME SCHEIKH: (*En montrant les deux cavaliers qui sont à ses côtés.*) Nous de Zahleh: on nous reconnaîtra aux cris des vaincus; nous ne laisserons pas pierre sur pierre. . . ."

"TROIS SCHEIKHS: Nous nous chargerons de Deïr-el-Kamar!

"SIXIEME SCHEIKH: Nous, de Beyrouth!

"SEPTIEME SCHEIKH: Nous, de Damas!

"HUITIEME SCHEIKH: Nous, de Tripoli!

"BEN-YACOUB: Bien! et je serai partout, moi! . . . oui, Damas, Beyrouth, Tripoli! la triple clef qu'il nous faut! . . . —Nous sommes les soldats, les élus du dieu Hackem. . . . Ceux qu'il a condamnés périront! . . . Ils périront par le fer, par l'eau, par le feu! . . . Mort aux chrétiens! mort aux giaours! . . .

"TOUS: Mort aux chrétiens! mort aux giaours!"

18. "LE CONSUL ANGLAIS: . . . C'est possible; mais, je vous avouerai, monsieur, que vos craintes me paraissent exagérées; et par contre. . . .

"LE CONSUL FRANÇAIS: Qu'importe, si elles nous amenaient à prévenir un grand malheur."

19. "LA D'JEMMALA: (*Agitant le drapeau.*) Voilà le symbole d'honneur et de courage de ces francs qui viennent nous braver jusque chez nous. . . .

"TOUS: A bas le drapeau! à bas!

"LA D'JEMMALA: Oui, car derrière ce haillon il y a un peuple infâme et lâche. . . .

"TOUS: Sous les pieds! sous les pieds!

"LA D'JEMMALA: Un peuple qui rit de Mahomet, le vrai prophète! . . .

"TOUS: Aux ruisseaux! aux ruisseaux!

"LA D'JEMMALA: Un peuple maudit que je voudrais abattre comme cette guenille, et fouler sous les talons comme ce haillon!"

20. This issue is reproduced in Jean-Pierre Seguin's *Canards du siècle passé*, 63–64.

21. "L'émir est de taille moyenne; sans avoir une figure remarquable, il y a une certaine majesté dans son visage; son teint est blanc, ou plutôt pâle, quoique un peu bruni par le soleil; il a le visage ovale, les traits réguliers, la barbe claire et d'un

châtain foncé; ses yeux d'un gris-bleu, sont beaux et très expressifs, il a le regard pensif et presque timide, mais quand il parle, ses yeux s'animent et étincellent."

22. "ABD-EL-KADER: Profanateurs de choses saintes, arrière!

"TOUS: Abd-el-Kader!

"ABD-EL-KADER: Oui, moi! . . . et le Franc est un noble peuple, puisqu'il peut trouver des défenseurs même parmi ses anciens ennemis!

"TOUS: (*Furieux.*) Le drapeau! le drapeau!

"ABD-EL-KADER: J'ai vu combattre les Français. . . . je sais comment ils triomphent ou meurent. . . . Je remplace le plus résolu d'entre eux en ce moment. . . . Je combattrai et mourrai pour ce drapeau! (*Cris.*) Voici ma poitrine, voici mon coeur, frappez, ou faites-moi place!

"(*Les rangs s'ouvrent. Abd-el-Kader passe.*)"

23. Confronted with the undeniable commercial status of boulevard theater, Gautier seems to have gradually lost interest in his post as theater critic of the official government newspaper, *Le Moniteur universel*, which he took up in 1855. By 1861, it was apparently commonly known that Gautier increasingly turned the duties of theater critic over to his son. According to the Goncourt brothers, "le père fait la tête et la queue de l'article. Le fils, tout encombré de bouquins, pioche l'historique et les dates du milieu" ("the father writes the beginning and end of the article. The son, loaded down with books, churns out the historical facts and dates").

24. "Une espèce de prophétesse noire, raison troublée par le soleil d'Afrique et les réverbérations des sables, folle sanguinaire et fanatique qui parcourt les tribus montée sur un cheval noir comme elle. . . ."

25. ". . . comme le génie du massacre. . . elle parcourut les rues en hurlant, tuant, pillant, saccageant . . . et comme la nuit éte sombre, elle fit mettre le feu aux quatre coins de la ville pour mieux voir."

26. "Djemmala est la personification monstrueuse de la superstition; c'est la nuit qui proteste contre la lumière; la race obscure tentant un dernier effort contre la race blanche."

27. "AU PALAIS DE BEN-YACOUB A SAIDA. Une magnifique salle dans le goût oriental; des arcades, au fond, fermées par de riches tentures; ces tentures se relèvent à volonté, et laissent voir une galerie ou terrasse qui court autour du palais. Des femmes, au fond, étendues sur des coussins."

28. "BEN-YACOUB: . . . mon amour est farouche, j'en conviens; mais c'est Dieu qu'il faut accuser . . . c'est à lui qu'il faut s'en prendre, et à ces rudes montagnes du Liban qui m'ont donné leur âpreté et leurs hauteurs! . . . je sens leur grandeur sauvage et leur abîme en moi! . . . je ne sais pas prier . . . mes passions sont des orages . . . l'air que je respire m'embrase . . . ce soleil qui me brûle m'a pétri de bronze et de fer comme une menace ou un danger! . . . je suis ainsi!"

29. "AÏSSA: On venait de retracer à mes yeux les horribles cruautés exercées contre les chrétiens dans la montagne. J'avais le coeur gros de larmes. Je me disais qu'on devait mieux prier dans la maison des martyrs; une église s'est présentée, et j'y suis entrée.

"ABD-EL-KADER: (*Tristement.*) Ton âme va de ce côté, mon enfant . . . je ne te blâme pas. Mais songe que tu es du sang de Mahomet. . . ."

30. ". . . en face des empires qui croulent et des civilisations mortes! . . . Oh! Mahomet, la race d'Islam s'en va, et ton nom s'efface même du coeur de ma fille! . . . Triste! triste! triste!"

31. "ABD-EL-KADER: (*Prenant son épée.*) . . . Napoléon III m'a donné cette épée . . . je me sentais assez grand pour l'accepter; je me sens assez digne pour m'en servir! . . . Je prouverai au sultan de France que cette main qu'il a touchée est sienne, que ce coeur qu'il a ému lui appartient, et qu'il a un serviteur dévoué et un soldat en moi. . . ."

32. "Ce musulmane machiavélique et rapace, qui n'a même point le fanatisme pour excuse, obéit aux instincts les plus pervers et les plus bas, aux passions les plus honteuses et les plus cruelles."

33. "La condamnation des enfants druses au balayage des rues a produit son effet. Je crois qu'on pourrait en profiter pour soulever Beyrouth."

34. "GEORGES: Enfin, des excès odieux ont éclaté du côté d'Hasbeiya . . . partout des hommes massacrés . . . des femmes enlevées, deshonorées, égorgées. . . . On ne tue pas seulement, on torture! . . . on prend son temps comme pour mieux faire l'horrible besogne!"

35. "C'est de veuves qui pleurent leur mari . . . d'enfants désespérés qui redemandent leur père! . . . c'est de têtes coupées que je parle . . . c'est du sang versé que je m'occupe, et j'en demande compte!"

36. "Les victimes sortent tumultueusement du sérail avec des cris épouvantables; elles se défendent encore; les uns leur femmes ou leurs filles, les autres leurs enfants nouveau-nés qu'elles pressent sur leur coeur. . . ."

37. "DAOUB-KAÏBAR: La loi les condamne, la loi les frappe . . . on laissera parler et agir la loi.
"GEORGES: Quelle loi? . . . Oui, quelle loi? est-ce la loi de Mahomet, qui justifie et glorifie l'assassinat commis sur un chrétien? . . . est-ce celle de votre dieu Hackem, qui ordonne l'extermination des infidèles?"

38. "GEORGES: Ne jurez pas . . . ce sont des chrétiens que vous avez devant vous: le Koran vous a d'avance délié des serments que vous pourriez nous faire."

39. "On a voulu voir dans les *Massacres de Syrie* une pièce à la fois politique et littéraire, un manifeste, une proclamation, j'allais presque ajouter une déclaration de guerre. Pour moi, je n'y ai vu qu'un drame énergique et puissant, une lutte acharnée entre deux rivaux de race et de religion diverses qui aiment la même femme; le tout ayant pour cadre un pays splendide, et *rappelant sans aucune exagération, dans leur vérité nue et avec une simplicité éloquente, des événements contemporains qui ont ému toute l'Europe.*"

40. It should be recalled that journalists showed no such reservations in calling attention to British isolation in these matters (see Chapter 4). While in this instance Séjour was undoubtedly motivated by concerns for dramatic effect rather than by any imperialist ideology, his representation could only serve to reinforce the emerging discourse of an irremediable difference between Christian Europe and Muslim Middle East.

41. When these memoirs were published in English translation in 1988, they appeared under the sensationalistic title *Murder, Mayhem, Pillage, and Plunder: The History of the Lebanon in the 18th and 19th Centuries*. As the text itself states,

the most accurate translation of the Arabic title would be a "response to a suggestion by beloved ones." In contrast to the convention for translations of European
works, moreover, the name of the translator rather than that of the author appears
on the binding of the volume. It would seem that the volume itself carries vestiges
of Orientalism.

42. In addition to the text of the letter, this edition includes contemporary
paintings, engravings, cartoons, and photographs of 'Abd al-Qadir.

Conclusion

1. For discussions of these issues, see Patrice Pavis, ed., *The Intercultural Performance Reader*; Bonnie Marranca and Gautam Dasgupta, eds., *Interculturalism
and Performance*; and Rustom Bharucha, *Theatre and the World: Performance and
the Politics of Culture*.

2. For an overview of the field, see Helen Gilbert and Joanne Tompkins,
eds., *Post-colonial Drama: Theory, Practice, Politics*.

Bibliography

A! A! A! [Abel Hugo, Armand Malitourne, Jean Adler]. *Traité du mélodrame.* Paris: Delaunay, Pelicier, Plancher, 1817.

Abd-el-Kader. *Lettre aux Français.* Translated by René R. Khawam. Paris: Phébus, 1977.

Abraham, Antoine J. *Lebanon at Mid-Century—Maronite-Druze Relations in Lebanon, 1840–1860: A Prelude to Arab Nationalism.* Washington, D.C.: University Press of America, 1981.

Alali, A. Odasuo, and Kenoye Kelvin Eke, eds. *Media Coverage of Terrorism: Methods of Diffusion.* Newbury Park, Calif.: Sage, 1991.

Albert, Maurice. *Les Théâtres des Boulevards (1789–1848).* Paris: Société Française d'Imprimerie et de Librairie, 1902.

Allévy, Marie-Antoinette. *La Mise en scène en France dans la première moitié du dix-neuvième siècle.* Paris: Droz, 1938.

Badir, Magdy Gabriel. *Voltaire et l'Islam.* Studies on Voltaire and the Eighteenth Century, vol. 125. Edited by Theodore Besterman. Banbury, Oxfordshire: Voltaire Foundation, 1974.

Bapst, Germain. *Essai sur l'histoire du théâtre: La Mise en scène, le décor, le costume, l'architecture, l'éclairage, l'hygiène.* Paris: Hachette, 1893.

Baroli, Marc. *La Vie quotidienne des Français en Algérie (1830–1914).* Paris: Hachette, 1967.

Barrows, Susanna. *Distorting Mirrors: Visions of the Crowd in Late Nineteenth-Century France.* New Haven, Conn.: Yale University Press, 1981.

Barthes, Roland. "Rhétorique de l'image." *Communications,* vol. 4 (1964): 40–51.

Baylé, Jacqueline. *Quand l'Algérie devenait française.* Paris: Fayard, 1981.

Beaulieu, Henri. *Les Théâtres du Boulevard du Crime de Nicolet à Déjazet (1752–1862).* Paris: H. Daragon, 1905.

Beaumont. Review of *Les Ruines de Babylone,* by Guilbert de Pixerécourt. *Journal du Soir,* October 31, 1810.

Becq de Fouquières, L. *L'Art de la mise en scène: essai d'esthétique théâtrale.* Paris: G. Charpentier, 1884.

Bellanger, Claude, and Jacques Godechot, Pierre Guiral, and Fernand Terrou, eds. *Histoire générale de la presse française.* Vol. 1, *Des origines à 1814.* Vol 2, *De 1815 à 1871.* Paris: Presses Universitaires de France, 1969.

Bentley, Eric. "Melodrama." In *The Life of the Drama.* New York: Atheneum, 1964.

Bernoyer, François. *Avec Bonaparte en Egypte et en Syrie, 1798–1800.* Paris: Curandera, 1981.

Bharucha, Rustom. *Theatre and the World: Performance and the Politics of Culture.*

London and New York: Routledge, 1993. (First published by Manohar Publications, India, 1990.)

Booth, Michael R. *English Melodrama*. London: Herbert Jenkins, 1965.

Bourdieu, Pierre. *Distinction: A Social Critique of the Judgement of Taste*. Translated by Richard Nice. Cambridge, Mass.: Harvard University Press, 1984. (Originally published as *La Distinction: Critique sociale du jugement*. Paris: Minuit, 1979.)

————. *The Logic of Practice*. Translated by Richard Nice. Cambridge, U.K.: Polity Press; Stanford, Calif.: Stanford University Press, 1990. (Originally published as *Le Sens pratique*. Paris: Editions de Minuit, 1980.)

Bradby, David, Louis James, Bernard Sharratt, eds. *Performance and Politics in Popular Drama: Aspects of Popular Entertainment in Theatre, Film, and Television, 1800–1976*. Cambridge: Cambridge University Press, 1980.

Bratton, J. S. "Theatre of War: The Crimea on the London Stage, 1854–5." In *Performance and Politics in Popular Drama*, ed. David Bradby et al. Cambridge and New York: Cambridge University Press, 1980.

Bratton, J. S., Richard Allen Cave, Breandan Gregory, Heidi J. Holder, and Michael Pickering. *Acts of Supremacy: The British Empire and the Stage, 1790–1930*. Manchester, U.K.: Manchester University Press, 1991.

Bratton, Jacky S., Jim Cook, and Christine Gledhill, eds. *Melodrama: Stage Picture Screen*. London: British Film Institute, 1994.

Brazier, Nicolas. *Chroniques de Petits Théâtres de Paris*. Paris: Rouveyre et Blond, 1883.

Brisbane, Era Mae. *Le Théâtre de Victor Séjour*. Master's thesis, Hunter College, 1942.

Brooks, Peter. "Melodrama, Body, Revolution." In *Melodrama: Stage Picture Screen*, ed. Jacky Bratton, Jim Cook, and Christine Gledhill. London: British Film Institute, 1994.

————. *The Melodramatic Imagination: Balzac, Henry James, Melodrama, and the Mode of Excess*. New Haven, Conn.: Yale University Press, 1976. Reprint. New York: Columbia University Press, 1984.

Brown, Frederick. *Theater and Revolution: The Culture of the French Stage*. New York: Viking Press, 1980.

Cabanis, André. *La Presse sous le Consulat et l'Empire (1799–1814)*. Paris: Société des Robespierristes/CNRS, 1975.

Cain, Georges. *Anciens Théâtres de Paris*. Paris: Charpentier et Fasquelle, 1906.

Calhoun, Craig, Edward LiPuma, and Moishe Postone, eds. *Bourdieu: Critical Perspectives*. Chicago: University of Chicago Press, 1993.

Carlson, Marvin. *The French Stage in the Nineteenth Century*. Metuchen, N.J.: Scarecrow Press, 1972.

————. *Places of Performance: The Semiotics of Theatre Architecture*. Ithaca, N.Y.: Cornell University Press, 1989.

————. *The Theatre of the French Revolution*. Ithaca, N.Y.: Cornell University Press, 1966.

Case, Sue-Ellen, and Janelle Reinelt, eds. *The Performance of Power: Theatrical Discourse and Politics*. Iowa City: University of Iowa Press, 1991.

Certeau, Michel de. *Heterologies: Discourse on the Other*. Translated by Brian Massumi. Minneapolis: University of Minnesota Press, 1986.

———. *L'Invention du quotidien*, vol.1: *Arts de faire*. Paris: 10/18, 1980. Translated by Steven Rendall as *The Practice of Everyday Life*. Berkeley and Los Angeles: University of California Press, 1984.

Charlemagne, Armand. "Le Mélodrame aux boulevards: Facétie littéraire, historique et dramatique." Paris: Imprimerie de la rue Beaurepaire, 1809

Chartier, Roger. *The Cultural Uses of Print in Early Modern France*, trans. Lydia Cochrane. Princeton, N.J.: Princeton University Press, 1987.

———. *Forms and Meanings: Texts, Performances, and Audiences from Codex to Computer*. Philadelphia: University of Pennsylvania Press, 1995.

Chartier, Roger, et al., eds. *L'Histoire de l'édition française*, vols. 2 and 3. Paris: Promodis, 1984, 1985.

Churchill, C. H. *The Druze and the Maronites under Turkish Rule: From 1840–1860*. London, 1862.

———. *Life of Abdel Kader*. London: Chapman and Hall, 1867.

Colnet. Review of *Les Ruines de Babylone*, by Guilbert de Pixerécourt. *Gazette de France*, October 31, 1810.

Davoine, Jean-Paul. "L'Epithète mélodramatique." *Revue des sciences humaines* 41, no. 162 (April–June 1976): 183–92.

Demarcy, Richard. *Eléments d'une sociologie du spectacle*. Paris: 10/18, 1973.

De Marinis, Marco. *The Semiotics of Performance*. Translated by Áine O'Healy. Bloomington and Indianapolis: Indiana University Press, 1993. (Originally published as *Semiotica del teatro: L'analisi testuale dello spettacolo*. Milan: Gruppo Editoriale Fabbri, Bompiani, Sonzogno, Etas S.p.A., 1982.)

Deschamps, Emile. "Letter to Guilbert de Pixerécourt," May 4, 1841. In Guilbert de Pixerécourt, *Théâtre choisi*, vol. 3. Geneva: Slatkine Reprints, 1971.

Descotes, Maurice. *Histoire de la critique dramatique en France*. Paris: Place, 1980.

———. *Le Public de théâtre et son histoire*. Paris: Presses Universitaires de France, 1964.

Douthwaite, Julia V. *Exotic Women: Literary Heroines and Cultural Strategies in Ancien Régime France*. Philadelphia: University of Pennsylvania Press, 1992.

Ducray-Duminil. "Notice sur *Coelina*." In Guilbert de Pixerécourt, *Théâtre choisi*, vol. 1. Geneva: Slatkine Reprints, 1971.

Dusaulchoy. Review of *Les Ruines de Babylone* by Guilbert de Pixerécourt. *Journal des spectacles*, October 31, 1810.

El-Nouty, Hassan. *Théâtre et pré-cinéma: Essai sur la problematique du spectacle au XIXe siècle*. Paris: Nizet, 1978.

Europe. Special issue on "Le Mélodrame." Nos. 703–4, November-Décember 1987.

Fabre, Michel. *From Harlem to Paris: Black American Writers in France (1840–1980)*. Urbana and Chicago: University of Illinois Press, 1991.

Fischer-Lichte, Erika. *The Semiotics of Theater*. Translated by Jeremy Gaines and Doris L. Jones. Bloomington and Indianapolis: Indiana University Press, 1992. Originally published as *Semiotik des Theaters*. Tübingen: Gunter Narr Verlag, 1983.

Fleury, Abraham. *The French Stage and the French People*, vol. 1. Edited by Th. Hook. London: H. Colburn, 1841.

Fulchur, Jane. *The Nation's Image: French Grand Opera as Politics and Politicized Art*. Cambridge: Cambridge University Press, 1987.

Gainor, J. Ellen, ed. *Imperialism and Theatre: Essays on World Theatre, Drama and Performance, 1795–1995*. London and N.Y.: Routledge, 1995.

Geoffroy. "Notice sur *Les Ruines de Babylone*." In Guilbert de Pixerécourt, *Théâtre choisi*, vol. 3. Geneva: Slatkine Reprints, 1971.

Gerould, Daniel. "Historical Simulation and Popular Entertainment: The *Potemkin* Mutiny from Reconstructed Newsreel to Black Sea Stunt Men." *The Drama Review* 33 (1989): 161–84.

———, ed. *Melodrama*. New York: New York Literary Forum, 1980.

Ghareeb, Edmund. *Split Vision: Arab Portrayal in the American Media*. Washington, D.C.: Institute of Middle Eastern and North African Affairs, 1977.

Gilbert, Helen, and Joanne Tompkins, eds. *Post-colonial Drama: Theory, Practice, Politics*. London and New York: Routledge, 1996.

Ginisty, Paul. *La Féerie*. Paris: Michaud, 1910.

———. *Le Mélodrame*. Paris: Michaud, 1910.

Gledhill, Christine, ed. *Home Is Where the Heart Is*. London: British Film Institute, 1987.

Goulemot, Jean-Marie. "De la Lecture comme production de sens." In *Pratiques de la lecture*, ed. Roger Chartier. Paris: Rivages, 1985.

Grimsted, David. *Melodrama Unveiled: American Theater and Culture, 1800–1850*. Chicago: University of Chicago Press, 1968.

Grosrichard, Alain. *La Structure du sérail: La Fiction du despotisme asiatique dans l'occident classique*. Paris: Seuil, 1979.

Guiral, Pierre. *Les Militaires à la Conquête de l'Algérie (1830–1857)*. Paris: Criterion, 1992.

Gunning, Tom. "The Horror of Opacity: The Melodrama of Sensation in the Plays of André de Lorde." In *Melodrama: Stage Picture Screen*, ed. Jacky Bratton, Jim Cook, and Christine Gledhill. London: British Film Institute, 1994.

Hadidi, Djavâd. *Voltaire et l'Islam*. Paris: Publications Orientalistes de France, 1974.

Hall, Catherine. "The Sweet Delights of Home." In *A History of Private Life*, vol. 4: *From the Fires of Revolution to the Great War*. Edited by Michelle Perrot. Translated by Arthur Goldhammer. Cambridge, Mass.: Belknap Press of Harvard University Press, 1990. (Originally published as *L'Histoire de la vie privée*, vol. 4: *De la Révolution à la Grande Guerre*. Paris: Editions du Seuil, 1987.)

Hallays-Dabot, Victor. *La Censure dramatique et le théâtre*. Paris: Dentu, 1871.

———. *L'Histoire de la censure théâtrale en France*. Paris: E. Dentu, 1862.

Hamiche, Daniel. *Le Théâtre et la Révolution: La Lutte de classes au théâtre en 1789 et en 1793*. Paris: 10/18, 1973.

Hartog, Willie. *Guilbert de Pixerécourt: Sa Vie, son mélodrame, sa technique, et son influence*. Paris: Champion, 1913.

Heath, Stephen. "Film and System: Terms of Analysis." *Screen* 16, no. 1 (1975).

Hébrard, Jean. "Les Nouveaux Lecteurs." In *L'Histoire de l'édition française*, vol. 3, ed. Roger Chartier et al. Paris: Promodis, 1985.

Heilman, Robert. *Tragedy and Melodrama: Versions of Experience*. Seattle: University of Washington Press, 1968.

Hemmings, F. W. J. *The Theatre Industry in Nineteenth-Century France*. Cambridge and New York: Cambridge University Press, 1993.

———. *Theatre and State in France, 1760–1905*. Cambridge and New York: Cambridge University Press, 1994.

Herman, Edward, and Gerry O'Sullivan. *The "Terrorism" Industry: The Experts and Institutions that Shape Our View of Terror*. New York: Pantheon, 1989.

Hourani, Albert. *A History of the Arab Peoples*. New York: Warner, 1991.

———. *Syria and Lebanon: Political Essay*. London: Oxford University Press, 1946.

Howarth, W. D. "Bonaparte on Stage: The Napoleonic Legend in Nineteenth-Century French Drama." In *Historical Drama*. Themes in Drama, no. 8. London and New York: Cambridge University Press, 1986.

Isherwood, Robert. *Farce and Fantasy: Popular Entertainment in Eighteenth-Century Paris*. New York and Oxford: Oxford University Press, 1986.

al-Jabarti, 'Abd al-Rahman. *Journal d'un notable du Caire durant l'expédition française 1798–1801*. Translated into French by Joseph Cuoq. Paris: Albin Michel, 1979.

Jacques le Souffleur. *Petit Dictionnaire des Coulisses*. Paris, 1835.

James, Louis. "Was Jerrold's Black Ey'd Susan More Popular than Wordsworth's Lucy?" In *Performance and Politics in Popular Drama*, ed. David Bradby et al. Cambridge and New York: Cambridge University Press, 1980.

JanMohamed, Abdul R. "Colonialist Literature." *Critical Inquiry* 12, no. 1 (1985): 59–87.

———. *Manichean Aesthetics: The Politics of Literature in Colonial Africa*. Amherst: University of Massachusetts Press: 1983.

Jenkins, Bruce. *Nationalism in France: Class and Nation since 1789*. Savage, Md.: Barnes & Noble, 1990.

Kaplan, E. Ann. *Motherhood and Representation: The Mother in Popular Culture and Drama*. London and New York: Routledge, 1992.

Krakovitch, Odile. *Hugo Censuré: La Liberté au théâtre au XIXe siècle*. Paris: Calmann-Lévy, 1985.

———. *Les Pièces de théâtre soumises à la censure (1800–1830)*. Paris: Archives Nationales, 1982.

———. "Robert Macaire ou la grande peur des censeurs." *L'Europe* 65, nos. 703–4 (1987): 49–60.

Lacapra, Dominick, and Steven L. Kaplan, eds. *Modern European Intellectual History: Reappraisals and New Perspectives*. Ithaca, N.Y.: Cornell University Press, 1982.

Lecomte, L.-Henry. *Histoire des théâtres de Paris*. 10 vols. Paris: Daragon, 1905–1913.

———. *Napoléon et l'Empire racontés par le théâtre, 1797–1899*. Paris: J. Raux, 1900.

———. *Napoléon et le monde dramatique*. Paris: H. Daragon, 1912.

Lefebvre, Georges. *Napoleon: From Tilsit to Waterloo, 1807–1815*. Translated by J. E. Anderson. New York: Columbia University Press, 1969. (Originally published as *Napoléon*. 5th ed. Paris: Presses Universitaires de France, 1965.)

Lekain. "Lettre à M. de ——," January 10, 1750. In *Mémoires de Lekain, précédés de*

réflexions sur cet acteur et sur l'art théâtral par M. Talma, 380–82. Paris, 1825.
Reprint. Geneva: Slatkine Reprints, 1968.

Lemonnier, Alphonse. *Les Petits Mystères de la vie théâtrale*. Paris, 1895.

Lowe, Lisa. *Critical Terrains: French and British Orientalisms*. Ithaca, N.Y.: Cornell University Press, 1991.

Lule, Jack. "The Myth of My Widow: A Dramatistic Analysis of News Portrayals of a Terrorist Victim." In *Media Coverage of Terrorism: Methods of Diffusion*, ed. A. Odasuo Alali and Kenoye Kelvin Eke. Newbury Park, Calif.: Sage, 1991.

Marranca, Bonnie, and Gautam Dasgupta, eds. *Interculturalism and Performance: Writings from PAJ*. New York: PAJ, 1991.

Mason, Jeffrey D. *Melodrama and the Myth of America*. Bloomington: Indiana University Press, 1993.

———. "The Politics of *Metamora*." In *The Performance of Power: Theatrical Discourse and Politics*, ed. Sue-Ellen Case and Janelle Reinelt. Iowa City: University of Iowa Press, 1991.

Mayer, David. "The Music of Melodrama." In *Performance and Politics in Popular Drama*, ed. David Bradby et al. Cambridge and New York: Cambridge University Press, 1980.

McConachie, Bruce A. *Melodramatic Formations: American Theatre and Society, 1820–1870*. Iowa City: University of Iowa Press, 1992.

McCormick, John. *Popular Theatres of Nineteenth-Century France*. London and New York: Routledge, 1993.

Meisel, Martin. *Realizations: Narrative, Pictorial, and Theatrical Arts in Nineteenth-Century England*. Princeton, N.J.: Princeton University Press, 1983

Metz, Christian. "On the Impression of Reality in the Cinema." In *Film Language: A Semiotics of the Cinema*. Translated by Michael Taylor. New York: Oxford University Press, 1974. (First published as "A propos de l'impression de realité au cinéma." *Cahiers du cinéma*, 166–67 [1965]: 74–83.)

Mishāqā, Mikhayil. *Murder, Mayhem, Pillage and Plunder: The History of the Lebanon in the 18th and 19th Centuries*. Translated by Wheeler M. Thackston, Jr. Albany: State University of New York Press, 1988.

Moiret, Joseph-Marie. *Mémoires sur l'Expédition d'Egypte*. Paris: Pierre Belfond, 1984.

Naugrette-Christophe, Catherine. "La Fin des promenades: Les Bouleversements de la carte des théâtres dans le Paris du Second Empire." In *Les Voies de la création théâtrale*, vol. 15: *Le Théâtre dans la ville*, ed. Elie Konigson. Paris: CNRS, 1987.

Nichols, Bill. *Representing Reality: Issues and Concepts in Documentary*. Bloomington and Indianapolis: Indiana University Press, 1991.

Odin, Roger. "L'Entrée du spectateur dans la fiction." In *La Théorie du film*, ed. Jacques Aumont and J. L. Leutrat, 198–213. Paris: Albatros, 1980.

———. "Pour une sémio-pragmatique du cinéma." *Iris* 1, no. 1 (1983): 67–81.

———. "Rhétorique du film de famille." In *Rhétoriques, Sémiotiques, Revue d'Esthétique* 1–2, 340–73. Paris: 10/18, 1979.

Parent, Françoise. "Nouvelles pratiques de lecture." In *L'Histoire de l'édition française*, vol. 2, ed. Roger Chartier et al. Paris: Promodis, 1984.

Pavis, Patrice, ed. *The Intercultural Performance Reader*. London and New York: Routledge, 1996.

———. *Theatre at the Crossroads of Culture*. Translated by Loren Kruger. London and New York: Routledge, 1992. Originally published as *Le Théâtre au croisement des cultures*. Paris: Corti, 1990.

Perrot, Michelle. "The Family Triumphant." In *A History of Private Life*, vol. 4: *From the Fires of Revolution to the Great War*. Edited by Michelle Perrot. Translated by Arthur Goldhammer. Cambridge, Mass.: Belknap Press of Harvard University Press, 1990. (Originally published as *L'Histoire de la vie privée*, vol. 4: *De la Révolution à la Grande Guerre*. Paris: Editions du Seuil, 1987.)

Peyronnet, Pierre. *La Mise en scène au XVIIIe siècle*. Paris: Nizet, 1974.

Picard, Jean-François. "Tableaux des Tirages de la Presse nationale de 1803 à 1944." In *Documents pour l'histoire de la Presse nationale aux XIXe et XXe siècles*. Edited by Pierre Albert. Paris: CNRS, 1976.

Pixerécourt, Guilbert de. "Dernières Réflexions de l'auteur sur le mélodrame." In *Théâtre choisi*, vol. 4. Geneva: Slatkine Reprints, 1971

———. *Les Maures d'Espagne, ou le Pouvoir de l'enfance*. In *Théâtre choisi*, vol. 2. Geneva: Slatkine Reprints, 1971.

———. *Les Ruines de Babylone, ou le Massacre des Barmecides*. In *Théâtre choisi*, vol. 3. Geneva: Slatkine Reprints, 1971.

———. "Souvenirs de la Révolution." In *Théâtre choisi*, vol. 2. Geneva: Slatkine Reprints, 1971.

Przybos, Julia. *L'Entreprise mélodramatique*. Paris: Corti, 1987.

Redmond, James, ed. *Melodrama*. Themes in Drama, no. 14. London and New York: Cambridge University Press, 1992.

Reid, Douglas A. "Popular Theatre in Victorian Birmingham." In *Performance and Politics in Popular Drama*, ed. David Bradby, Louis James, and Bernard Sharratt. Cambridge: Cambridge University Press, 1980.

Revue des sciences humaines 41, no. 162 (April–May 1976). Special issue on "Le Mélodrame."

Roach, Joseph. "Mardi Gras Indians and Others: Genealogies of American Performance." *Theatre Journal* 44 (1992): 461–83.

Rodmell, Graham E. *French Drama of the Revolutionary Years*. London and New York: Routledge, 1990.

Rojare. Review of *Les Ruines de Babylone*, by Guilbert de Pixerécourt. *Petites Affiches*, October 31, 1810.

Root-Bernstein, Michele. *Boulevard Theater and Revolution in Eighteenth-Century Paris*. Ann Arbor, Mich.: UMI Research Press, 1984.

Rosenberg, James L. "Melodrama." In *The Context and Craft of Drama: Critical Essays on the Nature of Drama and Theatre*, ed. Robert W. Corrigan and James L. Rosenberg. San Francisco: Chandler, 1964.

Rothenberg, Gunther E. *The Art of Warfare in the Age of Napoleon*. Bloomington: Indiana University Press, 1978.

Rougemont, Martine de. "Le *Mélodrame classique*: exercice de poétique rétrospective." *Revue des sciences humaines* 41, no. 162 (April–June 1976): 163–70.

———. *La Vie théâtrale en France au XVIIIe siècle*. Paris: Editions Champion, 1988.

Said, Edward. *Orientalism*. New York: Vintage, 1979. (First published by Pantheon, 1978.)

Salgue. Review of *Les Ruines de Babylone*, by Guilbert de Pixerécourt. *Journal des Arts*, November 4, 1810.

Saxon, Arthur H. *Enter Foot and Horse: A History of Hippodrama in England and France*. New Haven, Conn.: Yale University Press, 1968.

Seguin, Jean-Pierre. *Canards du siècle passé*. Paris: Horay, 1969.

———. *Les Canards illustrés du 19e siècle: Fascination du fait divers*. Paris: Musée-Galerie de la Seita, 1982. (Exhibition catalogue.)

———. *Nouvelles à sensation: Canards du XIXe siècle*. Paris: Armand Colin, 1959.

Séjour, Victor. *Les Massacres de la Syrie. Magasin Théâtral*. Paris: Barbré, 1861.

Smith, James L. *Melodrama*. London: Methuen, 1973.

Spurr, David. *The Rhetoric of Empire: Colonial Discourse in Journalism, Travel Writing, and Imperial Administration*. Durham, N.C.: Duke University Press, 1993.

Thiry, Jean. *Bonaparte en Egypte*. Paris: Berger-Levrault, 1973.

Thomasseau, Jean-Marie. *Le Mélodrame*. Paris: Presses Universitaires de France, 1984.

———. *Le Mélodrame sur les scènes parisiennes: De Coelina (1800) à l'Auberge des Adrets (1823)*. Lille: Service de reproduction des thèses, 1974.

Tomlinson, John. *Cultural Imperialism: A Critical Introduction*. Baltimore: Johns Hopkins University Press, 1991.

Ubersfeld, Anne. "Les Bons et le méchant." *Revue des sciences humaines* 41, no. 162 (April–June 1976): 193–203.

———. *L'Ecole du spectateur*. Paris: Editions sociales, 1981.

———. *Lire le théâtre*. 4th ed. Paris: Editions sociales, 1982.

———. *Le Roi et le bouffon*. Paris: Corti, 1974.

———. *Le Roman d'Hernani*. Paris: Mercure de France, 1985.

Valory et Montigny. *Zara, ou la Soeur de l'Arabe. Magasin Théâtral* 31 (1842).

Van Bellen, Eise Carel. *Les Origines du mélodrame*. Utrecht: Keminck and Zoon, 1927.

Vardac, Nicholas. *From Stage to Screen: Theatrical Method from Garrick to Griffith*. Cambridge, Mass.: Harvard University Press, 1949.

Vincent-Buffault, Anne. *The History of Tears: Sensibility and Sentimentality in France*. Translated by Teresa Bridgeman. New York: St. Martin's Press, 1991. (Originally published as *L'Histoire des larmes: XVIIIe–XIXe siècles*. Paris: Rivages, 1986.)

Voltaire. *Appel à toutes les nations: Des Divers Changements arrivés à l'art tragique*. 1761.

———. "Avis de l'éditeur." November 18, 1742. In *Oeuvres complètes*, 4:97–100. Paris: Garnier, 1877.

———. "Lettre au Pape Benoît XIV," August 17, 1745. In *Oeuvres complètes*, 4:101–2. Paris: Garnier, 1877.

———. *Mahomet le Prophète, ou le Fanatisme*. In *Oeuvres complètes*, 4:91–167. Paris: Garnier, 1877.

———. *Zaïre*. In *Oeuvres complètes*, 2:531–620. Paris: Garnier, 1877.

Welschinger, Henri. *La Censure sous le Premier Empire*. Paris: Charavay, 1882.

White, Hayden. 1980. "The Value of Narrativity in the Representation of Reality."
    Critical Inquiry 7, no. 1 (1980): 5–27.

Wicks, Charles Beaumont. *The Parisian Stage*, Parts 1–5. University of Alabama
    Studies, 1950–1979.

"Avertissement pour la présente édition." *Zaïre*, by Voltaire. In *Oeuvres complètes*,
    2:533–35. Paris: Garnier, 1877.

Review of *Zaïre*, by Voltaire. *Le Courrier de l'Europe*, October 10, 1810.

Acknowledgments

I would like to express my deepest appreciation to all the people who have served as guides on this expedition into the nineteenth century. At Berkeley, I had the good fortune to study with two scholars whose expertise and interests made it possible to envision and develop this project. Working with Bertrand Augst was always an adventure in ideas and a gift of resources. Masao Miyoshi's investigations into the relationship of power and culture in global contexts provided a constant stimulus for this research. In its original form as a dissertation, this project also benefited from the attentive reading of Michael Lucey and David Lloyd. My special thanks go to Sau-ling Wong for her unofficial mentoring and friendship and her invitation to teach in the Asian American Studies program—an experience that provided me with a cultural center from which all other examinations of culture can proceed.

A fellowship from the George D. Lurcy Foundation supported an invaluable year of study and research in France. The archival research that forms the foundation for this study was conducted during that year. It was also during this time that I had the opportunity to attend a seminar taught by Roger Chartier, whose generosity and patience with a mere beginner in the field of sociocultural history enabled my efforts to recover meanings from the past. I must also thank Jean Hébrard for sharing his particular knowledge of nineteenth-century cultural practices.

The final year of research and writing of *The Orient of the Boulevards* as a dissertation was supported by an American Fellowship from the American Association of University Women. A summer research grant from George Washington University allowed me to make one more trip to Paris to investigate the links between press and stage in nineteenth-century France.

Finally, I would like to thank Jerry Singerman for unveiling the mysteries of bringing a manuscript to press.

Index